Braddock's Campaign,1755

VIEW OF THE SCENE OF BRADDOCK'S DEFEAT

Braddock's Campaign, 1755

The Fort Duquesne Expedition during the French
& Indian War

ILLUSTRATED

Winthrop Sargent

LEONAUR

Braddock's Campaign, 1755
The Fort Duquesne Expedition during the French & Indian War
by Winthrop Sargent

ILLUSTRATED

First published under the title
The History of an Expedition against Fort Du Quesne in 1755
under Major-General Edward Braddock

Leonaur is an imprint of Oakpast Ltd

ISBN: 978-1-78282-774-0 (hardcover)
ISBN: 978-1-78282-775-7 (softcover)

http://www.leonaur.com

Contents

The March to War 9

Forts in the Wilderness 26

Settlers and Savages 46

The Gathering of Arms 80

General Braddock 90

The British Army 106

The Hour and the Man 115

The French Prepare 147

The British Movement 157

The Fatal Crossing 172

The Jaws of the Trap 185

The Retreat 194

Conclusions 209

Appendix No. 1 231

Appendix No. 2 239

Appendix No. 3 245

Appendix No. 4 250

GEN. BRADDOCK.

To
Joseph R. Ingersoll;
Through Whose Public Spirit
The Matter which Forms Its Basis was Procured
This Volume
Is Respectfully Dedicated.

FRENCH AND INDIAN WAR

MAP OF THE SCENE OF OPERATIONS.

CHAPTER 1

The March to War

On the night of the 30th of April, 1748, the preliminaries of what was boldly asserted to be a definitive and lasting peace, were signed by the diplomatic representatives of England, Holland, and France, at the city of Aix-la-Chapelle. Exhausted by the fatigues of a long, harassing, and unsatisfactory struggle, the two great parties in this arrangement embraced, if not eagerly, at least without reluctance, a scheme which would give to each an opportunity to extricate itself from any unprofitable enterprise or dangerous dilemma in which it had become involved, and to prepare, at leisure, plans for a future and more successful war. Lord Mahon says:

> Never, never, perhaps, did any war, after so many great events, and so large a loss of blood and treasure, end in replacing the nations engaged in it in nearly the same situation as they held at first.

The Earl of Chesterfield—the only man in the British Cabinet possessed of sufficient energy and capacity to have directed more successfully hostile measures, or to have procured more advantageous terms of peace—had been compelled to withdraw from power six months before: and to the ignorant or feeble hands which continued to hold the reins of government, much of the future, as well as the then existing blunders in the policy of the Crown—at least, so far as America was concerned—may safely be attributed, (see note following.)

★★★★★★

Hist. of Eng. from Peace of Utrecht, &c. So keenly was their disgrace felt by the English, that Charles Edward himself, then residing at Paris, could not view it without indignation. "If ever I ascend the throne of my ancestors," he exclaimed, "Europe shall see me use my utmost endeavours to force France, in her

9

turn, to send hostages to England."

★★★★★★

Certainly, no one versed in the political secrets of the day could, by any possibility, have believed that this peace was to be a lasting one. It was deficient in every element of coherence. Nothing was settled by the treaty: conquests all over the world were to be mutually restored; some trifling shiftings of territorial proprietorship on the part of the Italian and other minor princes engaged in the war were agreed upon; a few other articles, relative to European affairs, of little or no consequence in proportion to the cost at which they were effected, were inserted; and the treaty of Utrecht, as well as all former treaties, confirmed in existence. In short, matters were essentially placed *in statu quo ante bellum*, at a cost to England of £110,000,000.

But there were two circumstances, connected with the treaty of Aix-la-Chapelle, galling in the last degree to British pride and British interest: these were the surrender of Cape Breton to its former possessors, and the delivery of hostages until that was done. Accordingly, whilst the Earl of Sussex and Lord Cathcart awaited, at Paris, in easy but dishonourable captivity, the tardy messengers whose return should announce that once more the lilies were planted upon the bastions of Louisbourg, there glowed in the breast of every true Briton the burning embers of mortified vanity, the but half-smothered lust of fierce revenge. From the throng of Hanoverian favourites around their alienigenate king, down to the hardy New England fisherman who trimmed his light sail as he glided within sight of that apple of the American eye, curses both loud and deep were vented against the degrading terms they had submitted to. They had suffered not only disgrace and dishonour, but infinite loss; and they anxiously awaited the hour of vengeance. That hour was not fated to be long delayed.

It has been observed, that the treaty of 1748 left England in a state of mind but too ready to seize, with avidity, upon the first pretext for bettering its condition, and restoring to itself those rights which it had unjustly periled in that compact. Unfortunately for the peace of humanity, circumstances not so weak as to be considered mere pretexts, soon presented themselves, to provoke a renewal of the strife. It is, perhaps, not very expedient to go back to the ultimate causes of the war, and tracing their progress, event by event, finally, after the fashion of an inverted pyramid, taper this narrative down to the story of the single battle by which its epiphany was signalised. But a few brief comments upon the immediate and most glaring inducements

10

to a contest so important in its conduct, so momentous in its results, may not be out of place.

If ever there was a just cause of war, England had it in 1755. By the treaty of October, 1748, (Art. III.,) that of Utrecht (1713), and numerous others, were recognised and confirmed in all their parts; save, of course, such as might be modified by the pact in question—and were formally constituted its basis. By the treaty of Utrecht (Art. XII.,) "all Nova Scotia or Acadia, with its ancient limits, and all its dependencies, was ceded to the crown of Great Britain;" and, furthermore, it was provided (Art. XV.,) that "the subjects of France, inhabitants of Canada and elsewhere, should not disturb or molest in any manner whatever the five Indian nations which are subject to Great Britain, nor its other American allies." These articles were certainly incorporated into the treaty of Aix-la-Chapelle; but with neither stipulation were the French willing to comply.

The last clause would evidently always open to Great Britain a *casus belli;* for it was impossible for a year at a time to pass by without some troubles between the Iroquois and their Canadian neighbours; and in such cases each party, on the showing of the other, is inevitably the aggressor. But the provision respecting Nova Scotia was widely different. The restoration of Louisbourg, as matters then stood, was a point of equal importance to the settlers in Canada and the colonists of New England. Under its ancient lords, this nursing-mother of privateers would be powerful alike to preserve the French, and to destroy the English trade and fisheries in that part of the world. The annoyance, therefore, of the New England people was extreme and well founded; and at their earnest representations, the Home Government was finally instigated to adopt the only practical method left of peaceably dissipating the dangers with which they were threatened by the constantly increasing power and malignity of the French.

The armed occupation and settlement of the province of Nova Scotia, till then unnoticed or disregarded by the Ministry, became now a subject of consideration. In the spring of 1748, and during that and the ensuing year, several thousand colonists were sent thither by the government, at an expense of £70,000, and the town of Halifax was founded. But the French, who had hitherto evaded or disingenuously dallied with their obligations to yield up the peninsula—suppressing, wherever they could, the settlements of the English there, and constantly increasing their own strength by reinforcements—now openly resisted, under M. de la Corne, the progress of their rivals.

Thus, commenced that scene of constant dissension and strife which ensued between the original settlers, scattered over the land, and the subjects of the crown to which it lawfully pertained; whose melancholy termination was that enforced expatriation which posterity has consecrated to sorrow in the pages of Evangeline. That the Court of Versailles, through its subordinate officers, promoted and encouraged the sturdy denial of British sovereignty by these loyal-hearted Acadians, cannot at this day be doubted or denied; but the result of such a course was as fatal to the fair fame of the conquerors, as to the happiness of the conquered.

Nor did the French Government confine itself to an unavowed but well-supported resistance to the progress of Anglo-American power in the north only. Thirty years before, its grand scheme for uniting its colonies, from the Gulf of Mexico to the Bay of Fundy, by a chain of posts along the Mississippi, the Ohio, and the lakes, had begun to be tangibly developed: ever bent upon the fulfilment of these cherished ideas, already its encroaching grasp was extended, with many ramifications, from Canada to the Lower Mississippi. In 1731, Crown Point was unlawfully erected by the French within the limits of the Five Nations, and of New York: Niagara had been seized on in 1720. In truth, their policy seemed both rational and feasible. During a large portion of the year, the natural outlets of Canada were effectually sealed by the angry elements: supplies of troops or provisions—in fact, almost every intercourse whatever with Europe—were utterly shut out from its ports.

The facility of water communication between Canada and New Orleans, by the lakes and rivers of the West would, if made properly available, not only facilitate the secure transmission of supplies, but would inevitably throw the whole peltry trade of those regions into the hands of the French. It is no wonder, then, that they were desirous of procuring so manifest an advantage; but, unhappily for themselves, they grasped at too much, and lost the whole. Like the dog in the fable, they sacrificed not only the hoped-for gain, but all their present good, in the endeavour. (That the designs of the French were perfectly comprehended in the English colonies, is abundantly proved by Gov. Shirley's letter to Gov. Hamilton, of March 4th, 1754, printed in the Minutes of the Provincial Council of Pennsylvania, Vol. 6.)

To have opened a communication between their widely-separated establishments, by the way of the western lakes and the Illinois, would have been a comparatively safe, and by far the wiser mode of procedure for the French, under the circumstances of their position. So far as its ostensible objects were concerned, it would have perfectly answered the purpose, and the trade it would secure would have been prodigious: nor could the English, everything considered, have made any very effectual opposition. But to adopt this route would have left too wide a margin for British enterprise. The warlike tribes seated between the Illinois and the Alleghanies—the Inroad lands watered by the Muskingum, the Scioto, and other kindred streams, by whose marge arose the bark lodges of the Shawanoes and the Delawares—the gloomy forests, where—

Beneath the shade of melancholy boughs,

—the Six Nations wandered on their distant hunting-parties—these would have still remained open to the visits—subjected to the influence of their hated rivals. The notion of occupying the head-waters of the Ohio, and of planting a line of forts from Lake Erie, by the Le Boeuf, to the Alleghany, and thence down the Ohio to the Mississippi, was a more dangerous but a more fascinating vision. Its execution would probably be fraught with much hazard, but its results, if successful, were too precious to suffer the powers that were to resist the temptation. Out of the nettle danger they hoped to pluck the flower safety; and, at one time, it really seemed as though all their an-ticipations were to have been crowned with success. But the wisdom of Almighty Providence had ordered the event otherwise.

In an evil hour, then, for themselves, the French decided to persevere in the latter plan. While the Appallachian chain, it was thought, would serve at the same time as a bulwark against the British colonies, and as a well-marked and palpable boundary between the two nations, the whole body of the Western Indians would be thrown completely under their control. Already game had begun to be scarce, or to disappear ut-terly, east of the mountains, and the best furs were to be found upon the further side. With forts and trading-houses once established in their midst, it would not be difficult to prevent the savages from supplying the English dealers or receiving in turn their commodities. The peltry traffic, so profitable to European commerce, had already to be pursued on the frontiers; and it was not probable that the Indians would go thither to seek no better market than they could find at home.

The certain consequences, too, of thus virtually monopolizing the right to buy and sell with the savages, would be to secure, beyond a peradventure, their services against the English, in any difficulty that might occur. There is nothing the American aborigine learns more quickly than to abandon his rude native weapons of the chase—the bow or the flint-headed spear—for the fusil and gunpowder of the whites; and having become thus dependent on his neighbours for the means of subsistence, it has never been found difficult to point out other and less innocent employment for his arms. By thus building up a mighty power behind the English settlements, they would not only be in a position to terribly annoy, if not to entirely overcome them, in the event of war, but also to clog and embarrass their prosperity during time of peace.

A very great staple of that commerce which made America so valuable to Great Britain being utterly destroyed, its domestic increase, its foreign influence, would be materially affected. The agricultural productions of the colonies would likewise be touched; for, with the constant necessity, through an imminent danger, there must likewise be the constant presence of a portion of the population in arms; and thus, the tobacco plantations and the fields of maize would miss a master's hand and yield a diminished crop. It is unnecessary to consider here how many millions of money were yearly employed at this period in the trade between the mother country and her colonies—to how many thousands of souls it gave a support: nothing can be more evident than that such an attack upon the productiveness of the one must at once affect their value to the other, and thus render them, day by day, less important, and less self-capable of preservation. In short, as was well said in the House of Commons, the French held the colonies within their range of posts as in the two ends of a net, which, if tightened by degrees, would get them all into the body of it, and then drown them in the sea. (I. Entick, *The Contest in America between Great Britain and France.*)

It will be recollected, that for a long period the undefined western limits of the two English colonies of Pennsylvania and Virginia had occasioned much controversy and had induced considerable ill-feeling between those provinces. Their claims were conflicting; and no authorized power had yet reconciled their demands and assigned to each sovereignty final and determinate territorial bounds. So long, therefore, as the question remained open, and the precise confines of either province unestablished, it was impossible for settlers to know from which government they could procure a good title. For this reason, chiefly, the lands lying west of the Alleghanies, and upon the streams which unite to form the Ohio, had remained unvisited by any other Englishmen than the few traders who found their annual profit in selling to the savages in the neighbourhood of their homes.

To perplex matters still more, the associates known as the Ohio Company obtained, in 1749, a vague grant from the crown, vesting in them vast but undefined tracts of land bordering on, if not actually embracing, the very territory in dispute between Virginia, and Pennsylvania.

******

Perhaps the influence with the ministry of John Sargent, Thomas Walpole, and the other associates of the Ohio Company, whose prospects were entirely subverted by the presence of the French, may have contributed more powerfully than any other cause to the expedition against Fort Du Quesne.

******

All these circumstances combined to render more easy of execution the manoeuvres of the French in regard to the occupation of the forks of the Ohio, and they were availed of without delay. The history of their first settlement in that vicinity; of the unsuccessful mission of Washington to procure their departure; of the consequent collision that ensued between the two parties; and the English defeat at Fort Necessity; are prominent passages in history. It is from these occurrences that we are to date the original conception, the organisation and execution, and the disastrous results, of the expedition commanded by Major-General Braddock.

It is very true, that at the period in question both colonies claimed that the lands comprehended within the forks of the Ohio were included in their patents: yet, nevertheless, nothing can be more certain than that it rightfully appertained to neither Pennsylvania nor Virginia. The original patent, from James I. to the London and Plymouth Companies, which was relied upon by Virginia, had been legally overturned on a *quo warranto* in 1623.; and the tacit acquiescence of those companies in the grant of Maryland to Lord Baltimore by Charles I, in 1632, was considered to have barred their right to open the case anew, after the interval of an hundred years. The charter from the crown to William Penn, in 1681, would appear to cover the whole territory in dispute; but, hitherto, the proprietaries, to whom alone belonged the power of purchasing the soil from the Indians, had not come to any terms with their dusky neighbours.

The land, in fact, belonged absolutely to its savage inhabitants; and the utmost the province of Pennsylvania could claim was the exclusive right of purchasing it from them. Nor had the French any better title:

perhaps, if the comity of Christian nations were to be taken into the account, none so good. Thus, whatever it might be alleged, neither crown had as yet any right to the country west of the Alleghanies. But that was of small consideration: a block-house once established, and a garrison maintained thereon some specious pretext; a judicious distribution of red ochre, gewgaws, fire-arms, and rum; and it would be easy enough to get an absolute title from the Indians.

★★★★★★

Horace Walpole sneeringly dwells on the methods by which England and France seated themselves in America. "They enslaved, or assisted the wretched nations to butcher one another," says he, "instructed them in the use of fire-arms, brandy, and the New Testament, and at last, by scattered extension of forts and colonies, they have met to quarrel for the boundaries of empires, of which they can neither use nor occupy a twentieth part of the included territory." (I. *Mem. Geo. II.*, 343.) But "*we do not massacre,*" he adds, "we are such good Christians as only to cheat!" (III. *Corresp.* 136.)

★★★★★★

This was the end of the French, who were not disposed to admit any English pretensions that conflicted with their own interests. When, therefore, in 1752, on the first alarm of the threatened invasion of these regions, the Penns instructed their lieutenant-governor to lend all aid in his power to Governor Dinwiddie of Virginia, in the erection of a fortress that might thwart their designs, it was also provided that no rights of the proprietaries should be prejudiced thereby. Two years later, when there was actual likelihood of such a fortress being erected, and Dinwiddie had issued his proclamation, granting away two hundred thousand acres of the soil upon part of which Pittsburg now stands, a correspondence ensued between the two governments, in which that of Virginia, while denying the fact of the forks of the Ohio being within the jurisdiction of Pennsylvania, very honestly conceded that if on investigation this should prove to be the case, the rights of that colony should not be at all impaired.

★★★★★★

Minutes of Provincial Council of Pennsylvania, Vol. VI., I. Olden Time. I am happy in joining my testimony with that of Mr. Francis Parkman (Conspiracy of Pontiac), as to the extreme value of Mr. Craig's labours in regard to the earlier settlements beyond the Alleghanies. So far, in particular, as relates to Western Pennsylvania, his collections are worthy of much praise.

★★★★★★

Previously, however, to the actual occupation of this region, the French had been gradually strengthening their hands and drawing closer their lines in that quarter. Their scattered posts upon the Mississippi, though few in number and wide apart, gave them the command of that stream; and they had already a fortified establishment upon the Ohio, at the mouth of the Wabash River. In 1745, the Marquis de la Galissonière was appointed Governor-General of Canada. Penetrated at once with the immense advantage that would result from an arrangement that should not only open the communication of Canada with the mother country during those seasons when all its natural outlets were closed by ice and frost but would likewise restrain and cripple the English colonies upon the continent, he spared no toil to mature and put into shape the needful elements of its organisation.

It was he who, in 1748, despatched Bienville de Celoron, with three hundred men, on a tour of inspection along the Alleghany and the Ohio, depositing in various quarters leaden plates on which were inscribed a memorial of his master's title to those countries, and warning the English traders whom he encountered, that henceforth they were prohibited from visiting the Indians there. (I. *Olden Time*, II. *Histoire du Canada, par* F. X. Garneau, Craig's *Hist, of Pittsburg*.)

In 1750, by command of his successor, the Marquis de la Jonquière, harsher measures were resorted to. A body of troops under Joncaire visited the Ohio country, seizing the property and persons of such English traders as they found there. The former they confiscated; the latter they sent prisoners to France.

★★★★★★

Vide Lord Albemarle's letter to Lord Holdernesse, respecting the case of John Patton, Luke Irwin, and Thomas Bourke. I. Entick. The Marquis de la Jonquière arrived in Canada in August, 1749; and acting under positive instructions from his court, faithfully pursued the policy of his predecessor in regard to shutting out the English from the Ohio. Descended of a Catalonian family, he was born in Languedoc, in 1696; and died at Quebec, May 17th, 1752. He was a man of superb presence and undaunted resolution; but, withal, prone to avarice. His whole career gave abundant evidence of his courage and soldier-like bravery: but the world ridiculed the passion that induced him, on his dying bed, to begrudge the cost of wax candles while his

17

coffers were overflowing with millions of money. He enjoyed little peace towards the conclusion of his life, by occasion of his efforts to suppress the order of Jesuits in his government; and, indeed, this dispute is supposed to have shortened his days. (II. Garneau.)

★★★★★★

These scenes were the commencement of a tedious and unresulting diplomatic correspondence between the Earl of Albemarle, His Britannic Majesty's Ambassador at the Court of Versailles, and the French authorities, which was prolonged without intermission upon either side of St. George's channel, until the capture of the Alcide and the Lis, by Boscawen's fleet, compelled the Duc de Mirepoix to demand his passport, and war was openly waged.

★★★★★★

Roland-Michel Barrin, Marquis de la Galissonière, and a Lieutenant-General in the French service, was one of the ablest men of his time. As a scholar, a soldier, a statesman, his merit was deservedly esteemed. Born at Rochefort, Nov. 11, 1693, he entered the navy in 1710, in which he served with distinction until he was appointed to Canada. In that colony, his conduct was eminently conducive to the best interests of both the king and his people. The Swedish traveller, Du Kalm, bears abundant testimony to his scientific acquirements; while even his meagre appearance and deformed person added to his influence over the savages. "He must have a mighty soul," they said; "since, with such a base body, our Great Father has sent him such a distance to command us."

De la Galissonière did not remain in America long enough to carry out the course he had begun: he returned to France in 1749, where he was placed at the head of the department of nautical charts. He is best known in English history by his affair with the unfortunate Byng, in 1756, which resulted in the judicial murder of that excellent officer, in order thereby to screen the criminal derelictions of his superiors. He died at Nemours, Oct. 26, 1756, full of glory and honour, and loudly regretted by Louis XV., who was so sensible of his worth, that he had reserved for him the baton of a Marshal of France. *Biog. Univ.* (ed. 1816), Vol. XVI.

★★★★★★

In 1752, arrived in Canada, (to which government he had been appointed by the king on the recommendation of M. de la Galis-sonière), the Marquis de Duquesne de Monneville, a name destined to become indelibly impressed upon the history of that land whence the golden lilies of his nation, though watered by the best blood alike of friend and foe, were so soon to be extirpated. All of his antecedents that can be mentioned here are that he was a captain in the Royal Marines, and born of the blood of Abraham Duquesne, the famous admiral of Louis XIV. His abilities were good; and during his brief career he acquitted himself thoroughly of the duties of his position; but the haughtiness of his character, and the lack of affability in his manners, prevented his ever attaining any great degree of popularity with the Canadians. Nevertheless, he seems to have been possessed of some singularly generous dispositions.

In October, 1754, an English woman, nineteen years of age, ar-rived in Philadelphia from Quebec. Twelve years before, while yet almost an infant, she had been captured by the savages, and by them sold as a slave in Canada. In new scenes and the lapse of time, the names of her parents, the very place of her birth, had entirely passed from her memory; but she still clung to the sounds of the tongue of her native land, and dreamed of the day when she should be reunited to her unknown kindred. By some chance, her pitiful story reached the governor's ears; and, full of compassion, he at once purchased her freedom and furnished her with the means of returning to the British colonies. There she wandered from city to city, vainly publishing her narration, and seeking to discover those joys of kindred and of home that she had never known.

An act of this kind should, at any season, reflect credit upon the performer; but considering its particular occasion, when war was plainly looming in the horizon, to liberate and restore in this manner a person abundantly qualified to reveal so much of the local secrets of Quebec, must clothe the character of M. de Duquesne with the attri-bute of magnanimity, as well as of generosity, (*Penn. Gaz.*, No. 1319.) In the latter part of 1754, however, he demanded his recall by the gov-ernment, in order to return to the naval service, and to encounter the enemy upon a more familiar element. It will be sufficient in this place to add, that his instructions while in Canada, in regard to the Ohio, were of a piece with those of La Jonquière and Galissonière, and that he faithfully obeyed them.

★★★★★★

II. Garneau, liv. viii., c. 3. I have been not a little indebted to this valuable work (2nd ed. Quebec, 1852: three vols. 8vo.), which, indeed, is the best history extant of Canada from the earliest period to the present time. In particular, I have occasionally found notices of the history of individuals that I know not where else to look for. It is to be hoped that the new edition of the *Biographie Universelle*, now being published at Paris by Didot, will, in respect to the lives of French worthies, at least, be more particular than that which it is designed to supplant. It is unjust to the past age, that the names of such men as Duquesne, Dumas and Coutrecoeur, should be consigned to oblivion. Thus, we are left in ignorance of the period of Duquesne's death, and of all save a single circumstance in his later career. In 1758, M. Duquesne, being in France, was appointed to the command of all the forces, sea and land, in North America.

In March he sailed from Toulon, in command of a small squadron, which, however, was utterly discomfited by the English. His own ship, the *Foudroyant*, of 81 guns and one thousand men, was engaged, after a long chase in which their comrades had been almost lost sight of, by the *Monmouth*, Captain Gardiner, of 61 guns and 170 men. Captain Gardiner had served under the murdered Byng in the Mediterranean, and the combat was a compulsory one with him. On the eve of sailing on this cruise, whence he was never to return, he mentioned to his friends that there was something which weighed heavily on his soul; that Lord A—— had recently said to him, that he was one of the men who had brought disgrace upon the nation; and he was convinced that in this very voyage he should have an opportunity of testifying to his lordship the rate at which he estimated the national honour.

As his ship was going into action, he made a brief address to his crew: "That ship must be taken: she looks to be above our match, but Englishmen arc not to mind that; nor will I quit her while this ship can swim, or I have a soul left alive!" Accordingly, he closed with the *Foudroyant*, and lay on her quarter within pistol-shot for several hours, till her flag came down. Shot through the head, and death inevitable, he still retained comprehension enough to say to his first-lieutenant, that "the last favour he could ask of him was, never to give up the ship!" That gentleman pledged himself that he never would; and nailing the flag to the staff, he stood by it during the contest with a brace of pistols, resolved to slay the first man, friend or foe, who approached to pull it down. A more gallant or hardly-contested sea-fight than that of the *Monmouth* and *Foudroyant* was never fought.

★★★★★★

In January, 1753, four traders on the Kantucqui River, near the Ohio, were captured by a party of Caughnawagas, or French Indians from Canada, who divided their goods, to the value of several hundred pounds, among themselves. This was undoubtedly done in pursuance of instructions from Quebec. The captives were carried as slaves to Canada, where they remained until the summer of the succeeding year; their new lords refusing to suffer them to be ransomed under the price of a negro slave for each. The province of Pennsylvania at last, however, succeeded in purchasing their freedom for the sum of seventy-five pounds sterling; a rate which gave such umbrage to Ononraguiete, the chief *sachem* of the tribe, that he wrote a furious letter to the Indian Commissioner, declaring that for the future he should cause all prisoners to be murdered, since no higher ransom was to be paid for them. (*Penn. Gazette*, No. 1338. VI. *Col. Rec.*, 129.)

It was under the administration of Duquesne that the first steps were taken towards an armed occupation of the Ohio. It must not be forgotten, in referring to these proceedings, that so far as involved his duty to the king his master, and his interpretation of that sovereign's rights, his conduct was perfectly justifiable throughout. Though neither power possessed the least claim in justice to that territory, France as well as England had not hesitated during many years to refer to it as their absolute inheritance, and virtually to utterly ignore any title in its original occupants to the sovereignty of the soil.

No treaty with the Indians inhabiting it had ever been made, by which, even for the poor pittance of a few strings of beads or barrels of whiskey, they had ceded it to the stranger. It is true that the French assured them that their only object was to found trading-posts; that they had no idea of cutting down the woods, and tilling the fields, after the fashion of the English.

★★★★★★

Shortly before quitting his government, Duquesne held a secret conference with the deputies of the Six Nations, at Montreal, in which he reproached them with their willingness to surrender the control of the Ohio to the English rather than to the French. "Are you ignorant," said he, "of the difference between

21

the King of France and the English? Look at the forts which the king has built; you will find that under the very shadow of their walls, the beasts of the forest are hunted and slain; that they are, in fact, fixed in the places most frequented by you merely to gratify more conveniently your necessities. The English, on the contrary, no sooner occupy a post, than the woods fall before their hand—the earth is subjected to cultivation—the game disappears—and your people are speedily reduced to combat with starvation." In this speech, as M. Garneau well observes, the marquis has accurately stated the progress of the two civilizations.

★★★★★★

The savage was not to be thus gulled; and he viewed their first encroachments with as great repugnance as he did the more flagrant advances of the British, who boldly penetrated into the most secret recesses of his hunting-grounds, laying out the lines of a future settlement without the least form of a purchase from its outraged inhabitants. (Sparks' *Life of George Washington;* II. Garneau.) Nevertheless, regardless of the Indian title, the King of France had, so early as 1712, granted the district watered by the River Wabash in his letters patent creating the colony of Louisiana; and following the explorations of La Salle in 1679, had furthermore added all the streams flowing into the Mississippi that were known to this discoverer. This liberality was well matched by some of the English patents, which were bounded by the Atlantic Ocean on the east, and on the west by the Pacific.

It costs little to a monarch to be generous in this style; and no pope or king in Europe was backward in thus gratifying the importunities of his subjects. But when a nation undertakes to enforce such grants of a foreign soil, it behoves it to sagely consider whether, in so doing, the interests of its neighbour may not be threatened. This was precisely the case here: the English, whose claim was, where both were bad, no better than that of the French, saw, or thought they saw, in its fulfilment, the ruin of all that they then lawfully and actually held, and with wisdom resolved to oppose such a consummation.

★★★★★★

Governor Shirley of Massachusetts, whose opinion on such points must have weighed greatly with the people, frankly declared, in his letter to Governor Hamilton of Pennsylvania (March 4th, 1754), that the language of King James the First, in the patents of the London and Plymouth Companies, was "the only rule for the English Governors to judge of the limits of the colonies under their respective governments, in all disputes with the French Governors concerning the extent of His Majestie's territories upon this Continent, except in cases where the original limits declared in these Letters Patent may be altered by treaty or other agreement between the two Crowns; and those Patents extend the English territories within the 32nd and 48th degrees of northerly latitude, quite across this Continent, *viz.*: from the Atlantic Ocean to the South Sea; and I can't find that these eastern or western limits have been abridged by any treaty." *vide* Penn. *Col. Rec,* Vol. VI. Mr. Shirley had lately been acting at Paris as one of the British Commission to define the boundaries of Acadia and New England.

★★★★★★

Strong in all the resources of civil and military centralization, the government of Canada moved with a resolution and celerity that, for the time, set at defiance the efforts of their slow-footed and divided adversaries. By the end of 1753, a connected line of forts existed, extending from Montreal to what is now called French creek, in Pennsylvania, but which was named by the French the Rivière aux Boeufs, on account of the numbers of buffalo that were found in its vicinity. (Sparks' *Washington.*) The nationality of its first European settlers soon caused it to receive another title.

It was to this fort that in December, 1753, Major Washington repaired on a fruitless mission from the Governor of Virginia, to warn the trespassers to retire; and here it was that he observed the extensive preparations they had made for still further encroachments in the ensuing spring. (Sparks' *Washington.*) Fifty birchen canoes, and one hundred and seventy of pine, were, at that early stage of the winter, drawn up on the shore, ready for the opening of the streams; and numerous others were in progress of completion. In these the troops were to be floated down Le Boeuf and the Alleghany, on their way to the Ohio. For though but some six or seven hundred, of the expedition of two thousand men who had been sent in the preceding autumn to erect these posts, remained in garrison there during the winter, it was already settled that a large body was to arrive in the spring for the further operations alluded to.

The private scandal of the place and period attributed the building of these establishments and their dark train of consequent calamities to the same cause as had since long before the day of Helen of Troy, according to Flaccus, brought about the waste of human life and the overthrow of mighty empires. M. Pouchot, an officer of rank in Canada, does not scruple to insinuate that the new governor, shortly after his arrival in Quebec, became involved in an intrigue with a beautiful woman, the wife of a resident of that place. M. Bigot, who had recently passed from the Intendancy of Louisbourg to that of Canada, had in like manner contracted a liaison with a Madame Péan, the wife of the *aide-major* of the city.

Bigot being thus at the head of the commissary department of the colony, it was an easy affair for the governor and himself to arrange a plan by which the willing husbands of the ladies in question should be detached from an inconvenient vicinity to their partners. Accordingly, it was decided to give them lucrative employments in an expedition which, it was gravely whispered, was concocted for the express purpose of placing these gentlemen at a considerable distance from home; and to Péan was assigned the command of the forces which were marched in 1753.

The forts then built were furnished with numerous and expensive magazines of merchandise and provisions; a precaution necessary enough under the circumstances of their position, but which, in the manner in which the business was managed, must have afforded endless opportunities for the acquirement of ill-gotten gains. Together with the proper provisions and stores, all sorts of goods, always expensive, but here utterly useless, were purchased in the name of Louis XV., and sent, for his service, into the wilderness. Stuffs of silk and velvet, ladies' slippers and damask shoes, silk stockings, and the costly wines of Spain, figure largely in the category, and enable us to conceive how it came about that the French colonies cost the nation so much and returned it so little.

★★★★★★

In 1753, the exports of Canada amounted to but £68,000; its imports were £208,000, of which a great portion was on the government account, and did not enter into the ordinary channels of trade. The exports of the English provinces during the same year were £1,486,000; their imports, £983,000. In 1755, the Canadian imports were 5,203,272 *livres*; its exports but 1,515,730. And while the population of British America was 1,200,000 souls, that of all Canada, Cape Breton, and Louisiana, could not have exceeded 80,000. The policy of sustaining such a colony at such a cost was thus doubted by the most brilliant if not the profoundest writer of the day:

"*Le Canada coûtait beaucoup et rapportait très peu. Si la dixième partie de l'argent englouti dans cette colonic avait été employé à défricher nos terres incultes en France, on aurait fait un gain considérable; mais on avait voulu soutenir le Canada, et on à perdu cent années de peines avec tout l'argent prodigués sans retour. Pour comble de malheur on accusait des plus horrible brigandages presque tons ceux qui étaient employés au nom du Roi dans cette malheureuse colonie.*"

("Canada cost a lot and did not pay much. If the tenth part of the money engulfed in this colony had been used to clear our uncultivated lands in France, we would have made a considerable gain; but we had wanted to support Canada, and we lost a hundred years of punishment with all the money lavished on our return. To make matters worse, the most horrible robbers were accused of almost all those who were employed in the name of the king in this unfortunate colony.")
—*Voltaire.*

★★★★★★

In fact, it would seem that the colonial stewards of the king were not unfrequently but too wont to look upon their office in no other light than as a source of revenue to themselves; and when, like Uriah the Hittite, the lords and masters of these new Bath-shebas were sent down to the host, they doubtless felt no compunction in making their absence as remunerative to themselves as possible. From Pouchot's position and character, it is not unjust to admit the truth of the facts upon which he bases his conclusions: but ignorant as, from the very nature of his subordinate rank, he must have been of the state arrangements and politic designs of the former governors and the Court of Versailles, it is easy to perceive how erroneous were his inferences. It may be true enough that the husband of each fair Evadne was named to a high command in the new expedition, but nothing can be more absurd than to imagine that to procure their absence was the primary motive to its undertaking.

★★★★★★

Mémoires sur la Dernière Guerre de l'Amérique Septentrionale, par M. Pouchot. (Yverdon, 1781), Vol. 1. These two volumes contain much curious and authentic information respecting the subject to which they relate. The author was born at Grenoble, in 1712, and at the age of twenty-two was an officer in the regiment of Béarn. His talents as an engineer, cultivated under such masters as Vauban and Cohorn, early pointed him out to favourable notice, and in season he acquired a captaincy in that regiment, and was created a knight of St. Louis. He came to America on the breaking out of the war of 1755 and gained much honor by the part he took therein, particularly in the defence of Forts Niagara and Levis, where he was in command. He was slain in Corsica, 8th May, 1769, during the warfare between the French and the natives of the island His memoirs, prepared by himself for publication, did not see the light for several years after his death. They are accompanied with explanatory notes, apparently by a well-informed hand. My opinion of their value is confirmed by that of M. Garneau.

★★★★★★

Forts in the Wilderness

It must not be supposed that the detachment ordered to Lake Erie and the new forts by Duquesne consisted entirely of regular troops. There were, at that time, probably not more than one thousand regular soldiers in all Canada. But an exceedingly well-organised militia, and the hardy, active, semi-Indian class, half-trappers, half-traders, who dwelt on the outskirts of French civilization, furnished material for any enterprise involving war or adventure. Woodsmen by education, full of courage and vivacity by birth, they formed an admirable band for such ends as they were now engaged in. To this day, the *coureurs des bois* are of the primest favourites of the Indians, with whom they intermarry and assimilate, and at whom they "never laugh:" they were, therefore, just the men required for a business that must depend for success mainly on the goodwill of the savages. (Schoolcraft: *Red Races of America*.)

Returning to Williamsburgh from his bootless errand on the 16th of January, 1754, Washington made his report to the Governor of Virginia; when it was instantly resolved, in compliance with the king's directions, to fit out an expedition which should proceed with all haste to the confluence of the Alleghany and the Monongahela, where the Ohio Company had already commenced to build a fortified trading-house, and there to erect such works as might, for the season, prevent any further enterprise on the part of the French. For this object, the Assembly of Virginia voted the sum of £10,000, and the party was put under the control of Colonel Joshua Frey, who, dying on the 31st

26

of May, was succeeded in office by Washington, the second in command. His instructions were to capture, kill, or destroy all persons who should endeavour to impede his operations. Aid was also requested from the neighbouring provinces; but none seems to have reached Virginia in time; and she is thus entitled to the honor of having single-handed first entered the lists against France, to struggle for the mastery of the continent.

******

Mr. Wheeler, in his *History of North Carolina* (Vol. 1), states that in compliance with Gov. Dinwiddie's request, the president of that province "issued his proclamation for the legislature to assemble at Wilmington on the 19th February, 1754; who met and appropriated £1000 to the raising and paying such troops as might be raised to send to the aid of Virginia. Col. James Innes of New Hanover marched at the head of a detachment, and joined the troops raised by Virginia and Maryland. But there being no provision made by Virginia for supplies or conveniences, the expedition was countermanded, and Col. Innes returned with his men to North Carolina."

Besides these North Carolina troops, three of the king's Independent Companies, two from New York and one from Carolina, had been ordered to Virginia. As they were paid by the king, but retained in the colonies for local protection, it was usual for the provinces to contribute to their victualling expenses on any extraordinary service in which they might be employed; which Virginia, on this occasion, refused to do. II. *Penn. Archives.*

******

The little army with which the beginning of all this was to be accomplished, was to consist of but four hundred men. In January, 1754, William Trent was commissioned to enlist one hundred; he succeeded in raising but seventy, with whom he instantly marched for the Ohio: the remaining three hundred were not raised so soon. They were furnished with ten cannon and eighty barrels of powder, and would, it was hoped, have succeeded in throwing up a couple of forts before the arrival of the French. If that were found impossible. Governor Dinwiddie looked to their attacking and destroying the enemy by a *coup de main.*

******

The cannon sent towards the Ohio were four-pounders, selected from thirty pieces presented by the king to his colony of Virginia. They went from Alexandria to Will's Creek, and thence in wagons. Small arms and accoutrements were also provided by Dinwiddie; with thirty tents and six months' provision of flour, pork, and beef. The uniform was a red coat and breeches; and a half-pint of rum *per diem* was allowed each man. The pay was as follows: To a colonel, 15*s. per diem*—to a lieutenant-colonel, 12*s.* 6*d*; a major, 10*s.*; a captain, 8*s.*; a lieutenant, 4*s.*; an ensign, 3*s.* The privates received 8*d. per diem* and a pistole bounty. *Vide* Dinwiddie's letter, in VI. Penn. *Col. Rec.*

★★★★★★

In the meanwhile, however, the French had not been idle. Nearly a year before, in the spring of 1753, they had built, at Presqu'-Isle on Lake Erie, a strong fort of chestnut logs, fifteen feet high, and one hundred and twenty feet square, with a block-house on each side. Leaving a strong garrison here, they marched to the Rivière aux Boeufs, where they erected another fort, cutting a wagon-road, twenty-one feet in width, between it and that at Presqu'-Isle. Pie re garrisons were maintained during the winter of 1753-4, and here strong reinforcements from Canada were directed to rendezvous in the spring of 1754, fully prepared to march to and occupy the head of the Ohio. (VI. *Col. Rec.*)

★★★★★★

It is possible that the French had some sort of an establishment at Presqu'-Isle so early as 1749; the ruins of the fort of 1753 are still perceptible within the limits of the town of Erie. It was provided with bastions, a well and a ditch; and was the headquarters of communication between Canada and the Ohio. Thirteen miles distant was the fort *de la Rivière aux Boeufs*, on the spot where now stands the village of Waterford (Erie County, Penn.). A small lake, and a stream rising from it to fall into French Creek, still preserve the memory of the long-vanished buffalo, which once fed on its fertile meadows. The last post on the route to the Ohio was on the Alleghany at the mouth of French Creek (where now is the village of Franklin), and was called Venango, being a corruption of *In-nun-gah*, the name by which the Senecas knew the latter stream. Its ruins are still to be seen. It was 400 feet square, with embankments which are yet eight feet in height, and furnished with four bastions, a large block-house, a stockade, and a ditch, seven feet deep, and fifteen wide, fed through a subterraneous channel of fifty yards by a neighboring rivulet. See Day's *Hist. Col. Penn.*

For this purpose, a corps of some 800 Canadians, under M. Marin, had been carefully raised and accoutred. Every man was amply provided with the needful equipments, while to each of the officers, naively observes an old chronicler in his enumeration of the good cheer provided for the detachment, was allotted a bottle of wine every day, two gallons of brandy a month, and food in proportion. (I. Pouchot.) Being thus prepared, M. de Contrecoeur (who succeeded in the command at French creek to Legardeur de St. Pierre, the one-eyed old warrior who had received Washington), set out betimes in the spring of 1754.

On the 17th of April, at the head of from five hundred to a thousand men, with eighteen pieces of artillery, he appeared before the incomplete and defenceless works which occupied the spot where now stands the great city of Pittsburgh. Ensign Ward, with his forty-one men, was in no condition to resist such a force. Without a struggle he was compelled to reluctantly abandon his post to the enemy and was suffered to retire unmolested to his own country. The French set at once about the strengthening and perfection of their conquest. Under the directions of Mercier, a captain in the artillery, new works were added and the former made more complete: till, by the middle of May, 1754, it was placed in a position to defy any force that could then be brought against it.

★★★★★★

On the fall of Fort Necessity, M. le Chevalier de Mercier went back to Canada, whence he was presently sent to France with an account of the campaign on the Ohio. Here his advice was much regarded at Versailles; and in 1755, he returned with Vaudreuil and Dieskau to America. His counsels were received by the latter with implicit faith, and eventually influenced Dieskau to measures which ended in his utter defeat at Lake George, 8th Sept., 1755. In August, 1756, he directed with great skill the works with which M. de Montcalm besieged Oswego, and on the surrender of that place, according to Pouchot, secreted to his own use a large share of the public property.

In March, 1757, he was sent by M. de Vaudreuil to demand the surrender of Fort William-Henry, but received a peremptory denial from Major Eyres, its governor. (*Vide* Pouchot and Mante.) This first architect of Fort Du Quesne seems to have been an accomplished officer, but a leech on the public purse.

He was probably one of that large tribe of locusts who went to Canada determined to make a fortune *quocunque modo*.

★★★★★★

Its breastworks were probably calculated to resist such small field-pieces as those which Washington had with him, as they were made in part, at least, of earth, and were two fathoms in thickness at the base. (II. Sparks' *Washington*.) A force of some eight hundred or a thousand men garrisoned the post, officered by such men as Laforce, Drouillon, de Villiers, Jumonville, Chauvignerie, de Longueil, and many others, whose names were war-cries along the border; and from Contrecoeur, who commanded the whole, it now for the first time received its title of Fort Du Quesne. (Dc Contrecoeur's summons to Ensign Ward is given at large in VI. Penn. *Col. Rec.*)

Washington was at Will's Creek when the tidings reached him of Ward's discomfiture; and acting promptly, on the same principle which had governed his mind in originally urging the very measure that was thus defeated, he was resolved to proceed to the mouth of the Red-Stone Creek, and there to erect a fortification under whose shelter he should await such things as time might bring forth. With his scanty force, it was impossible to think of the re-investment of Fort Du Quesne and its new garrison until the arrival of the reinforcements which were constantly expected; but he wished to be as near to the French as he possibly could get, and this spot offered too many advantages to be passed over. By tedious marches, and suffering under the greatest deprivations of food, raiment, and stores, he had arrived at the Great Meadow, when, on the 28th May, he encountered a detachment of thirty-five men under M. de Jumonville, sent out from Fort Du Quesne as ambassadors, as was alleged by M. de Contrecoeur, to warn him to withdraw.

Considering all that we can learn of the characters of the two French officers, and the circumstances of their position, it is to be regretted that there seems some cause to believe the truth of this story. Contrecoeur's treatment of Ward had not been in anywise treacherous or unmanly: his demeanour on other occasions seems to have been creditable and fair; and it is difficult to believe that he would have wilfully put his hand to a deliberate falsehood, to be echoed not only by all his brother officers, but throughout France and Europe. But, granting the doubtful story that Jumonville was entrusted with such a commission, he bore about him no reason to inspire Washington with the prescience of the fact.

Fort Cumberand and Will's Creek

An ambassador with thirty-five armed men at his heels in an enemy's country, with the army of his friends behind, his foe in front, and the shouts and clamour of victory still ringing through the air, was an anomalous character on that stage; and we humbly conceive that it was perfectly fair and just in Washington to defeat and destroy his party in any manner of lawful war. Certainly, no sane Englishman could have doubted Jumonville's object was other than to gain scalps or intelligence: probably it partook as much or more of the nature of both as of that of a formal embassy.

The strength of his party, and the impressions entertained of its designs by the Indians who were cognisant of its departure and brought the intelligence to the Americans—impressions, the justice of which was confirmed by the recorded testimony of officers of his own nation—these facts abundantly warranted Washington in treating him as an enemy in arms. (I. Pouchot.)

★★★★★★

Since both the French and the English have published their own stories, it is but fair to give the Indian version of this affair. At a council held at Philadelphia, in December, 1754, Scarroyaddy their leader pointedly dwelt on the efforts Jumonville had previously made to seduce him from the English (whom he was on the way to join), and how he rewarded these insidious overtures by at once informing Washington of their whereabouts, and aiding in the combat by way, as he told Washington, of "a little bloodying the edge of the hatchet."

John Davison, the interpreter, who was also in the battle, added that "there were but eight Indians, who did most of the execution that was done. Coll. Washington and the Half-King differed much in judgment, and on the colonel's refusing to take his advice, the English and Indians separated. Afterwards the Indians discovered the French in an hollow, and hid themselves, lying on their bellies behind a hill; afterwards they discovered Coll. Washington on the opposite side of the hollow in the grey of the morning, and when the English fired, which they did in great confusion, the Indians came out of their cover and closed with the French, and killed them with their tomahawks, on which the French surrendered." VI. *Col. Rec.*

★★★★★★

Washington could not but remember that Contrecoeur had but a few weeks before, by dint of superior power, ejected Ward from Fort

Assassination of Jumonville

Du Quesne (the first scene, by the way, of overt hostility in the long and bloody drama that was about to be enacted); and even at this day there is little reason to believe that he would have hesitated for one moment in the commission of any act which he supposed came within the line of his duty and the service of the king. Be this as it may, however, Washington, on the 24th of May, received notice from a friendly Indian that a secret expedition had started from Fort Du Quesne two days before, with intent to strike the first English they might see. Thus forewarned, he engaged them on the 28th, when Jumonville was slain in a manner too often detailed to need repetition here.

★★★★★★

Adam Stephen of Virginia, who served with distinction under Braddock and in the war of the Revolution, gives a contemporaneous and interesting notice of this skirmish, which seems to have escaped the notice of the historian. On May 10th, Capt. Stephen was detached with a reconnoitring party towards Fort Du Quesne, whence, his vicinity being discovered, Jumonville was despatched against him. Stephen fell back before his superior foe till he rejoined Washington, who, at 11 o'clock at night, through a heavily-pouring rain, went forth with forty men to the attack. The French were lodged in bark cabins about five miles from Washington's position; but so dark was the night, and so bewildering the storm, that it was not until four the next morning that they drew near the enemy.

Here it was found not only that seven men were lost on the journey, but that their pieces and ammunition were so wet as to be in a measure useless. They therefore charged the French with fixed bayonets, receiving their fire as they advanced, and not returning it fill they were at close quarters. Stephen adds, that three Indian men and two boys came up with the English during the battle; and that he himself made the first prisoner, capturing the Ensign M. Drouillon, "a pert fellow." *Penn. Gaz.*, No. 1343.

★★★★★★

In detailing this event to his Court, M. de Duquesne gave his own version of the affair, the correctness of which was ever denied by the English and questioned by officers of even his own army. Insomuch as he was taken by surprise, the French insisted that Jumonville's death was not only a base act, but a cowardly assassination; and for years, even down to our own times, their authors have continued to misrep-

French encampment attacked by George Washington

resent the occurrence, and to do an injustice to him who was incapable of acting unjustly to another. Chief among them was M. Thomas, an accomplished *littérateur* of the day, and a member of the Academy, who, in 1759, published his *Jumonville*, a lengthy poem in four *cantos*, in which he not only painted the death of that soldier in the most tragic colours, but traces all the subsequent misfortunes of the English to that unpardonable act. His unseen shade is made to stand beside Washington on the ramparts of Fort Necessity, freezing his blood with supernatural fear, and calling into life poetic serpents to hiss and gnaw within his breast; or gliding through the lines of his brethren, points at his bleeding wounds yet unrevenged

—and cries aloud—to battle!

Pursued thus by the inevitable sword of an avenging Nemesis, the woes of the British during the next five years—the heavy visitation of what the poet is pleased to consider retributive justice, is finely given: "*O malheureux Anglais!*" he exclaims; "Oh, wretched people!" (*Oeuvres Comp. de Thomas par* M. Saint-Surin, *tom.* V.)

★★★★★★

Mr. Sparks (II. Writings of Washington), has gone at length into the question of the death of Jumonville and has thoroughly cleared up the clouds that in some minds had obscured the morning brightness of Washington's fame. He does not notice, however, M. Pouchot's version of the affair, which is too significant to be passed over here. This writer says that Jumonville was sent with a letter summoning the English commander to retire. Being taken by surprise and finding the enemy's strength so much superior to his own, he endeavoured to show them the despatch of which he was the bearer; but they, unwilling to compromise themselves by a parley, poured in a volley, slaying Jumonville and some others.

The remainder were made prisoners. (Pouchot, Vol. I.) His editor, it is true, adds a note of dissent to the insinuation that Jumonville had any hostile intentions; but the evidence of a brother officer, whose ideas were derived from personal communications with those who were present at the fort at the time, must be received with some deference.

It is a little curious, that while the French made so much capital out of this occurrence, their version of its nature was very little considered in England. M. Thomas, for instance, opens his

Night Conference at Fort Necessity

preface with the declaration that his theme is *"l'assassinat de M. de Jumonville en Amérique, et la vengeance de ce meurtre,"* ("the assassination of Mr. de Jumonville in America, and the revenge of this murder.") During fourteen years after the event, its mere mention had not reached the ears of one of the greatest political gossips of the period in London. In July, 1768, Horace Walpole had never heard of it, and was only then in possession of the news, through the intervention of Voltaire, who had made it a subject of national reproach in his letters. (V. *Walpole's Correspondence*, ed. Lond. 1840.) It is due to a French historian, however, to add that there is an impartial account of the affair from the pen of M. Garneau. After considering the statements of either side, he says—

"Il est probable qu'il y a du vrai dans les deux versions; mais que l'attaque fut si précipitée qu'on ne put rien démêler. Washington n'avançait qu'en tremblant tant il avait pour d'être surpris, et il voulait tout prévenir même en courant le risque de combattre des fantômes. Ce n'est que de cette manière qu'on peut expliquer pourquoi Washington avec des forces si supérieures montra une si grande ardeur pour surprendre Jumonville au point du jour comme si c'eût été un ennemi fort à craindre? Au reste la mort de Jumonville n'amena pas la guerre, car déjà elle était résolue, mais elle la précipita."

("It is likely that there is truth in both versions; but that the attack was so precipitous that nothing could be disentangled. Washington was moving forward only trembling so much he had to be surprised, and he wanted to warn everything even when running the risk of fighting ghosts. Only in this way can it be explained why Washington with such superior forces showed so great a zeal to surprise Jumonville at daybreak as if it had been an enemy to be feared? Besides, the death of Jumonville did not bring the war, because already it was resolved, but it precipitated it.") II. *Hist, du Can.*

The historical statements of M. Thomas's work are ridiculously false: the only fact it contains is that Jumonville was really dead.

★★★★★★

A terrified soldier, escaping the fate of his fellows, returned to the fort with the sad tidings of Jumonville's discomfiture; and a council of war, to deliberate on what next should be done, was instantly assembled by Contrecoeur. Here the opinions of all were given in writing. The fiery Coulon-Villiers (known for his prowess as *Le Grand Villiers*), burning to avenge after the fashion of the savages his brother's death, was for violent and vindictive measures: the more safe and moderate advice of M. de Mercier prevailed. (I. Pouchot.) The desire professed on this occasion, to avoid everything which might be construed into an indefensible violation of the letter of the Treaty of Utrecht, when its spirit and meaning were already infringed by his very presence on the ground, shows how clearly the Frenchman anticipated the approaching war; and his anxiety to preserve, if not peace, at least appearances with the world. Villiers, with some six hundred men, was despatched to meet Washington, and Mercier accompanied him as second in command. (The accounts of their number vary from three to nine hundred men, besides Indians. Among the latter were many Delawares and others who had hitherto lived on terms of personal friendship with the English. *Vide* Min. Penn. Col. Council, Vol. VI.)

On the 29th of June, Washington, who was then at Gist's plantation, received intelligence of their advance; and his council of war resolved to await the attack at that spot. Entrenchments were at once undertaken; two detached parties under Captains Lewis and Polson were recalled; and an express sent to the Great Meadows to summon Captain Mackay, with the Independent Company from South Carolina. Mackay marched into camp that night, and the next morning Lewis and Polson came in. Apprised now of the enemy's overwhelming force, a second council on the 30th of June resolved, with one voice, to retreat to their former position at the Great Meadows. Two miserable teams and a few pack-horses being all their means of transporting their ammunition, the officers at once added their own steeds to the train; and, leaving half his baggage behind, Washington, for four pistoles, hired some of the soldiers to carry the remainder.

For twelve weary miles over the Alleghanies did the Virginians drag with their own hands the seven swivels that formed their park; the Independents obstinately refusing to bear any share of the burthen, whether of drawing guns, carrying ammunition, or clearing the road. On the 1st of July, the party arrived at the Great Meadows in such a state of fatigue that, unless their stores were abandoned, it was absolutely necessary for them to pause there for a few days. They had a plenty of milch-cows for beef, but no salt to cure their meat, so it was not possible to lay in a stock of salt provisions; and as for bread, though they had been eight days without it, the convoy from the settlements brought but a few bags of flour, not more than enough for five days. But learning that the two Independent Companies of New York were

George Washington and Christopher Gist

arrived at Annapolis on the 20th of June, they concluded to make a stand here, in hope of receiving a speedy reinforcement.

The spot selected for the works was well chosen; and to these rude defences was given the suggestive title of Fort Necessity. To Robert Stobo, a captain in the Virginia Regiment, the merit of being their contriver is attributable. The fort was a log breast-work 100 feet square, surrounded in part by a shallow ditch; and was commenced immediately on Washington's arrival. As day broke on the morning of the 3rd of July, the near approaches of the enemy were proclaimed by some of their scouts shooting down an English sentry; and at 11 a.m., the whole force came in sight and invested the petty fortress. Expecting to be stormed, the Independents were posted in the ditch, the Virginians being drawn up within their lines, intending to retain their fire till it was certain to take effect.

The enemy not adopting this course, however, but sheltering themselves among the trees that crowned a neighboring hill, the men were withdrawn to the cover of their works, and a dropping, desultory fire was kept up on either side during all the day. When night fell, and their ammunition (which only amounted to a handful of ball each, and powder in proportion), was nearly exhausted, the French repeatedly called a parley, which at last was listened to by the incredulous English; and a capitulation was speedily arranged. (MS. Gov. Sharpe's *Corresp.* in Md. Hist. Soc.)

To the besieged terms were proffered, not to be lightly rejected by men in their position: for two bags of flour and a little bacon now constituted all the provisions of 300 men; their guns were wet and foul, and there were but two screws in the party with which to clean them; and, to crown all, one-half the garrison was drunk. Yet even in this strait the capitulation produced by Captain Van Braam, who, being the only officer (save one who was wounded), that could speak French, was selected as his plenipotentiary, was considerably modified by Washington. The French stipulated for the surrender of the artillery and ammunition; the English insisted on retaining the one and destroying the other; and even this was acquiesced in.

★★★★★★

These guns, which were probably merely spiked and abandoned, were in later years bored out or otherwise restored to their former condition. For a long time, they lay on the Great Meadows, useless and disregarded. After the Revolution, however, when bands of settlers commenced to travel towards the

West, it was a favourite amusement to discharge these cannon: The Meadow being a usual halting-place. They were finally transported to Kentucky by some enterprising pioneers, and their subsequent fate is unknown.

★★★★★★

The cattle, etc., had already fallen into the enemy's hands. The articles of surrender, however, while they conceded all honours of war to the garrison, contained one awkward provision to which Washington unwittingly put his hand, in terms admitting that Jumonville's death was an assassination. This expression, by "the too great condescension of Van Braam," had been suffered to stand on the paper; and as his leader was compelled to take his oral version of their nature (for it was now nearly midnight, and the falling rain prevented a candle's burning more than a moment at a time), which substituted the word "death" for this odious phrase; it was not until afterwards that its real language was discovered. (II. Sparks' *Washington;* Stobo's *Memoirs*; Capt. Stephen's letter in *Penn. Gaz.*, No. 1339; Col. Innes to Gov. Hamilton, VI. *Col. Rec;* where also a correct copy of the capitulation will be found. II. *Olden Time.*)

In the meanwhile, the negotiator, Captain Jacob Van Braam, together with Captain Stobo, both Virginian officers, were given up to the enemy as pledges of the faithful performance of the articles of surrender.

★★★★★★

Robert Stobo was born at Glasgow, 1727, of respectable parentage, and was settled in Virginia as a merchant when the French troubles began in 1754. Dinwiddie giving him a company in Frey's regiment, he took an active part in Washington's campaign. It is not impossible he was one of "those raw, surly, and tyrannical Scots, several of them mere boys from behind the counters of the factors here," with whom, according to Maury (*Huguenot Family*), the governor filled the corps.

As the stipulations for which he remained a hostage were not complied with, he was, with his brother captain, Van Braam, sent from Du Quesne to Canada, but not before he had contrived to transmit a plan of its works to the English. His letters and drawings being found in Braddock's cabinet, excited no little odium against him. At last he escaped from captivity (whether with or without Van Braam is not certainly known to the writer), and after a series of romantic adventures, reached England.

His *Memoirs* were there published, a reprint of which has lately been given at Pittsburg, by Mr. Neville Craig, to whose notes the preceding remarks are due. The only remaining feature in his story that has been discovered is the fact that on June 5th, 1760, he was made a captain in the 15th Foot (Amherst's Regiment), then serving in America; which position he held as late as 1765. He was an eccentric creature; an acquaintance of David Hume and a friend of Smollett, to whom he is said to have sate for the character of the immortal Lismahago.

As for Van Braam, his career is still more obscure. Denounced as a traitor for his agency in the capitulation of Fort Necessity, it must not be forgotten that three weeks before the surrender, Washington (to whom he had served as interpreter on the mission of 1753), pronounced him "an experienced, good officer, and very worthy of the command he has enjoyed;" that he consented to going as a hostage to the French, with the certainty of his fraud being soon discovered by his own party, had he committed one; that he was detained rather as a prisoner than a hostage; and that he risked his life to return to the English.

These facts do not exculpate him from the charge of imbecility, but they are inconsistent with the assumption of his deliberate treason. In 1770, too, it would appear that he claimed and obtained his share of the Virginia bounty lands, with Washington as Commissioner; and on 14th June, 1777, was made Major of the Third Battalion of the 60th Foot, or Royal Americans, then stationed in the West Indies.

★★★★★★

On the following morning, the fourth of July, 1754, with drums beating and colours flying, the little garrison evacuated its feeble entrenchments, and sadly turned their faces homewards. Probably the memory of this day, whose return, twenty-one years after, was destined to open to him the gates of immortal fame, was for a season marked in Washington's calendar as the blackest, the most melancholy epoch of his life. His visions of future fame in the service of his native land seemed to have received a dangerous, perhaps a fatal, downfall: nor could the reflections that its immediate memory must have adduced have been of a very cheering character. In spite of the stipulation of the French commander, the Indians hung on the skirts of his diminished band, plundering the baggage, and committing a hundred annoyances and mischiefs. The medical stores they entirely destroyed;

thus, cruelly aggravating the unhappy condition of the wretches, who, sick and wounded, and without a horse to assist them, were to traverse fifty miles of inhospitable forests, ere they could reach the nearest halting-place on Will's Creek.

The number of savages, hitherto regarded as friendly to the colonies, whom he recognised enlisted under the standard of the enemy, was another source of regret. And so long as the French preserved their local superiority, he very well knew how little hope there was of these fickle people returning to their ancient friendships: nor was he blind to the unconcealed disgust at the result of the campaign of even those whose lot was immutably cast with the English.

★★★★★★

The celebrated Seneca chief Thanacrishon (better known as the Half-King), complained bitterly to Conrad Weiser of Washington's conduct.

"The Colonel," he said, "was a good-natured man, but had no experience; he took upon him to command the Indians as his slaves, and would have them every day upon the scout, and to attack the enemy by themselves, but would by no means take advice from the Indians. He lay in one place from one full moon to the other, without making any fortifications, except that little thing on the Meadow; whereas, had he taken advice, and built such fortifications as he (the Half-King) advised him, he might easily have beat off the French. But the French in the engagement acted like cowards, and the English like fools."— *Enquiry into the Causes of the Alienation of the Delaware and Shawanese Indians, &c.* (Lond. 1759).

This volume, whose rarity is greater than even its value and importance, was the work of Charles Thomson, subsequently Secretary of the Congress; but in 175G, when he prepared his material, an usher in the Quaker grammar school at Philadelphia. He writes in honest but bitter opposition to the Penns, on which account some allowances must be made in perusing his book. This Half-King, who was so free of his censure, was a pretty shrewd fellow. It was he who advised Ensign Ward, when summoned by M. de Contrecoeur to surrender his post, to reply that his rank did not invest him with sufficient power so to do, and to desire a delay until his chief commander might arrive; a suggestion which, though ineffectual in practice, argues considerable astuteness on the part of its proposer. See II.

Sparks' *Washington*.

★★★★★★

And above all other annoyances, the discovery of the unenviable and unmerited position in which Van Braam's "evil intentions or negligence" had placed his character, must have stung him to the quick. With reason, then, on the morning of Washington's departure from Fort Necessity, dark visions swam before his eyes. He saw before but the frowning forests; behind, the scene of his own and his country's defeat. "At that moment," observes Mr. Bancroft, "in the whole valley of the Mississippi to its headsprings in the Alleghanies, no standard floated but that of France," Destroying, as he says, not only the cannon surrendered by the English, but also the smaller piece reserved by the garrison as a point of military etiquette, but which it was incompetent to drag away; and knocking in the heads of the liquor-casks, to prevent a savage debauch, "the Great Villiers" departed on the same day as his adversaries, but in an opposite direction.

★★★★★★

In 1756, M. de Villiers took an active part in the capture of Oswego, (I. Garneau: I. Pouchot.) Till 1759, he would seem to have still been employed in that region, where he was one of the defenders and probably of the captives of Niagara: after which he is lost sight of. There were six brothers of the Villiers family killed in Canada during this war, fighting for France; each of whom was distinguished by some local surname. The seventh and last, also in the service, appears alone to have escaped. I. Forster's *Bossu*. From the language of M. Thomas (*Jumonv.*, ch. I.) we are at liberty to conjecture that they were natives of Old France.

★★★★★★

Gracing his triumph with the Virginia standard, which in the confusion had been left at the fort, he turned his steps toward Du Quesne, where he arrived on the 7th of July; having destroyed all the English settlements on the way and detaching also M. de la Chauvignerie for the same purpose. This circumstance in itself shows that the country had not utterly escaped the notice of colonists from the eastward, although it is more than probable that many of the houses so burned were trading-stations, or shelters recently erected for the convenience of some of Trent's or Washington's troops. On his journey, too, he encountered the place where his brother had fallen; and where mangled corpses, their skulls bare and bloody from the knife, still strewed the

45

ground with shocking memorials of that scene of slaughter.

A decent, if not a Christian burial, in earth best consecrated by the life-blood of a soldier, was bestowed upon their remains; and the grave of Jumonville is still shown to the curious traveller, who pauses, "by lonely contemplation led," to muse upon the spot where, like Philip's son, the future statesman and sage loosened the tangled web of policy with his sword; and invoking the *ultima ratio regum* to decide whether to a Guelf or a Bourbon North America should owe allegiance, the hands of the Father of his Country were for the first time steeped in human blood. (*Journal* of M. de Villiers; II. *Olden Time;* Sharp' MS. *Corresp.* The whole French and Indian loss at Fort Necessity is stated here to have been but one cadet and two privates killed and seventeen dangerously wounded.)

In the meantime, since their arrival in the spring the garrison under M. de Contrecoeur had experienced much privation and suffering. An expensive and abundant supply of provisions and stores had at an early day been despatched to this post from Canada, under a strong escort; but the difficulties incident on the portage at Niagara produced an unwelcome and unlooked-for delay. The want of horses and suitable equipages to transport them from the fort at Presqu'-Isle to the Ohio was also a great embarrassment. Four hundred of the party expired on the route, either from scurvy or from the fatigues of bearing all this burthen upon their shoulders.

The provisions of the escort were soon expended, and the magazines intended for their comrades were put into requisition. Then their contents became known, and every one took freely from them such wares as pleased his fancy. The officers were clad in rich velvets and drank to their fill of the rare wines with which, by the knavish connivance of the authorities with some unknown parties in interest, the detachment was charged. A scene of general waste and confusion ensued; and while the troops at Fort Du Quesne profited slightly enough by the costly engagements that had been criminally made for their benefit, the convoy which was to return to Canada arrived there brilliantly equipped, and with a report amply covering all their delinquencies. (I. *Pouchot.*)

CHAPTER 3

Settlers and Savages

If the reception of the tidings of the compulsory evacuation of the Ohio territories by the English gave any satisfaction in France, the feeling was far otherwise in London. Unwelcome enough was this news to a country whose commercial prosperity was so largely identified with the success of its colonial system; nor were the witticisms of the young Comte d'Estaing (himself destined in time to direct heavy and successful blows against British dominion in America), sufficient to restore the good-humor of the people. "*Pardieu, Messieurs*," said he to the English courtiers, "*ce seroit bien ridicule, de faire casser la tête à dix milles hommes pour quelques douzaines de chapeaux,*" ("it would be very ridiculous to have ten thousand men break their heads for a few dozen hats.") (IV. Mahon's *Letters of Chesterfield.*)

It was all very well to balance thus satirically the life of a man against the skin of a beaver; but the fur-trade on the Ohio, now lost to the English, was worth, though but in its infancy, no less than £40,000 a-year. (*Penn. Gaz.,* No. 1344.) The privation of such a profit, not less than the manner in which it was lost, was eminently calculated to excite indignation; and ample details of the whole, forwarded to London by Governor Dinwiddie and others, speedily brought about the inception of those vigorous measures which it is the province of these pages in part to chronicle. In the month of August, 1754, the surrender of Fort Necessity and the conduct of its commander were freely commented on in the highest political circles.

Walpole, (*Corresp.*) wrote:

The French have tied up the hands of an excellent fanfaron, a Major Washington, whom they took, and engaged not to serve for a year.

In several places, the same writer repeats the anecdote of Washington's despatch on this occasion:

'I have heard the bullets whistle; and believe me there is something charming in the sound.' On hearing of this letter, the king said sensibly, 'He would not say so, if he had been used to hear many.' (I. Walpole's *Memoirs of George II.*; Walpole to Sir H. Mann, V. *Corresp.*; II. Sparks' *Washington.*)

And the Duke of Cumberland avowed that:

Rather than lose one foot of ground in America, he would oppose the enemies of his country in that part of the world himself. (*Penn. Gaz.*, No. 1342.)

But the vacillating organisation of the Ministry prevented, for a season, any fruit ripening from these warlike blossoms. The recent death of Henry Pelham, the only brother of the Duke of Newcastle, and an excellent cabinet minister, had occasioned a remodelling of that body; and for some months, so considerable and uncertain were their various alterations, there was nothing but change and inconsistency displayed in the conduct of the official and salaried advisers of the Crown. Newcastle, however, with his great fortune and enormous borough-interest, remained always at the head of affairs.

Ambitious, but incapable, his combined ignorance and vanity cause him too often to appear in the memoirs of the period rather in the character of a ridiculous buffoon than that of a politic statesman; yet even to his understanding the necessity of a prompt movement was evident. Such was his natural imbecility, however, and his mean jealousy of all men in whom by any chance his imagination could foresee future rivals to himself, that a long and dangerous delay elapsed before anything like form and coherence was given to the proposed measures.

Previously to considering these proceedings, nevertheless, and having now shown, in their natural course, the circumstances which had induced this crisis, it may not be amiss to dwell for a moment upon the position of affairs in those colonies for whose immediate protection so much treasure was to be lavished, so many lives spent. The provinces most directly affected by the presence of the French upon the Ohio were those of Virginia and Pennsylvania. In the former, everything was ripe for war. Though its laws, forbidding the employment of the militia beyond their own confines, had prevented that body being called upon for the occupation of a region whose situation was well believed by many to be without its jurisdiction, this infant state had gallantly volunteered four hundred men for the undertaking, whose ill-success was crowned by the surrender of Fort Necessity. A martial spirit pervaded the land; and the governor was a man sagacious in his views and devoted to the interests of his nation.

★★★★★★

Very few colonial governors have obtained the popular verdict in their praise, and certainly Robert Dinwiddie was not one of that scanty number. His disputes with his Assembly in regard to his exaction of fees warranted by law but obsolete in practice, and his difficulties with Washington, have left an unpleasant impression of his character on the American mind. Yet he was an officer not unworthy of commendation. Remarkable integrity and vigilance in other employments, had procured him the government of Virginia; and the records of the day show very clearly how untiring were his efforts to secure the colony from a foreign foe.

A Scot by birth, he perhaps retained too many of the prejudices of that people; but he was not without their virtues; and as though in accordance with his armorial device—*ubi libertas, ibi patria*—he liberally aided in the protection and encouragement of knowledge and education, without which liberty so soon degenerates into license. The library of William and Mary College still preserves the evidences of his generosity; and Dinwiddie County, in the State of Virginia, perpetuates the memory of his name.

★★★★★★

With the exception of the constant quarrels (incident almost to the very existence of a colony), on the subject of money between him and his Assembly, the people and their rulers were generally united and strong in their views of foreign policy, and, what was of even greater importance, were firmly bound together by the common ties of domestic associations.

The case was not similar in Pennsylvania. Its population at this period exceeded three hundred thousand souls; its products, almost exclusively agricultural, were sufficient to employ five hundred vessels, mostly owned in its capital, that annually bore away to other lands provisions sufficient to subsist one hundred thousand men.

★★★★★★

I am aware that Mr. James S. Pringle, in a valuable paper read before the Historical Society of Pennsylvania in May, 1854, states the population of the province, in 1753, to have been but 250,000. Governor Morris, in March, 1755, computes it at the number above mentioned; though probably even his calculation was but conjectural. VI. *Col. Rec.*

★★★★★★

The character of this population was, however, as various as its numbers. In the vicinity of Philadelphia, it is true, the descendants of the original Quaker settlers, with all their purity of morals and all the civilization that could have reasonably been expected to arise from their pacific tenets, still prevailed. But farther from the wealthier and more ancient settlements were to be found large establishments of Scotch-Irish and Germans, each strongly preserving the peculiar idiosyncrasies of their national origin. The Germans, in particular, clinging tenaciously together, are even to this day far from being undistinguishably absorbed in the mass of their fellow-citizens; but then, dwelling as it were aloof from other settlements, they formed a clearly-defined and distinct population. A description of the manner in which one of these settlements was formed may not be devoid of interest.

On Christmas-day, 1709, ten ships set sail from London for New York, freighted with some 4000 Protestant and expatriated Germans, who had been supported in London by the bounty of Queen Anne, and were now sent by that benevolent sovereign to seek new homes in a new world. On their arrival, they were soon dispersed over the whole province, many seating themselves at Schoharie upon lands which belonged to others. Discountenanced in their conduct by Governor Burnet, and embarrassed by the opposition of the lawful owners of the soil, they were finally induced, in 1723, to set forth once more on their wanderings. Like the Israelites of old, their spies had gone down before them and searched out the fatness of the land and had brought back glowing accounts of the regions on the Swatara Creek in Pennsylvania, and the parts adjacent.

Cutting wagon-roads then from the Schoharie to the Susquehannah, they transported their effects through the unbroken forest, and in their rude canoes floated down the river to the mouth of Swatara Creek; their herds following along the shore. Thus, were founded the Swatara and Tulpehocking settlements. This was in the spring of 1723; it was not until 1732 that Thomas Penn purchased the country comprehending portions of Berks and Lebanon counties from the Indians; and, in the meanwhile, the settlements had continued to increase, not only against the will of the Proprietary, but to the annoyance and indignation of the savages, who beheld their hunting-grounds thus forcibly possessed by strangers. (Register of Conrad Weiser: *Penn. Hist. Soc. Coll.*, Vol. I.)

Intermingled with the rest at this time were numbers of English churchmen and Irish Catholics, all contributing to swell the mass of conflicting tongues and creeds that already was in itself sufficient to account for a certain degree of absence of mutual sympathy which so long seems to have prevailed among the people of Pennsylvania. In no manner did the exceeding difference of condition and feelings develop itself more plainly than in their intercourse with the Indians. By all the ties of their faith, as well as through their comparative freedom from the troubles incident on a near neighbourhood with the red men, the influential Quakers were, as a general thing, persuaded of the propriety of treating them in the same honourable manner prescribed by the founder of the province and their own great apostle.

With the frontier settlers, the case was otherwise. A hardy race, often of a temper too prone to inflict an injury, and always prompt to resent one, they were constantly, either in individual instances, or as a people, embroiled with their neighbours. Of the most important Indian tribes who were to be found about this period within the limits of Pennsylvania, and whose conduct and views would most materially influence the scattered remnants of other nations that still existed there, were the Delawares and the Shawanoes. The former had once been a powerful and a warlike tribe; but before the arrival of William Penn they were subdued by the Six Nations of the north, whose hunting-parties roamed at will, as feudal suzerains of old, through the whole region as far as the Ohio and the Chesapeake Bay.

They were compelled by their conquerors to put on petticoats and acknowledge themselves women; terms so degrading that nothing but the extreme awe inspired by the prowess of the confederates of the lakes could have induced submission to—and they were not permitted in any way to exercise the privileges of an independent people. When, therefore, Penn, after purchasing from the Iroquois the land upon which he proposed establishing the seat of his budding empire, made furthermore a point of buying the same lands from their occupants and ancient masters, he acted towards the Delawares with a politic propriety not less just in the abstract than soothing and grateful to their pride. Henceforth the Delawares and the Quakers were as brothers; and the Shawanoes, an alien tribe supposed to have found their way thitherward from the everglades of Florida, participated in these sentiments. No land was to be occupied by the whites until it had been granted by the Proprietary; and the latter's title must rest upon a previous concession from the Indians.

But these halcyon days were not long to endure. As time wore on, and new settlers, impelled by adverse fortune or allured by the fertility of its soil, migrated to Pennsylvania from other shores, the rights of the Indian became more and more disregarded. His lands would be occupied by a stranger, destitute of the shadow of a title, the reverberations of whose gun or the baying of whose hounds would frighten off the game (the flocks and herds of the savage), into still deeper recesses of the forest; and his pride would receive a constant shock from the imperious bearing and, oftentimes, the brutal behaviour of the unlicensed and unwelcome guest.

The proprietary government, it is true, sometimes endeavoured to restrain its subjects within due bounds; but too frequently it was itself guilty of misconduct not less flagrant. It would too often connive at white settlements upon lands belonging to the aborigines; or worse still, engage in some disgraceful, dishonest swindle, by which the savage would be cheated out of his inheritance. By these means, it is not wonderful that his dispositions were gradually becoming hostile to the Europeans, and that his ancient confidence in their friendly professions was impaired.

When, in 1741, that devoted New England philanthropist, John Sergeant, bore to the Shawanoes on the Susquehannah the tidings of salvation, they rejected with disdain his pious overtures. They had learned to hate the religion whose votaries corrupted their health, cheated them of their substance, and debauched their women. (Hopkins's *Mem. of Housatannuk Inds.*; Thomson's *Alienation*, &c.) And when the wiser and more foreseeing among them complained of the outrages they were subjected to by the traders, they met with but scanty redress. In 1727, the deputies of the Six Nations, who represented as well their own tribes as the subject Delawares, complained to Governor Gordon, at Philadelphia, of the traders who came among them, getting all their skins at trifling prices.

They get so little for them, that they cannot live; and can scarce procure powder and shot to bring more. That the traders bring very little of these, but instead bring rum, which they sell very dear.

They further urged that no more settlements should be made on the Susquehannah above Paxton; and that no more rum should be sold there to the Indians; and that none of the traders to the Ohio should be suffered to carry rum. To all which the governor replied, that in regard to new settlements, as his people increased they must necessarily spread; and as to the traders—

They know it is the custom of all to buy as cheap and to sell as dear as they can, and that every man must be on his guard and make the best bargain he can: the English cheat the Indians, and the Indians cheat the English; and that they were at perfect liberty to destroy without compensation all the rum that was brought among them, as the provincial laws forbade it being carried thither. (Thomson.)

52

A General Map of the River OHIO

OF THE N.W. TERRITORY OF THE UNITED STATES

PITTSBURGH

Allegany R.

M. Kees Port

Camp occupied in 1792 by Genl. Wayne against the Indians

OHIO RIVER

Yellow Creek

Long Island

Mingo Bottom

Grave Creek

Perhaps the governors could not do any more than they did to restrain the excesses of the traders; but all that they did do was ineffectual; the abuse continued to operate, undiminished by time.

★★★★★★

See the governor's message in 1744: "I cannot but be apprehensive that the Indian trade, as it is now carried on, will involve us in some fatal quarrel with the Indians. Our traders, in defiance of the law, carry spirituous liquors among them, and take the advantage of their inordinate appetite for it to cheat them of their skins and their *wampum*, which is their money, and often to debauch their wives into the bargain. Is it to be wondered at then if, when they recover from their drunken fit, they should take some severe revenges?"—*Votes of Penn. Assembly*, Vol. III. These traders generally consisted, according to the report of the same legislature, in 1754, of the vilest of their own inhabitants, or of transported convicts from Great Britain and Ireland.

★★★★★★

The result of the infamous Walking Treaty—as shameless a fraud as ever was perpetrated—had occasioned a great and natural discontent on the part of the unfortunates so unjustly and, as all will now concede, so illegally ousted from their homes. The story of this transaction is briefly as follows:

In 1686, as was alleged by the proprietaries and admitted by most of the Indians, Penn had purchased from the Delawares a tract of land comprehended within certain boundaries. The line was to begin at a certain spruce-tree on the River Delaware, above the mouth of Neshamony Creek; thence by a course west-north-west to the Neshamony; thence back into the woods as far as a man could walk in a day and a half; thence to the Delaware again, and so down to the place of beginning. No steps were taken to lay out this land until some sixty years afterward, when, upon mature consideration of the subject, it was decided by the proprietary to take formal possession of it.

Accordingly, every preparation was made to secure as good a bargain as possible. A road was surveyed for the walk; expeditious means of crossing the intersecting streams were provided; and the swiftest pedestrians in the province were engaged to accomplish as great a distance as might be compassed within the time limited. This having been attained, the next point was to run the line to the Delaware; and here, whatever may be thought of the mode in which the first part of the business had been transacted, a glaring wrong was perpetrated by the government. In the original deed, a blank had been left for the direction which the proposed line should take: and as the topography of this country could not, in 1686, have been accurately known, this seems not unnatural.

But now, by a foul advantage of this omission, it was resolved to run the line, not by the nearest course to the river, which would have been east-south-east, or parallel to that by which they set out, but by a north-east course for a hundred miles and more, till it struck the Delaware near the mouth of Lackawaxen Creek, far above Easton. A fortunate westerly bend in the channel enabled them to effect this, and to cover by their deed at least a million of acres, when, by a fairer computation, three hundred and fifty thousand should have confined their claim. (Thomson.)

Their best lands, and even their accustomed villages being invaded by this enormous fraud, the Indians on the Delaware evinced a decided inclination not to submit to it. To provide against any evil consequences on this head, a number of deputies from the Six Nations were, in 1742, invited to visit Philadelphia, nominally to transact public business of a mutual importance, but really to persuade them to overawe the Delawares into acquiescence in the chicanery that had been practised upon them. Accordingly, after having been conciliated with a few hundred pounds' worth of presents, they were requested to prevail on their cousins the Delawares to remove from the lands in the forks of the river, which, it was pretended, their fathers had sold and been paid for long before. The chiefs of this tribe being assembled in the council-chamber, were then earnestly addressed by the speaker of the Six Nations.

In homely but forcible phrase he reproached them with their misconduct. He said:

> They deserved to be taken by the hair of their heads and shaken severely, till they recovered their senses and became sober. But how came you to take upon you to sell lands at all? *We* conquered you; *we* made women of you; you know you are women and can no more sell land than women; nor is it fit you should have the power of selling lands, since you would abuse it. This land that you claim is gone through your guts: you have been furnished with clothes, meat, and drink by the goods paid you for it, and now you want it again, like children as you are!
> But what makes you sell lands in the dark? Did you ever tell us

that you had sold this land? Did *we* ever receive any part, oven the value of a pipe-shank, from you for it?. . . For all these reasons, we charge you to remove instantly: we don't give you the liberty to think about it. You are women. Take the advice of a wise man and remove immediately. You may return to the other side of Delaware, where you came from; but we do not know whether, considering how you have demeaned yourselves, you will be permitted to live there, or whether you have not swallowed that land down your throats as well as the land on this side. We therefore assign you two places to go, either to Wyomen or Shamokin. You may go to either of these places, and then we shall have you more under our eye and shall see how you behave. Don't deliberate, but remove at once, and take this belt of *wampum*.

Having thus satisfactorily closed all debate, the speaker summarily ejected "his cousins the Delawares" from the apartment. (Thompson.)

It was impossible for the Indians to disobey so potent a decree, and they removed as they were bidden. But the acquirement of their fields, so inexpensive at the beginning, in the end cost very dear. From that moment, they were ready to listen to the overtures of the French, and to contemplate with no great displeasure the discomfiture of both the Iroquois and the English. For it was not within the bounds of human endurance unmoved to see their wives and little ones starving by their side, and to feel themselves the sharp pangs of poverty and famine, while the whites were feasting on the fatness of their ancient inheritance.

It is useless to tell a rudely-reasoning and famishing barbarian, or, for the matter of that, a sage philosopher in the same condition, as did the deputies of the Six Nations at Philadelphia, that he or his ancestors had long ago sold the millions of acres along the Delaware, which they once occupied; and had enjoyed the full benefit of the 'two guns, six stroud-water coats, six blankets, six duffel watch-coats, and four kettles,' that were said to have been paid to them by William Penn. (Thompson.) An undisciplined feeling of natural equity, stimulated perhaps by hunger, advised them that such a price, if the story of its ever having been paid at all were true, was a poor compensation for the abandonment of a region abounding at the time in game and yielding ready crops of maize and pumpkins, for their new and dreary homes.

Conrad Weiser, that strange compound, to whom Indian life and the Indian tongue were perhaps more familiar than English, gives a piteous account of their condition in the winter of 1737, when he passed from Tulpehocking in Pennsylvania on his way to New York. Scattered through the forests, they would fix their camps near a grove of sugar-maple trees, the juice of which constituted the only magazine of food upon which they could with any certainty rely. Here the children searched along the lowlands and the banks of streams for nuts and esculent roots, or crowded weeping with their mothers around the traveller, in whose exhausted pouch yet remained a few crumbs of corn-meal.

★★★★★★

The turkey-pea has a single stalk, grows to a height of eight or ten inches, and bears a small pod. It is found in rich, loose soils; appears among the first plants in the spring and produces on the root small tubers of the size of a hazel-nut, on which the turkeys feed. The Indians are fond of and collect them in considerable quantities.—*Hunter.*

★★★★★★

A handful of maize steeped in a pot of ash-lye to make a kind of soup, constituted to them a most luxurious but unwonted dish. In the meantime, the husbands and fathers of the party, disdaining to rob their families of the miserable pittance which preserved them from death though not from starving, would range for weeks at a time through all the region between the Shamokin and the upper waters of the Susquehannah in fruitless search of game. By day he scouted through the dense spruce-forests, beneath those evergreen boughs which the sun's rays rarely pierced; every sense painfully on the alert lest the tread of a deer or the distant flight of a mountain grouse should escape his observation; or lest, by a misstep, he should be cast headlong down some precipitous chasm, or slipping between treacherous logs, be chilled in the icy torrent of the dark, deepflowing streams.

Cold and hungry, he would lie down at nightfall crouched beneath a pile of boughs, the snow drifting the while in fierce wreaths about his sleeping form; and in the morning awake, stiff and cold, to find his fire still burning in the hole, two or three feet deep, that it had melted during the night in the snow. With returning light, the labours of the chase are resumed. In vain he threads the Dia-dachlu or Wandering River (as he named Lycoming Creek); its fords at this season waist deep, its current swift and powerful and icy cold; or the fierce Oscohu, mountain-born, flowing between fringing maples. Carefully avoiding the weird ravine which superstition invested with mysterious horrors as the home of the *Otkon*, an evil spirit who delighted in blood and was only to be appeased by magical sacrifices, he would shudderingly gaze from the brow of a distant hill at the skulls which, bleaching in the winter's storms, declared at once the extent of the demon's power and the place of his abode.

Then turning to the north, he penetrates to the summit of the hill where, according to tradition, pumpkins, corn, and tobacco first grew for the benefit of humanity; but only to find that they grew there no longer. Exhausted and weary, the poor wretch turns his face homewards, and with languid gait—*sperans meliora*—seeks his camp by the waterside; diverging perchance on the way to visit the beaver-dam at the confluence of the Towanda and Lycoming Creeks, where once within his own memory many pipes of tobacco had been smoked before "his grandfathers the beavers." Now not a sign of their presence remained. To supply the insatiable maw of traffic, not only the males of the colony, but even the females, generally so sacred in the eyes of an Indian, had long since yielded up their skins; and the pool was silent and unbroken.

With a sinking heart he invokes the Great Spirit to come to his relief lest he perish, or to give him a reason why he and his people should thus suffer; and in a vision of the night, "when deep sleep falleth on men, fear comes upon him and trembling which makes all his bones to shake." A spirit passes before his face, and he hears the words of the *manitou*, pronouncing the doom of his race. Humbled in soul, but callous through long endurance, he returns empty-handed to his camp, happy if he finds there some benevolent stranger, differing from his colour in being a Christian not only in name but indeed, who, as he divides his few remaining ounces of corn-bread with weeping, starving women and children, murmurs within himself blessings on His name "who hath made in His wisdom thistles to grow instead of barley in this land, and the owners thereof to lose their life."

★★★★★★

There is not the least exaggeration in this sketch; every statement in it is literally true. *Vide* Weiser's *Narrative of a journey* in 1737, published in I. Coll. *Penn. Hist. Soc.*, 17. In the revelation referred to, God declared to the Indians: "You inquire after the cause why game has become scarce. I will tell you. You kill if for the sake of the skins, which you give for strong liquor, and drown your senses and kill one another, and carry on a dreadful debauchery. Therefore, have I driven the wild animals out of the country, for they are mine. If you will do good and cease from your sins, I will bring them back. If not, I will destroy you from of the earth." Weiser asked if they put faith in this vision. "They answered, yes; some believed it would happen so: others also believed it but gave themselves no concern about it. Time will show, said they, what is to happen to us. Rum will kill us and leave the land clear for the Europeans without strife or purchase."

★★★★★★

How changed was the Indian's condition since fifty years before! Then, save his own domestic broils, he had no enemies to contend with. Game was not slaughtered for the skin only, and food was therefore comparatively abundant. The twanging bow-string then answered all his purposes of destruction; the detonations of musketry had not yet broken the silence of his hunting-grounds and frightened off both bird and beast, and they were therefore easily accessible. Above all, rum, that scourge of the red race, was not familiar to his taste, and he was therefore independent. Cruel he was, and revengeful; and his social condition was marked with all those blemishes which almost prevent our regretting the means by which he has been destroyed in the reflection of the utter worthlessness of his existence to the rest of the world: but we must not forget that, so far as he was concerned, his lot was only injured by the approach of civilization.

Now, he is vanished; passed away, with all his atrocious faults and noble virtues, from the memory of the land, like a hideous dream: then, he was its owner, its master, and was happy. The Indian has no original wants that civilization can gratify; no aspirations that barbarism cannot fulfil. His fields are tilled by the woman with whom he vouchsafes to share his couch; his lodge is raised upon poles hewed from the nearest forest and covered with the spoils of the chase; his most glorious furniture is the scalps that dry in the smoke of his *wigwam*. His ornaments are arms, his pastime is war; his highest luxury consists in repletion. What to him are the rich marts of commerce, the narrow streets, the busy hum of crowded cities!

Coarse are his meals—the fortune of the chase;
Amidst the running stream he slakes his thirst;
Toils all the day, and at the approach of night,
On the first friendly bank ho throws him down,

Or rests his head upon a rock till morn:
Then rises fresh, pursues his wonted game;
And if, the following day, he chance to find
A new repast, or an untasted spring,
Blesses his stars, and thinks it luxury.

A glance, now, at the character and condition of the white settlers of those days, will not be out of place; and so different were they from the people of this generation; that the sketch may not be uninteresting. The diversity of national origin of the early population of Pennsylvania has already been noticed: there was a still greater difference in their intellectual and moral developments. Setting aside the shoals of convicts turned loose upon its borders from the English gaols, there were hundreds of other colonists arriving every year, whose presence, though necessary, perhaps, to the ultimate prosperity of the growing State, could not have been calculated to promote the immediate refinement and elevation of its character.

In every colony there must be a class of settlers who shall there serve the same purpose as Linnaeus beautifully attributes to the lichens and mosses of the physical world, when he aptly describes them as the bond-slaves of nature: they must form, upon the yet wild and unseated rock, the earliest soil from which, in time, the choicest of Nature's creations shall spring. Individuals must fall, and die, and be forgotten, as the leaves in the forest, their remains commingling with the mother earth, through long and tedious time, ere the solitude and gloom of the wilderness shall give place to the temples of luxury and civilization. Thus, it is ever in this world; each man, each plant, each insect, living or dying, has a part to play, a place to fill. Change, eternal change, the imperishable secret of Nature, is the only immutable measure of all her laws.

It is not designed in this place to dwell upon the particular establishments that were from time to time made by English, Scotch-Irish, or Germans, in the various parts of the province; but a few words respecting their distinctive characters will be of service as tending to show the causes of the conduct and sentiment of the people under peculiar circumstances. In each of these classes were to be found men of education, intelligence, and virtue. The English naturally preponderated in characters of this stamp. The amiable, honest, benevolent followers of Penn, who flocked to the shores of the Delaware as to a haven of refuge, comprehended within their ranks a degree of mental and moral cultivation which would have reflected credit upon any people in the world; the wealth, too, of the province, and the control of the Assembly, were chiefly in their hands.

Other English, of various denominations, were to be found, not inferior in station or capacity to the disciples of Fox; and although, at one time or another, the Presbyterians thought themselves neglected, or the churchmen took umbrage at the Quaker rule, yet, on the whole, we may safely conclude that there has rarely been an instance of religious power having been used with so much mildness. Certainly, had the societies of either the Church of England or the Westminster Assembly been in the position of the Quakers, there is no reason to believe they would have acted with a like tolerance to their fellow-citizens, while the poor Indian would have suffered terribly in the exchange.

The Scotch-Irish, as they were called, were emigrants from the northern part of the sister-kingdom, descendants of the Scottish colonies planted there by Cromwell. They were a hardy, brave, hot-headed race; excitable in temper, unrestrainable in passion, invincible in prejudice. Their hand opened as impetuously to a friend as it clenched against an enemy. They loathed the Pope as sincerely as they venerated Calvin or Knox; and they did not particularly respect the Quakers. If often rude and lawless, it was partly the fault of their position.

They hated the Indian, while they despised him; and it does not seem, in their dealings with this race, as though there were any sentiments of honor or magnanimity in their bosoms that could hold way against the furious tide of passionate, blind resentment. Impatient of restraint, rebellious against anything that in their eyes bore the semblance of injustice, we find these men readiest among the ready on the battlefields of the revolution. If they had faults, a lack of patriotism or of courage was not among the number.

We have already alluded to a lawless settlement of the Germans upon the Susquehannah; and indeed, the province soon became a chosen harbour for these people, who appear to have migrated from Germany in very much the same sort as they do at this day. The wanderers were generally of the lower orders—peasants, mechanics, or sometimes small farmers or tradesmen. Selling their useless possessions at home, they would embark together in droves for the promised land. Many were so poor (and not of the Germans alone, but of all nations emigrating to America), that it was a very customary thing for a passenger to sell his or her labour for a term of years to the captain of the vessel as a payment for the passage. These the captain, upon his arrival, would in turn dispose of to inhabitants of the province. Thus, as slaves, or servants for a fixed period, the unfortunate emigrants wore on their life of toil.

More fortunate were many who had not found a necessity of resort to this shift; but brought with them to the New World, if little pecuniary wealth, at least free limbs. These, adhering together in a foreign land, preserved their language and national characteristics for a surprisingly long period. Phlegmatic, parsimonious, industrious, and honest, their constant care was to accumulate wealth and to avoid disturbance. Being chiefly of the inferior classes at home, the first German settlers were not remarkable for any very elevated notions either in religion or politics; nor, indeed, is it a matter for surprise, that among all the frontier settlers (to whom, as a class, the remarks which are now being made are generally applicable), a higher value should be set on physical than on mental endowments; on skill in hunting, or the practical arts of daily life, and bravery in war, than on any polite accomplishments or taste in the fine arts.

Thus, many of the vulgar superstitions which had at one time held a place in the minds of the highest classes of the Old World, and which were still nourished among its peasantry, were transplanted to the wildernesses of America. Here, in the gloomy, silent shadows of a virgin forest, whose solitude was as yet uncheered by the murmurs of the honey-bee or the pleasant warbling of singing birds—those invariable attendants upon the axe of the woodsman—the nightly howling of the dog, who bayed at the moon; the shrill, startling whoop of the owl, from some stridulous bough overhanging his camp-fire and bending to the evening breeze; the sinister croak of the raven, perched on the hollow oak, were notes of prophetic woe that filled the bosom of the pioneer with dismal forebodings. (*Virgil.*)

In dreams, he foresaw the good or ill success of his undertakings; and after the fashion of the ancients, prosperity or misfortune would appear to him in the semblance of a female form. Over the low door of the German's cottage one would be sure to find nailed the horseshoe, fatal to witches; and love-spells and barbarous charms against the dangers of the field were familiar to their lips. Absurd incantations were held in supreme repute as infallible remedies for haemorrhage, toothache, or the fatal battle-stroke; nor was a belief in witches and ghosts yet banished from the popular faith. The silver bullet, however, was rarely found necessary for the overthrow of a witch.

The German who suspected his fireplace of being a resort for such characters, readily expelled them by burning alive a young dog or two therein. Nor did the black cat, that old companion of sorcery, escape unscathed; but, earless and tailless, wandered through the neighbourhood, a monument of the use to which its blood had been put in the treatment of St. Anthony's fire.

★★★★★★

I cite almost the very words of the intelligent and pious Joseph Doddridge, D.D.; a backwoodsman by birth, who lived and died among the people he taught. His *Notes of the Settlement, &c., of the Western Parts of Virginia and Pennsylvania* (Wellsburgh, Va., 1824), is one of the most interesting works we have upon the subject and will be often referred to in this volume.

★★★★★★

But recently escaped from the galling oppression of their ancestral homes, the German settlers were as little disposed as able to yield a perfect obedience to the minor requirements of laws of which they neither understood the language nor comprehended the objects; and from their own lips we learn how, as of old, when in Israel there was no king, every man did in those days what seemed good in his own eyes. (Conrad Weiser, Coll. *Penn. Hist. Soc.*, Vol. I.; Doddridge.) And if any reliance is to be placed upon the testimony of competent and intelligent witnesses, the earliest German colonists evinced, in the hour of necessity, a conduct which shows very clearly how vague was their comprehension of the new duties they had assumed.

In 1753, Franklin, writing to Peter Collinson, declared that the Germans in Pennsylvania, being generally the most ignorant of their own countrymen, were perfectly intoxicated with the unwonted possession of a political power: which they exercised, even upon their own preachers, with equal bigotry and tyranny. Keeping apart from the English, they preserved with tenacity the usages of their native land. Their conversation was carried on in German; their children were educated in ignorance of any other tongue; their books, their newspapers, their deeds and legal instruments even, were in German. He continues:

The French who watch all advantages, are now themselves making a German settlement back of us in the Illinois country, and by means of these Germans they may in time come to a good understanding with ours; and, indeed, in the last war the Germans showed a general disposition that seemed to bode us no good. For, when the English, who were not Quakers, alarmed by the danger arising from the defenceless state of our country, entered unanimously into an association, and within this government and the lower counties raised, armed, and disciplined near ten thousand men, the Germans, except a very few in proportion to their number, refused to engage in it; giving out, one amongst another, and even in print, that if they were quiet the French, should they take the country, would not molest them; at the same time abusing the Philadelphians for fitting out privateers against the enemy; and representing the trouble, hazard, and expense of defending the province as a greater inconvenience than any that might be expected from a change of government. (Sparks' Franklin, Vol. VII.)

★★★★★★

In 1755, Franklin energetically addressed the British public in favour of excluding any more Germans from the colonies. "Since detachments of English from Britain sent to America," said he, "will have their places at home so soon supplied, and increase so largely here, why should the Palatine boors be suffered to swarm into our settlements, and by herding together establish their language and manners, to the exclusion of ours?" XXV. *Gent. Mag.,* 485.

That the intelligent and educated portion of the German population did not clearly comprehend and honestly conform to the requirements of their novel condition, is not insinuated: yet, even in 1754, when Henry Muhlenberg and a number of the most influential and respected Germans in the province (men of pure hearts, unblemished lives, and pious souls), addressed themselves to Gov. Morris, loyally pledging their fidelity to the King, they admit that there were "a few ignorant, unmannerly people lately come amongst us," who entertained contrary sentiments. II. *Penn. Arch.*

★★★★★★

It is not with any desire to cast unmerited reproach upon the character of any people that these remarks are offered: the investigation has been made purely in a spirit of seeking after historical truth, where the student can never be considered at liberty to disregard the evidences that stare him in the face. But, after all, nothing that has been said is in conflict with the usual course of human nature. Many of the earliest settlers were doubtless in some respects better men than their descendants; but they were still far from being perfect. They were not less governed by circumstances than human beings usually are: their judgment was as likely to err or be warped by passion.

If the Quakers were sincere, pious, and benevolent, it does not follow that they should be willing to consent to what they conceived to be an unfair system of taxation: if the Germans were frugal and industrious, it does not necessarily involve the fact that they should wipe out in a moment from their minds the memory of the distant homes they had just left; or that they should enter, heart and soul, into the merits of a controversy in which they had no previous interest. It was natural enough, then, that they should be indisposed to peril their new-born independence and scanty fortunes in a quarrel between George and Louis; being utterly indifferent whether either succeeded, so long as they themselves might enjoy repose. But when they conceived it necessary to fight, the Germans acted with ample spirit, as was abundantly testified in the war of the Revolution.

But while the masses of the people sought homes in regions yet unsettled, they generally kept the frontier lines considerably before them. Along the borders, however, was to be found a population consisting indifferently of the children of every nation but uniting here in habits and customs peculiarly their own. Wherever a fertile bottom was spread along the banks of the stream, or a warm, sheltered champaign stretched beneath the covert of a range of hills, the steady, monotonous fall of the woodsman's axe would soon be heard through the long morning hours.

Presently a dull crash would echo through the forest, as some monarch of the grove fell prostrate, to rise no more. Ere long, the circle of the sky would begin to expand above the spot, and the sunlight, for the first time during untold ages, bathe the earth beneath in a continuous flood of warmth and brightness. A deadening once made, a few acres of rustling corn would raise their heads and reveal their golden treasures to the autumnal wind; while all around, mute mourners at the scene, tall, ghostly trees, the springs of whose life had been destroyed by the girdling axe, exalted their phantom forms and stretched sadly forth their skeleton arms.

★★★★★★

A *deadening*, in the rustic patois of Pennsylvania, signifies the effect produced on the trees by girdling, or cutting a ring about their trunks. The bark being thus completely severed, the sap ceases to communicate, and the tree loses all its foliage and soon dies. A *clearing*, according to the same authority, denotes a spot where the forest is cut down, and nothing but the stumps remain. The ghastly aspect of the former process would doubtless render it objectionable to the eyes of a landscape gardener; but none such were probably to be found in the backwoods; and the facility with which a tract could thus be prepared for agricultural purposes, was no small inducement to the settler. A good woodsman will soon deaden a number of acres, which by the next seed-time will be ready for cultivation.

★★★★★★

Vainly they yearned for the nymph, the tutelary divinity of their shade. Still deeper in the forest gloom, by some distant spring or lonely mountain tarn, the homeless Dryad bewailed the leafy shrine which she should see no more.

During the dull, dark days of early winter or approaching spring, the smoke of the consuming dead trees mounted slowly on the air and lost itself in the cold grey above. But when summer returned, the settler would find perhaps a score of like clearings going on around him; and as many evening fire-sides welcomed the return of autumn. It did not take long to build a house in those days. Logs were felled and hewed of the proper length and arranged with friendly aid into the frame-work of a one-roomed log-cabin. A roof of puncheons, rudely shaped with the broad-axe, was placed upon it, and an outside chimney of stone and sticks, filled in with clay, adorned one end of the edifice.

The interstices between the logs were then plastered up with mud and moss: a door, and an aperture for a window added, and, if the building were a luxurious one, a puncheon floor: and the house was done. A block or two served for stools; a broad slab of timber for a table; a rude frame-work for a couch. Here in one chamber would sleep all the family—men, women, and children, married or single, young or old: here was their kitchen; here did they eat. In some more elegant establishments, a double-cabin, or even a loft, was to be found. A few wooden bowls and trenchers, some spoons carved from a horn, a calabash and an iron pot, with two or three forks and knives, completed the simple furniture.

China, or even ordinary delf-ware, was unknown in those times; a few pack-horses in their annual journey were the only means of communication with the sea-board. For food, the chief reliance was upon the product of the chase, the corn, pumpkins, and potatoes which were cultivated upon the little farm, and the invariable dish of pork. No settler was without his drove of swine; and "hog and hommony" is still a proverbial expression for western fare. Their cows yielded them milk; and corn-meal, either ground by hand or pounded in a wooden mortar, furnished their only bread. In times of scarcity, such as were of too frequent occurrence, when the granary was exhausted, the children were comforted with lean venison under the name of bread, till a new harvest should come around.

Nor was their costume less primitive than their diet. Petticoats and dresses of linsey-woolsey (a cloth, home-woven, of wool and flax) filled the wardrobe of the country maiden, innocent, save on state occasions, of superfluous shoes and stockings; while the men were clad in a coarse linsey or buckskin hunting-shirt, with breeches, leggins, and *moccasins*. Their cattle were of too much value living, to be slaughtered either for their flesh or their skins, and the hide of the wild deer, tanned by their own hands, was compelled to supply the place of leather.

Hardy as they were, however, the first settlers suffered greatly from the inclemencies of the weather; against which neither their clothing nor their dwellings afforded a sufficient protection. The seasons were then far more severe than, even in the same country, they are at present. The summers were shorter, and more damp and cold; the winters earlier, and more stern. Rheumatic affections, and the usual train of disorders consequent upon exposure, were common afflictions; and doubtless owing to the extreme ignorance which prevailed in matters of medical science, there were very many lives needlessly sacrificed from a want of proper treatment.

But, after their own fashion, they were a happy race, these backwoodsmen. Reckless of future danger, unconscious of prospective woe, they lived very much in the present. Full of animal spirits, the blood coursing through their veins under spur of the excitement of a constant peril, that at bed or at board, at seed-time and in the harvest-field, was ever by their side, they embarked eagerly in every homely sport or rustic revelry. The most unartificial frolic was partaken of with a zest that would astonish the tranquil tastes of one bred among more civilized scenes. Athletic games—wrestling, running, or shooting at a mark—were the friendly arenas wherein each strove to bear away an honourable fame.

The boys were taught to throw the tomahawk with unerring aim; to imitate the cries of the creatures of the forest with a fidelity that would deceive the most practised ear, or to properly wield a rifle. Other education they rarely had; for no schoolhouse, for many long years to come, was destined to raise its low roof among them; no church, no clergyman taught them to think of higher aims. Sunday came, indeed, a day of rest for the weary, but a day of mirth and amusement to the young and gay; nor was it, with all, distinguished in even this extent from the other days of the week. Yet it must not be supposed that it found the people plunged in dishonourable vice or excessive immorality. On the contrary, they were perhaps less so than the inhabitants of many Christian cities.

Profane they undoubtedly were; in their most ordinary conversation, "they clothed themselves with curses as with a garment," and, in the gust of passion, were careless of the destruction of limb or life. But lying and cheating were abhorred among them, and a coward was the scorn of the community. Their sons were brave and their daughters were virtuous. The loss of female chastity was a calamity that involved dishonour; and instances of its violation or seduction were of rare occurrence, and usually swiftly and bloodily revenged. Seldom was it for other cause than a family feud that a youthful couple found any impediment in the path to matrimony; and such dissensions were not likely to endure in a neighbourhood bound together in a common danger.

Indeed, the gaiety it produced was frequently a sufficient inducement for a young man, able to support her, to take unto himself a wife. Then the whole country-side would assemble at the bride's dwelling, and, with copious libations of whiskey, in which the happy pair set them the example, exhaust the night in merriment and sport. To the scraping of an old violin, four-handed reels or Virginia jigs would endure till morning dawned or the performer's strength failed him. As evening wore on, the blushing fair, with her lover by her side, would clamber up the ladder which led from the lower chamber, filled with a boisterous crowd, to the loft above, where the nuptial couch was spread; and at a later hour, a substantial meal of pork, cabbage, and whiskey would be served up to them in their privacy. Preposterous as all this appears at this day, it was then the custom of the country, and as such, honoured in the observance.

The most important feature of a new settlement, was, however, its fort. This was simply a place of resort for the people when the Indians were expected, and consisted of a range of contiguous log cabins, protected by a stockade and perhaps a blockhouse or two. It was chiefly in the summer and fall that the approach of the savage was to be dreaded;

and at this season families in exposed positions were compelled to leave their farms and remove with their furniture to the fort. Parties of armed men would sally out by day, and in turn cultivate each plantation, with scouts at a distance to warn them of the presence of the foe. Every precaution that the swarthy warrior himself could adopt was resorted to by his no less wily antagonist. The earth beneath, the bushes around, the skies above, were carefully interrogated; and a broken twig, the impress of a *moccasined* foot upon the dewy sod, or a distant column of smoke faintly ascending to the heavens, were infallible "Indian signs" to the uneasy husband or father.

Then women and children would be quickly brought within shelter; cattle and furniture placed in safety, and a few of the most adventurous spirits thrown out to observe or interrupt the progress of the suspected danger. But let the panic once spread, and the alarm of a general Indian onslaught along the frontiers get headway, and in a moment plantations and settlements were abandoned. The popular terror, like wildfire, communicating to every quarter, would crowd the inland towns with anxious, careworn faces, and leave to the torch of the invader the scenes of their late prosperity.

But occasions such as these, were, fortunately, not frequent; and when the snows of winter had begun to fall, and the improvident savage could no longer find sustenance in the fields tilled by his wife's hoe, he was conceived to have occupation enough in the quest of game and in endeavouring to avoid starvation; and all fear of an attack faded away. Then the settler, ensconced once more in his own cottage, would linger over the fire during the long winter evenings, framing articulate sounds in the wild wailings of the northern blast, that piled up the deep snow-drift against his wooden walls, or striving to decipher the phantasmagoria which played among the lingering embers. Perchance the fierce howlings of a distant wolf would call his thoughts to his own fold; and floundering through the snow, he would sally forth into the darkness to assure himself that his treasured herds were in safety. Shaking the white masses from his burly form, he would soon resume his station by the ample hearth, and

In social scenes of gay delight
Beguile the dreary winter night.

Some simple story of the chase, or a yet more thrilling tale of personal adventure, would arise. With open ears and busy hands, the little family would gather around or within the roaring chimney; one boy mending the lock of a gun, another adjusting the barb of an arrow or the spring of a trap, and sighing for the day when he too might bear a rifle and be acknowledged a man—

When young and old in circle
Around the firebrands close;
When the girls are weaving baskets
And the lads are shaping bows:

—the sire would, for the hundredth time perhaps, narrate to un-wearied ears some ancient fable of far beyond sea: of knights and giants, and beauteous ladies ravished from their bowers; or, with innumerable variations of incident, recite his valiant deeds who conquered Cormo-ran. Then, from some half-lit corner, where the flickering flame from the hearth (their only light), shaped monstrous, grotesque shadows on the irregular log-walls, the sound of female voices would rise; and to the monotonous accompaniment of the unceasing shuttle, would be sung in low, subdued tones a ballad of "bold Robin Hood that merrye outlawe;" whose deeds furnished to these people the staple of their poetry. Little skill or art was necessary to please a willing ear:

They chant their artless notes in simple guise;
They tune their hearts, by far the noblest aim:

and the cruelties of Barbara Allen, or the plaintive strains of 'Wil-low, willow, willow,' were enough to excite every emotion that these rough breasts could feel. Such ballads were naively enough, but not unaptly, styled 'love-songs about murder.'

★★★★★★'

Doddridge, from whom the above sketch is faithfully drawn, gives a singular description of the garb which the young men sometimes assumed in times of Indian excitement. It consisted simply of a pair of *moccasins*, leggins that reached to the thigh, and a breech-cloth twisted through a belt so as to suffer a skirt some eight or nine inches broad to fall down before and be-hind. The body, embarrassed by perhaps as scanty clothing as has been worn since the days of Adam, was thus perfectly free for action. "The young warrior," continues the worthy divine, "instead of being abashed by this nudity, was proud of his Indi-an-like dress. In some few instances, I have seen them go into places of public worship in this dress. Their appearance, how-ever, did not add much to the devotion of the young ladies."

★★★★★★

Such as has been described is a fair picture of the domestic scenery of the various portions of the land in the middle of the 18th century. On the one hand were the Anglo-Americans, eagerly pushing forward their borders, careless of the lowering brows or half-uttered threats of the Indians; on the other were savage tribes who had little love for the French, it is true, but whose dispositions were ripe for trouble with the English. So deeply rooted, indeed, was the lurking disaffection towards their ancient allies, that so early as 1744, the Iroquois had warned the Governor of Pennsylvania that in the event of another French war the Delawares and Shawanoes would inevitably be found in the ranks of the enemy. The latter had in fact for many years previously spared no pains to bring the Shawanoes into their interest. (*Votes of Penn. Assembly*, Vol. III.; Thomson.)

Nevertheless, the presence of the French upon the Ohio was exceedingly unwelcome to all the Indian nations. The Iroquois, as well as the Delawares and Shawanoes, made some overtures, in 1753, of removing by force of arms the party under M. de Contrecoeur, after two separate messages had been vainly sent to persuade him to withdraw: and a deputation was despatched to Virginia and Pennsylvania to desire the countenance of those provinces in the anticipated troubles and to put matters on a right footing between all parties. At Carlisle they met the provincial commissioners, whom they urgently pressed to call back the whites already settled on the western side of the Alleghanies, where as yet the Indians had sold not a foot of land. (Thompson.)

And though nothing came of this temper, which, if properly managed, might have been used to immense advantage by the English, yet it serves to show how powerfully old predilections and national traditions conspired to make these people still disposed to friendship with the English and hatred to the French. But, as has been well observed, the Indian is to a certain extent a venal character. The nature of his existence had by this time compelled him to look to the whites for powder and ball; for rum and tobacco; for blankets and vermilion. The simple weapons of other days were no longer sufficient to enable him to pursue successfully his prey.

Unless he would starve, he must resort to the store-houses of the trader; and once there, soft words and flattering gifts would be very apt to bring his will into the control of the donor. The lustre of the benefaction last received seldom fails to obscure all that preceded it;

71

and like a child with a new toy, he loses all appreciation of former favours in the contemplation of his present enjoyment. In this manner the French worked upon the savages who visited them at Fort Du Quesne. The needy warrior, who went empty-handed, would return to his companions gratified with a new blanket, gun and ammunition, and flaunting in the unwonted attire of a laced coat and hat and a shirt streaming with ribbons. Then he would contrast the generosity of the French with the niggardliness of the English; and the event would be that his fellows would all hasten to participate in the precious harvest that awaited them.

★★★★★★

The two Ohio journals of Post exhibit very strongly this feature of Indian character. In the one, just such a scene as is above described was enacted; poor Post himself being compelled to bear the odium of his employer's meanness. But by and by the tide changed; the stock at the fort perhaps ran low, and the bribes of the English told powerfully on the savages; and Post made a second journey to endeavour to detach them from the service of the enemy. Then he found the tables turned; nor could even the presence of the French captain restrain the expressions of contempt with which the chieftains spoke of him.

"He has boasted much of his fighting," said they; "now let us see his fighting. We have often ventured our lives for him and had scarcely a loaf of bread when we came to him, and now he thinks we should jump to serve him." It must not be forgotten that it was to the presents and kind words of the Quakers, who first set on foot these negotiations, that the merit of prevailing upon the Indians to leave unopposed General Forbes's route to Fort Du Quesne, and the consequent fall of that important post, are justly due.

★★★★★★

The Canadian Government certainly dealt with an open hand; in this respect possessing an immense advantage over its rivals, whose bounty, diluted through a dozen provinces, could never be brought to bear on a given point with the same efficacy that attended the operations of one centralized power.

What finally tended perhaps more than anything else to alienate the Indians of Western Pennsylvania from the people of that province was the injudicious conduct of the proprietary commissioners at the Congress of Albany, where, on the 19th of June, 1754, all the English colonies were actually or constructively represented, and where the Six Nations were present to join in the deliberations concerning their common interests. (Commissioners from all the New England colonies, from New York, Pennsylvania and Delaware, and Maryland, were in attendance; and Virginia and Carolina desired to be considered as present. II. *Doc. Hist. N.Y.*) In their warrant for convening this Congress, it is gratifying to observe how clearly some of the causes of Indian discontent were comprehended by the Lords of Trade; and how alive they were to the critical condition of the English interest. Smooth words and liberal gifts are recommended as a cure for past sorrows; and it was most imperatively urged that the allegations of fraudulent occupation of their land should be promptly and satisfactorily investigated. Liberal gifts, too, were sent from the Crown to buy the good-will of its dangerous allies. (VI. *Col. Rec,* 14. And see the proceedings of this conference, as preserved in the Johnson MSS., and published under the care of Dr. O'Callaghan in the second volume of the *Documentary History of New York.*)

On this occasion the Six Nations (claiming, it will be recollected, to be the absolute proprietors of the country in question, as well as protectors of their weaker nephews, the Delawares), made a forcible reply to the reproach by the Commissioners that the French had been permitted to build forts on the Ohio. Old Hendrick, that doughty Mohawk warrior (who the next year sealed with his life his devotion to the English by the pleasant waters of Horicon), answered that the conduct of the French had received no favour at their hands, he said:

> The Governor of Virginia and the Governor of Canada are both quarrelling about lands which belong to us: and such a quarrel as this may end in our destruction. They fight who shall have the land. The Governors of Virginia and Pennsylvania have made paths through our country to trade and build houses, without acquainting us with it. They should first have asked our consent to build there, as was done when Oswego was built. (II. *Doc. Hist. N.Y.*)

This statement of the old Mohawk, like many other Indian speeches, was true but in part; and the commissioners, in turn, while they confessed that they ever had, and still acknowledged, the Ohio country to belong to the red men, reminded them that for thirty years traders from Pennsylvania had, without interruption, been in the custom of visiting the tribes dwelling there. All that was now intended, it was said, was to protect them in the free enjoyment of their own property, and to drive away the intruding Frenchman. By these speeches, and a judicious distribution of gifts, their savage ire was so far subdued, that ere the council closed some of the Six Nations were actually prevailed upon to sell to the proprietaries of Pennsylvania all the land in controversy!

This fatal purchase, comprehending about 7,000,000 acres, was bounded on the north by a line to be drawn north-west by west from Shamokin, on the Susquehannah, to Lake Erie; on the east, by the Susquehannah; on the south and west, by the furthest limits of the province. It included not only the hunting-grounds of the Delawares, the Nanticokes, the Tuteloes, and other lesser tribes, but the very villages of the Shawanoes and Delawares, of the Ohio; who could not yet have forgotten that, by precisely similar means, they had been driven hither from their former homes; and they now were to anticipate nothing less than the same fate.

It is possible that there might have existed, in some age or country, a race base enough to submit to these degrading conditions; but no sane man could have anticipated such a tame surrender from the American savage. The tribes actually dwelling there were not consulted in the business. They had no deputies at the council to join in the sale; and the whole transaction was smuggled through in an unjust, underhanded manner. The chiefs of the Iroquois who conducted it were not authorised to act for their people in the premises; and, when it came to light, the negotiation was solemnly repudiated by the Grand Council of Onondaga. (Thomson.)

All their discontents thus fanned into a flame, the Ohio Indians honourably determined to fight to the last in defence of their liberties; and in revenging this last and crowning outrage, to wipe away the well-remembered wrongs, real and fancied, which had rankled in their bosoms for years. For their own protection, the tribes, on the Susquehannah formed a league, which was strengthened by daily accessions of straggling families, scattered, as chance or fancy dictated, along the brook-sides or under the edge of some forest-glade of that umbrose, scaturiginous land.

At the head of this federacy was placed Tadeuskund, a Delaware chieftain, well known in border history; who, after dallying a space with either party, finally yielded to the pressure of the times, and joined with his race in the warfare against the English. (Thomson.)

★★★★★★

74

A MINGO INDIAN OF OHIO COUNTRY

Heckewelder's *Hist. Account of Indian Nations.* The latter author would lead us to suppose that the Wyoming chief never actually took up arms; but Thomson, who knew him well, is explicit on this point; and in the political tract called the Plaindealer, No. III. (Phil., 1764), is an undeniable instance of his prowess against the settlers of Northampton County. A memoir of Tadeuskund, the last *sagamore* of the Lenape, who remained east of the Alleghanies, whose consequence was so great as to win him the title of the "King of the Delawares," is given in Heckewelder, *ut sup.* He was burned in his lodge, in the spring of 1763. In the language of Uncas, that grandest of Cooper's portraitures, "he lingered to die by the rivers of his nation, whose streams fell into the sea. His eyes were on the rising, not on the setting sun."

★★★★★★

What share the Iroquois had in bringing about this conjuncture, can never, it is probable, be with certainty known. Zeisberger, in Ettwein's narrative, it is true, openly charges the Six Nations with having secretly placed the hatchet in the hands of the Delawares, bidding them to strike; and afterwards turning treacherously against them for this very conduct.

★★★★★★

I. Bull. *Hist. Soc. Penn.*, No. 3. The Rev. John Ettwein was a Moravian missionary for many years among the savages. He died a bishop of that church, at Bethlehem, Pennsylvania, in 1802, in the 73rd year of his age. Rev. David Zeisberger was a devout brother of the same order, who went hand and soul with Heckewelder in his heroic labours.

★★★★★★

But perhaps a just version of the affair would be to suppose that individual warriors of the Six Nations, acting on their own impulses (which in many instances were abundantly hostile to the English), egged on the Ohio Indians and the rest to a step which was never recommended by the confederates in their national capacity. Subsequently, the Iroquois reluctantly, but vigorously, entered into the measures of Sir William Johnson, and were of great service in the ensuing contest.

As ill-blood in the human system first discovers itself in eruptions and disorders, the malignity and unfriendly dispositions of the border tribes soon began to be manifested in preparations for war, in casual rencontres, and other sporadic acts of violence. Then, indeed, the proprietary government, having unavailingly sought, with insufficient means, to appease the ire of the foes whom hitherto it had looked on almost as subjects, vainly having tempted them to

——*Unthread the rude eye of rebellion,*
And welcome home again discarded Faith,

undertook, as to a court of last resort, to bring the delinquents before the tribunal of their lords, the Six Nations. These, entering warmly into the merits of the case, peremptorily charged the Delawares to forthwith repent, while yet there was time; to lay aside their arms, and make their peace for past offences: "Get sober," said they, in the metaphorical manner of Indian speech; "your actions have been those of a drunken man." But the palmy days of yore were gone, when the trembling Delaware stood cowering, like a whipped hound, before the frown of an Iroquois, and quaked to his inmost soul at the awful voice of the undying fire. A blind, unhesitating submission to the imperious, unreasonable mandates of the tribes that had so long oppressed and insulted his nation, was no longer written on his heart. He had resolved to throw off the petticoat, and to again assume the proud rank of a warrior of the once dreaded Lenni Lenape—'a son of the Great Unamis'—among the children of the forest; and to the words of the Iroquois, he returned scoff for scoff and scorn for scorn.

★★★★★★

The true title of the gallant tribe whom we call the Delawares was Lenni Lenape—"original people"—for they claimed to be of the pure, unmixed race, with which the earth was first populated, and would proudly boast, "We are the grandfathers of nations." The river whose banks was their chosen seat they named the *Lenapewihittuck*, or, "the rapid stream of the Lenape." And when the English renominated it in honour of Lord De la Warre, the people, with whose name its own was previously wedded, were still continued in the same connection. Heckewelder gives a most interesting account of the history of the Lenape.

★★★★★★

The tribes on the Susquehannah said to the deputies who had borne them the injurious behests of the Six Nations:

We are men, we are men and warriors. We will acknowledge no superiors upon earth. We are men and are determined to be no longer ruled over by you as women. We are warriors and are determined to cut off all the English save those that make their escape from us in ships. So, say no more to us on that head, lest we make women of you as you have done of us. (Thomson.)

Their day of serfdom had gone by; and from that time forth, the Delawares were once more an independent nation. Nothing could now be done with them by threats; but it was soon discovered that long habits of association still preserved their effect; and the friendly influence of the Six Nations being led to bear on them by Sir William Johnson, the best beloved of all the white men, they were eventually brought into measures of peace. To follow this theme further, would be to transcend the proper limits of our narrative. Suffice it to observe here, that many of the Iroquois themselves joined heart and hand in the original designs of the Delawares and would never consent to come into the national views of their own people.

Even while the Six Nations were openly at war with the French, many of their warriors were in arms at Fort Du Quesne against the English, and using all their influence to bring other Indians into the same views. When the Delawares began to waver in the hasty course they had adopted; we find these men using every argument to hold them firm; and it is curious to observe with what contemptuous in-difference the lately subservient, "petticoated" Delaware had already begun to treat "their uncles the Iroquois." When Post brought over-tures to Logstown, near Fort Du Quesne, the Delawares received him kindly; but one of the Iroquois who were there, an old Onondaga warrior, bitterly resented his presence:

I don't know this *Swannock* (or Englishman), it may be that *you* know him. I, and the Shawanoes, and our fathers the French do not know him. I stand here, (stamping his foot), as a man on his own ground. Therefore I, and the Shawanoes, and our fathers, don't like that a *Swannock* come on our ground.

This allusion to the ancient claim of sovereignty by the Six Na-tions was too much for Delaware patience to endure, and one of them instantly rose and replied:

That man speaks not as a man: he endeavours to frighten us by saying that this is his ground. He dreams. He and his father have certainly drank too much liquor: they are drunk. Pray let them go to sleep till they are sober. You don't know what your own nation (the Iroquois), do at home; how much they have to say to the *Swannocks*. You are quite rotten: you stink, (*i.e.* Your sentiments are offensive.) You do nothing but smoke your pipe

78

here. Go to sleep with your father, and when you are sober we will speak to you. (Thomson.)

Nevertheless, if they slew the English, it was not for love of the French. Equally jealous of both parties, all the savage desired was to see his old hunting-grounds unpolluted by the armies of the stranger, untrodden save by its native denizens; and so that this object was attained, the defeat of either or both would not seriously discompose him: to him, the success of either was a matter of as little importance—*que le chien mange le loup ou que le loup mange le chien*, (that the dog eats the wolf or that the wolf eats the dog.) With accurate perception, he gloomily dwelt on the idea that the permanent occupation of his lands was the real object of their controversy, and he bitterly vowed this should never be.

★★★★★★

"D—n you," said Shamokin Daniel, a Delaware warrior on the Ohio, to the English, "why don't you and the French fight on the sea? You come here only to cheat the poor Indians and take their lands from them!" There was more of truth than of elegance in this pithy address, but it was echoed by his fellows: "The French say they are come only to defend us and our lands from the English, and the English say the same thing about the French; but the land is ours and not theirs." Thomson.

★★★★★★

But alas for the poor savage! Driven before the ever-onward surge of civilization, that may recede for a moment, but only to return with a mightier force, his shattered tribes—prostrated by the inherent defects in their own character and debilitated by Christian vices, their naturally ferocious tempers sharpened by the use of rum, the presence of poverty, and the memory of better days—have continued and shall continue to retire more and more westwardly, till already the scanty remnants of the people whose fathers are buried by the broad waters of the Delaware, who daily gazed upon the Atlantic waves freshening in the light of the morning; now linger out a precarious life on the distant prairie whose face is wasted, as with fire, by the caravan of the emigrant; and pitch their lodges on declivities whose waters flow down into another ocean. Already with prophetic ear they hearken to the chafings of those billows which are the limit of an existence that has held a continent in its span: already they foresee the day when the wild cry of the sea-fowl, circling over the faint, murmuring waves of the ultimate Pacific, shall drown the parting sigh of the last of the Lenni Lenape!

Such then was the condition and disposition of Indian sentiment in Pennsylvania previous to and during the earlier stages of the war. We have seen how readily, in the summer of 1754, Major Washington had obtained the services of a large body of savages against the French: and we may judge from this fact alone how practicable it would have been to have enlisted them on the same side during the whole contest. It was impossible for a fight to come off at their very doors without their taking a share in it, on one side or another; and £10,000 well and liberally expended in presents at Fort Cumberland, with a fair-dealing or at least a plausible exposition of the designs of the English concerning their lands, would have bound all the Pennsylvania Indians in a common interest.

Had such a consummation been effected, the scalp of every Frenchman on the Ohio would have been smoke-dried in the *wig-wams* of Shamokin, or festooning the hoop-poles of Shenango, years before the British ensign was fated to be displayed upon the ramparts of Fort Du Quesne. But a different policy was unfortunately pursued, as will presently have to be noticed; and the bloody trophies which by hundreds graced the horrid triumph of the savage, were torn from the bodies of the English. In the meantime, let us resume the thread of our story.

CHAPTER 4

The Gathering of Arms

When, in August, 1754, the tidings of the fall of Fort Necessity reached London, the exigencies of the case compelled the ministry to an energetic action. The affairs of the American colonies were at that time committed to the care of the Secretary of State for the Southern Province, assisted by the Board of Trade. (I. Walpole's Memoirs of George II.) Since the days of Sir Robert Walpole, this Board had lingered out a supine, sinecure existence. The Secretary during all this period was the Duke of Newcastle, who, like the Old Man of the Sea in the Arabian tale, clinging about the neck of power with a tenacity that effectually prevented any policy but such as his own jealousy of merit or time-serving selfishness dictated, had hitherto carefully suppressed any indication of a desire on the part of his colleagues or subordinates to deserve the public approbation by the exercise of a capacity to promote the public good.

The records of the Board of Trade were crowded with packages of

A Plan of the Fort and Barracks at Mount Pleasant in Maryland

References

A. The Commanding Officers House
B. ... House of ... is 15 feet by 24 each
C. ... Guard Room ... 24 feet by 9.
D. ... Ward Room .... 15 feet by 9
E. Magazine
F. Sally Port
G. Company Parade
H. Officers Quarters
I. Mens Barracks
K. Commissary House
L. Hospital
M. Places of ...
N. Fort Yards 25 feet by 40
O. Fort Gate 8 feet
P. P... Barrada
Q. ... Gate
R. ...
S T. Watercourses

Wills Creek

Branch of the River Potomack

Ground of Virginia

Scale of Feet

Fort Cumberland

Wills Creek

remonstrances from the colonies, its tables were covered with bundles of unread representations and unnoticed memorials. It seems indeed to have existed for no other object than, in the language of Mr. Pitt, to register the edicts of one too powerful subject. Of the nature of American affairs, of the requirements and circumstances of the provinces he misruled with absolute sway, of their very geography he was ludicrously ignorant.

★★★★★★

When General Ligonier hinted some defence to him for Annapolis, he replied with his evasive, lisping hum—"Annapolis, Annapolis! Oh! yes, Annapolis must be defended; to be sure, Annapolis should be defended—where is Annapolis?" (T. Walpole's *Geo. II.*).

"He was generally laughed at," says Smollett, "as an ape in politics, whose office and influence served only to render his folly the more notorious."

At the beginning of the war, he was once thrown into a vast fright by a story that 30,000 French had marched from Acadia to Cape Breton.

"Where did they find transports?" was asked.

"Transports!" cried he; "I tell you they marched by land."

"By land to the island of Cape Breton!"

"What, is Cape Breton an island? Are you sure of that?" And away he posted, with an "Egad! I will go directly and tell the king that Cape Breton is an island!"

The weaknesses of this man afforded an endless theme to the sarcasm of Smollett's muse. In another place, his manner of farewell to a general departing for America is exquisitely satired; "Pray, when does your Excellency sail? For God's sake have a care of your health and eat stewed prunes on the passage—next to your own precious health, pray, your Excellency, take care of the Five Nations—our good friends, the Five Nations—the Toryrories, the Maccolmacks, the Out-of-the-ways, the Crickets, and the Kickshaws. Let 'em have plenty of blankets, and stinkibus, and *wampum*; and your Excellency won't fail to scour the kettle, and boil the chain, and bury the tree, and plant the hatchet, ha!"

In Bubb Dodington's *Diary*, will be found other instances of the duke's silliness.

★★★★★★

In the language of the great critic and satirist of the day, he was the strangest phenomenon that ever appeared in the political world.

A statesman without capacity, or the smallest tincture of human learning; a secretary who could not write; a financier who did not understand the multiplication-table; and the treasurer of a vast empire who never could balance accounts with his own butler.

It is not surprising, then, that such a character should neglect or blunder through his duties, careless of the result so long as his own importance at court was not diminished. But fortunately for Britain as well as America, the presidency of the Board of Trade was filled at this juncture by the Earl of Halifax, a man of parts and ambition, who was neither disposed to slumber on his post, nor to omit any opportunity of strengthening his own official power by enlarging the scope of his duties. We may fairly attribute to his energy the adoption in the cabinet of a resolution no longer tamely to submit to encroachments that, unless speedily checked, would inevitably turn all the channel of Indian trade from our borders, and immuring the colonies between the sea-board and the mountains, leave them to wither and perish; as a pool turned aside from its parent stream and enclosed with embankments, dries up beneath the rays of the sun.

Nevertheless, in the first steps taken by the ministry on this matter, Halifax was not consulted. The king had already held two councils upon American affairs, and instructions had been sent out to the provincial governors to repel any French encroachments force by force.

★★★★★★

It is His Majesty's command, that in case the subjects of any foreign prince should presume to make any encroachments in the limits of His Majesty's dominions, or to erect forts on his Majesty's lands, or to commit any other act of hostility; and should, upon a requisition made to them to desist from such proceedings, persist in them, they should draw forth the armed force of their provinces, and use their best endeavours to repel force by force. (I. Entick.)

★★★★★★

This policy had been decided upon; it was known how ingloriously its first practical workings under Washington had failed. Fired with the consciousness that, vigorous measures to regain the ground thus lost must immediately ensue, Newcastle resolved to arrogate the entire merit and patronage of the plan to himself. Like the Athenian weaver, he would fain retain for his own glorification every part in which there was the least opportunity of gaining distinction, however incompetent he might be to fulfil it. Summoning to his secret counsels the Lord Chancellor Hardwicke and the Earl of Holdernesse, he endeavoured in vain to fructify a conception which might subserve at once the public good and his private gain.

But natural incapacity, joined with talents which, though great, were transplanted for the occasion to an alien soil, could effect nothing. To organise military measures, military men must be consulted; to act with advantage in the colonies, some little knowledge of colonial affairs was required; and the Duke of Cumberland, the head of the army, and the Earl of Halifax, the best authority on plantation questions, were both studiously excluded from the deliberations of the *triumvirate*.

Independent of any other reason of jealousy, it was evident that, in such an undertaking, the properest persons to direct its appointments were Cumberland and Halifax; and this was enough to alarm the Duke of Newcastle. His policy was to cook up, from the information of obscurer men, some scheme in which himself should shine the *magnus Apollo*, the dispenser of favour, and the sole original of reward. He first, therefore, summoned to his aid a Mr. Horatio Gates, a young English officer, who had recently served with reputation in America; and desired his advice.

★★★★★★

Horatio Gates, afterwards so distinguished in American history, is said to have been the son of a respectable victualler in Kensington, and the godson of Horace Walpole. This latter circumstance may account for Walpole's knowledge of the details of the interview with Newcastle, which he certainly did not arrive at through the minister. Gates was born in 1728. Soon after his return to England from Nova Scotia, he must have gone back to America; since we find him in command of the King's New York Independent Company under Braddock. It is believed these companies were formed of the regiments disbanded in 1748-9.

Those stationed in Carolina were the remains of Oglethorpe's old regiment (*Penn. Gaz.*, No. 1338); and it may be noticed here that while a part of his former command was thus posted in his vicinity, others followed Oglethorpe to his new colony, and became founders of the State of Georgia. The Independents do not seem to have had any field-officers; consequently, promotion must soon have lifted Gates from this sphere, since we find him, in 1759, acting as aide, with the rank of major, to Hopson, or his successor, Barrington, at the reduction of Martinico. In July, 1760, he was brigade-major, under Monckton, at Fort Pitt. (III. Shippen MSS.)

★★★★★★

Gates modestly avowed his youth and inexperience; pleaded that he had seen nothing of America save the parts of Nova Scotia in which his regiment had been quartered, and his consequent incompetence to devise such an important operation. He professed his willingness to answer any questions that might be put to him; but he was too astute to be led into the enunciation of any grand system, the burthen of which he well knew would, in case of failure, break down his own shoulders, while all the praise of success would accrue to his superiors. In short, he utterly declined acting as he was desired.

The trio next fell upon a Quaker gentleman, a Mr. Hanbury, whose connections were such that he happened to know a little about America, though nothing, probably, of warfare; and at his suggestion, Virginia was selected as the basis of operations, and it was determined to entrust the whole conduct of the business to Horatio Sharpe, Lord Baltimore's Lieutenant-Governor of Maryland. Though Sharpe was a lieutenant-colonel in the Royal Army, he had never been engaged. (This grade—which, however, was local, and confined to the West Indies—Sharpe received July 5th, 1751. He held it so late as 1778.) But when the contrivers of his promotion laid their plan before the king, it was accompanied with a declaration that he had served through the whole of the last war, and was well known to possess the good opinion of the Duke of Cumberland: The latter replied:

So good, that if Sharpe had been consulted, I am sure he would have refused.

In the meanwhile, however, his appointment was forwarded to him by the hands of Governor Arthur Dobbs, of North Carolina. (The governor, with his son, Captain Dobbs, had arrived at Hampton Roads, Oct. 1, 1754, in the *Garland*, after a stormy trip, in which the ship lost her main and mizzen-masts. They brought with them, also, £10,000 in specie for Virginia.) His instructions would seem to have contemplated nothing beyond the capture of Fort Du Quesne by a provincial force, although there was an intimation of a considerable body of regulars being shortly sent over from Great Britain. Proceed-

ROBERT DINWADDIE

ing at once to Williamsburg, he concerted with Dinwiddie and Dobbs his measures to effect the desired end. It was concluded to raise immediately 700 men, with whom, and the three Independent companies, the French fort should be attacked and reduced, ere reinforcements could be brought thither from Canada or Louisiana.

This effected, that post and another which he thought it would be necessary to erect on a small island in the river, were to be held for the king. To garrison these and the fort at Will's Creek would require all his forces, and he concluded it would be useless for them to attempt anything further against the enemy on Le Boeuf and Lake Erie "without they be supported by such a body of troops from home as he dared not presume to hope for the direction of." But his enlistments went on slowly; and at Will's Creek, where his men were to rendezvous, he learned that the French strength on the Ohio was much increased by the arrival of a number of Ottawas, Adirondacks, and Caughnawaga Indians; and he therefore abandoned all hope of striking an immediate blow.

As had been intimated to Sharpe, more effectual means were on the tapis; but he was not destined to control them. The most that his supporters could urge to the king in his favour was, that if not remarkably able, he was at least a very honest man. The monarch shrewdly replied:

A little less honesty, and a little more ability, might, upon the present occasion, better serve our turn.

It was decided to make, forthwith, a general movement; and for once Newcastle was compelled to yield to the counsels of abler men. At all events, it is certain that Cumberland's influence was eventually paramount in the formation of the scheme finally adopted.

★★★★★★

I. Walp. *Geo. II.* MS. Sharpe's *Corresp.* VI. *Col. Rec.* Though Sharpe's views in regard to the campaign seem to have been very sagacious, yet it appears clearly, from this correspondence, that it was to his and Dinwiddie's suggestions that the royal order settling the comparative rank of provincial and regular officers was attributable—a step fraught with dangerous consequences to the best interests of the crown.

★★★★★★

Rather with a view, we may believe, to conciliate by a show of confidence, than to obtain the benefit of his advice, Newcastle sought

Fort Le Boeuf

to communicate the details of his plans to Mr. Pitt; but the disappointed statesman gave him a curt interruption:

> Your Grace, I suppose, knows, that I have no capacity for these things; and therefore, I do not desire to be informed about them.

While all these intrigues were going on, the ambassadors of the two powers—the Duc de Mirepoix and the Earl of Albemarle, two very fine gentlemen, but sadly deficient in the qualifications necessary for the place and the moment—were frittering away their time in idle negotiations and empty professions of pacific intentions. Neither kingdom set the least practical store by these assurances, but busily went on arming for the steps they respectively purposed taking. Strong reinforcements were prepared in France for its American possessions, with instructions to hold, *à la main forte,* all they had hitherto acquired; while, on the other hand, the English ministry ordered their governors to thrust out every intruder they found upon their backlands, at whatever cost.

Some anxiety was also manifested to enlist the services of the Indians; who had, as was well known in London, relaxed in their friendship. From Virginia, Dinwiddie had written, in August, 1754, to the other colonies for aid in men and money to defend their common cause; while to England he had applied for ordnance. This last demand was gratified by a present of two thousand stand of arms and accoutrements. Indeed, it was upon Virginia that the hopes of the crown chiefly reposed; for Pennsylvania politics, as will presently be shown, were not such as to inspire much confidence in the military capacity of that wealthy province.

While the eloquent Whitfield, and other religious lecturers at Philadelphia, availed themselves of the presence of the enemy on their frontiers to lend an additional fervour to their exhortations, (*Penn. Gaz.,* No. 1341), the Cabinet of London were preparing more effective fulminations against the French. The Duke of Cumberland (who, whatever may have been his other demerits, was certainly possessed of a military capacity) had been now called into the councils of the king; and, under his moulding hand, the preparations for an expedition whose destination was, as yet, kept secret from the public, began to assume some form and coherency. It was soon known, however, that two regiments of the line were designed for Virginia—the colony to which public attention had chiefly been attracted.

Nothing was, as yet, said of their ulterior movements; and it was a perfectly reasonable thing for Great Britain to station so small a force in her plantations—a force which, according to Horace Walpole, was too insignificant to be of any service if the French intended to stand firm, but far too large to be exposed to the certain destruction of health and constitution of an American climate. (Letter to Sir H. Mann, Oct. 6, 1754. III. *Walp. Corresp.*) For the charges of this expedition. Parliament, on the 28th of November, 1754, voted the following sums, (*Univ. Mag.*, 1755):

For two regiments of foot to be raised for North America; . .	£40,350 15s.
For defraying the charges of the officers appointed to go with the forces commanded by General Braddock;	£7338 2s. 6d.
For defraying the charges of the officers appointed to attend the hospital for the expedition commanded by General Braddock;	£1779 7s. 6d.
	£19,468 5s.

CHAPTER 5

General Braddock

Of the personal history of the gentleman to whom the command in Virginia had thus been entrusted, little or nothing more than what is contained in the public records of the period has, with unwearied care and research, been discovered to reward the student's curiosity. Before his name had become immortal in the scanty annals of the defeat and disgrace of British arms, Braddock had not done anything to earn himself a place in the chronicles of the times. Even the writers of memoirs, those gleaners in the fields of history had not stooped to bind up such a poppy blossom in their sheaves: no "snapper up of unconsidered trifles" had sketched his biography.

And so great, so horrible was the *inignoscible* disaster that crowned his existence, that only in vouchsafing him a soldier's death does it fall short of tragic perfection. Then, when the minds of men were exasperate with the thrill of national dishonour, for the first and last time does Braddock's name appear staining with its shameful characters the pages of history. Yet even the most bitter of those who sate in judgment on him, allow him certain merits. Walpole says:

> Desperate in his fortune, brutal in his behaviour, obstinate in his sentiments, he was still intrepid and capable.

Though a man of wit, his associations had probably not been such as to give him any place in the memorials of the literary characters of the day previous to his campaign in America; and perhaps for the very reason, that merely as an officer of the Guards and the *elève* of the Duke of Cumberland, he was well known to a certain portion of the court and city, and totally unknown to the rest of the world, his conduct finds no place in the social history of the period. Though a professed man of pleasure, it is not likely that the aristocratic doors of Boodle's or White's were opened to an Irish adventurer; yet even there he would hardly have come in contact with many of "the mob of gentlemen who write with ease." The few noble *literati* of the time— the Walpoles, the Selwyns, and the Herveys—do not seem to have had much personal acquaintance with him. It was at some place of lower resort that he pursued Fortune and staked his little means at gleek, passage, or the E O table. Still, even such were not the accustomed haunts of the garreteers of Grubstreet or the *habitués* of the King's Coffee-House. (A place in Covent Garden Market, well known to houseless bards.) Thus, whether—

> *Obliged by hunger—or request of friends—*

—the chronicler took his pen in hand, he was not often apt to find food for his meditations in the behaviour of Braddock. It is in a letter of Mr, Shirley, his military secretary, written in all the confidence of friendship to Governor Morris, that the strongest picture of his character is to be found. Shirley was evidently, like all of his race, a man of ability and of ambition, and it was upon the observations of several months that his remarks were grounded:

> We have a general, most judiciously chosen for being disquali-fied for the service he is in, in almost every respect. He may be brave, for aught I know, and he is honest in pecuniary matters.

Benjamin Franklin, that sagacious and keen observer of human nature, sums up in a few words his opinion of Braddock's capacity.

> This general was, I think, a brave man, and might probably have made a figure as a good officer in some European war. But he had too much self-confidence, too high an opinion of the va-

MONONGAHELA,
July 8th 1755.
From a contemporary plan by
Patrick Mackellar, Engineer.

British.
Wagons.
Cattle & Packhorses.
French & Indians.

500 · 1000 YARDS.

Turtle Creek

Fraser's Ho.

Hollow Way

R. Monongahela

lidity of regular troops, too mean a one of both Americans and Indians. (Sparks' *Franklin*; VI. Col. Rec.: And Franklin's notion is followed by Lord Mahon, IV. *Hist. Eng.*)

Not dissimilar to this view is that of the English historian Entick, who, besides being a contemporary of Braddock, seems to have had access to very good sources of information in the preparation of his volumes.

> It has also been hinted, that much of the disappointment in this expedition was owing to the general himself, in point of conduct. The plan was laid, and his instructions settled in such a manner, as to put him always on his guard against ambuscades, which were to be expected in a march through woods, deserts, and morasses.
> But this gentleman, placing all his success upon the single point of courage and discipline, behaved in that haughty, positive, and reserved way, that he soon disgusted the people over whom he was to command. His soldiers could not relish his severity in matters of discipline: and, not considering the nature of an American battle, he showed such contempt towards the Provincial forces, because they could not go through their exercise with the same dexterity and ability as a regiment of Guards in Hyde Park, that he drew upon himself their general resentment. (I. Entick.)

From the confused and imperfect data that are obtainable at this day, it would seem that Braddock was an officer well versed in military science and tactics according to the system that then prevailed; a rigid martinet, utterly unforgiving to a neglect of duty; and a brave, unflinching soldier. It was never said during his life that he ever bade his men follow danger where he was not greedy to lead the way; and it will be seen in the course of these pages that he was as prompt himself to face perils and to encounter hardships as to exact a like readiness from those under his control. In short, his military character was precisely calculated to meet the approbation of the raiser of such a creature as the brutal Hawley; and, indeed, there were very many points of resemblance between these favourites: in the rebellion of 1745, the latter had even commanded the identical troops which Braddock now led.

But Hawley proved himself in the field a braggart and a poltroon, and if his defeat at the rout of Falkirk was not as fatal in its consequences as that of the Monongahela, it was infinitely more igno-minious to the general who with bloody rowels led a shameful flight. Braddock, whatever his defects, was too much of an Irishman ever to show the white feather. In private life, he was what would now be termed dissolute; he was prone to the debaucheries of his day and class, the bottle and the gaming-table; he was imperious, arrogant, and self-opinionated. But if dimmed by the vices of his profession, his character was also brightened by many of its virtues.

When or where Edward Braddock was born, there is no means of ascertaining. Dr. Goldsmith, with a poet's license, speaks of his family as one of the best in the kingdom, (Goldsmith's *Misc. Works*), and it is said to have been of Irish extraction; but even this is doubtful. (The name, certainly, does not seem to appear at all in the *Rotuli Hiberniae*, published by the Record Commission.) The name is certainly of Sax-on, rather than Celtic or Erse, origin; and so, indeed, is it asserted, in a sort of monody, apparently by a friend, published immediately after his death, in which its derivation is said to be from two Saxon words, signifying Broad Oak.

It is possible his father or grandfather may have been one of those English adherents of William of Orange, who found, in Irish confis-cated estates, the reward of their Protestant zeal; and this would, in a measure, account for the favour which some of the members of this family seem to have encountered at the hands of the House of Ha-nover. All that can now be discovered in this regard, however, is that, during the past century, with the exception of the father of the hero of this volume and his immediate posterity, there were none of the name who rose into public notice; and before and after that period, it is unknown in British history.

★★★★★★

There was a Sergeant Braddock in General Forbes's army in 1758, and the name occasionally occurs among the lists of London bankrupts and traders that adorn the columns of Syl-vanus Urban. But at present the Post-Office Directory shows that there is not one of that name resident in the 'royal city.' A highly respectable family in New Jersey, however, still bear, as I am told, the name of Braddock; and it likewise occurs in the Philadelphia and Pittsburg directories.

★★★★★★

His father, who was also named Edward Braddock, must have been born about the middle of the seventeenth century, since we find him

Native Indians in an ambush during Braddock's march to the Monongahela in 1755

a lieutenant in the Coldstream Guards at least as early as 1684. In 1690, he was their senior captain; on the 1st of October, 1702, he got his majority; and on the 10th of January, 1704, was appointed their lieutenant-colonel. He was gazetted a brigadier on the 1st of January, 1707, and a major-general on the 1st of January, 1709. In September, 1715, he retired from the service, and died at Bath, on the 15th of June, 1725. (*Gent. Mag.* 1707-10; II. MacKinnon's *Hist. Coldstreams*; III. Goldsmith's *Misc. Works*.)

This "honest, brave old gentleman, who had experienced some undeserved hardships in life," is buried there, in the Abbey Church of St. Peter and St Paul.

★★★★★★

I. *Gent. Mag.* (1731), 397. This seems to have been the fashionable place of sepulture for strangers: the reader will recollect Sir Lucius and his "I'm told there is very snug lying in the Abbey."

★★★★★★

The old general must have been in at least comfortable circumstances, since he left to his two daughters the sum of £6000: to his only son, in all probability, a much larger amount descended. This son was the Edward Braddock with whom we have now to do. One of the daughters, Fanny Braddock, committed suicide at Bath on the 8th of September, 1731. Her sister, also unmarried, had died some years before. Mistress Fanny Braddock—as the fashion of the day styled all unmarried women—was a lady singularly gifted with attractions of person and of mind, and was, by her sister's death, in 1728-9, in possession of a competent fortune. But, yielding to an undisciplined impulse, she sacrificed the latter to relieve the necessities of the man whom she loved; and the former speedily lost their lustre in the eyes of the gay throng whose esteem she coveted.

Without a stain upon her honour, she at length sank into a condition of despair, and at the gaming-tables—then the frequent resort of ladies of fashion in England, as now on the continent—she soon dissipated away the scanty remains of her patrimony. Wearied of life, unable longer to endure the painful contrast of her position as governess in the family of a respectable tradesman with the brilliant place she lately occupied, she resolved on self-destruction. During the long night-watches in her lonely chamber, her mind reverted to his infamy who had broken her heart and squandered her fortune. To drive away these mournful reveries, she took down a book and essayed to read. The volume was the *Orlando Furioso of Ariosto*; and she opened it at that passage of the ninth *canto* where Olympia mourns the perfidy that had shut every avenue of hope from her soul.

The fatal similarity of fortune weighed upon her mind and confirmed her in her unhappy resolve. With a firm step and unwavering will, she passed through the portals of the house of life, and in a moment more, was beyond the reach of human sympathy or human censure.

Nothing could increase the feelings of disgust with which the conduct of Edward Braddock, on this sad occasion, must inspire the reader. That, through her levities or his own misconduct, his affections should have been long since alienated from his sister, seems natural enough; but there must have been an inborn, consummate brutality, to guide the tongue which could frame no other expression of sorrow than:

Poor Fanny! I always thought she would play till she would be forced to tuck herself up!

★★★★★★

III. Walp. *Corresp.* Walpole tells us, that before making away with herself, she wrote, with her diamond, these lines (from *Garth's Dispensary, Canto* III.) upon her window-pane:

To die is landing on some silent shore,
Where billows never break, nor tempests roar:
Ere well we feel the friendly stroke, 'tis o'er.
The wise, through thought, th' insults of Death defy;
The fools, through blest insensibility.
'T is what the guilty fear, the pious crave;
Sought by the wretch and vanquished by the brave.
It eases lovers, sets the captive free;
And, though a tyrant, offers liberty.

The truth is, that, speaking twenty years after the event, the great letter-writer was led away by a similarity of sentiment and expression. The actual inscription was this:

O, death! thou pleasing end to human woe!
Thou cure for life! thou greatest good below!
Still mayst thou fly the coward and the slave,
And thy soft slumbers only bless the brave.
See I. Hone's *Every-Day Book.*

★★★★★★

No sensibility could exist in his heart who could, for the sake of a scurvy pun, jest upon the manner of a sister's death, and say that she had adopted this plan 'to tie herself up from cards!'

******

XXXII. *Gent. Mag.*, .542. *To tie one's self up from play*, was a cant phrase for incurring some obligation which should act as a restraint upon gambling. Thus, there was an instance of the Duke of Bolton receiving a hundred guineas from Beau Nash on a contract to repay £10,000 if he should ever lose as much at one sitting; and the duke actually soon found occasion, at Newmarket, to comply with his bargain, (III. Goldsmith's *Misc. Works.*)

******

Surely on this occasion Walpole was justified in terming Braddock "a very Iroquois in disposition!"

There is another anecdote which does not any more tend to give one a very elevated conception of his character. It seems that his virtues, such as they were, had won the favour of a certain Mrs. Upton, on whose infamous wages he was not ashamed to live. By constant applications, he had kept this poor fool's exchequer so dry, that one day she frankly answered a demand for money by pulling out her purse with but twelve or fourteen shillings in it. With the keen eye of an experienced forager, Braddock saw cause to suspect this was not all its contents. "Let me see that!" he cried and snatched it from her hand.

In the other end he found five guineas. Coolly emptying all the money into his pocket, he tossed the empty purse into his mistress's lap. "Did you mean to cheat me?" cried he; and he turned his back upon the house to see her no more. (III. Walp. *Corresp.*) This shabby transaction was a subject of town-talk in the coffee-houses and lobbies of the day; and was cleverly seized by Fielding and brought upon the Drury Lane boards in 1732, in a witty but licentious play, called the *Covent-Garden Tragedy*. Captain Bilkum (by whom, it is said, Braddock was meant) is made to thus deny the consolations of "the humming bowl," (A.I. sc.6):

> *Oh! 'tis not in the power of punch to ease*
> *My grief-stung soul, since Hecatissa's false;*
> *Since she could hide a poor half-guinea from me!*
> *Oh! had I searched her pockets ere I rose,*
> *I had not left a single shilling in them!*

If, indeed, the immortal satirist designed the whole of his character of Bilkum as a paraphrase of Braddock's, he could have held him but in the light of one of those hired ruffians whose office it is to awe into silence the poor cully whom their partners have robbed. This is going infinitely too far: an occasional solitary instance, such as has been cited, may have stained his reputation, but it was not a specimen of his general character. There were many better things in him than that: and perhaps it is pressing closely the limits of moderation to say that he kept his flight so near the ground that he could have stooped to such a scene of self-degradation. His faults were evidently considered by men of worth rather as foibles than vices: his intimacies were with persons of character and honour; and in many respects he was worthy of their confidence, though his excesses must often have lost it. It was thus that he became embroiled with Colonel Gumley, an old comrade and friend, whose sister was married to Pulteney, Earl of Bath; and a duel was the result.

As they met on the ground, Gumley, knowing very well the state of his opponent's finances, coolly tossed him his purse. "Braddock," said he, "you are a poor dog! Here, take my purse: if you kill me, you will have to run away; and then you will not have a shilling to support you."

His infuriated adversary was galled to madness by this new provocation; he lost all command of his temper, and quickly saw his sword fly from his hand; but he was still too proud to ask his life at the victor's hand. (III. Walp. *Corresp.*) Another duel between Braddock and Colonel Waller is recorded, fought with sword and pistol in Hyde Park, on the 26th of May, 1718: but of its cause or consequences nothing can be traced. (*Origin and History of the Coldstream Guards*, by Col. Daniel MacKinnon. Vol. II.)

As may be judged from the date of his first commission, Edward Braddock must have been born towards the close of the seventeenth century. On the 11th of October, 1710, he entered the army with the rank of Ensign in the grenadier company of the Coldstream Guards; and on the 1st of August, 1716, was appointed a lieutenant. (II. MacKinnon's *Coldstreams.*) In the columns of the *Gentleman's Magazine* his steps may be traced as follows:—On the 30th of October, 1734, Lieutenant Braddock was gazetted to a captain-lieutenancy. (IV. *Gent. Mag.* 628; II. MacKinnon.) On the 10th of February, 1736, he was appointed to a captaincy in the Second Regiment of Foot-Guards, (II. MacKinnon), and on April 2nd, 1743, he had risen to the rank of a lieutenant-colonel in the line and was further advanced to be the second major of this regiment. (XIII. *Gent. Mag.* 219; II. MacKinnon.)

At that period, as at present, the household troops were considered the choicest portions of the army, and a commission in their ranks could not be esteemed a light favour.

The Duke of Cumberland, the Captain-General of the British Army (a dignity in which the great Churchill and the good Ormond were his only predecessors), had been Colonel of the Second and was now in command of the First Regiment; and William Anne, Earl of Albemarle, was Colonel of the Second, or Coldstreams, to which Braddock was attached. It is more than probable, however, that his father's position in the regiment may have facilitated the young ensign's entrance; and it may be worth noting that the total period of service in this regiment of father and son did not fall short of seventy years, during all which period the name of Edward Braddock appeared on its roster. Nor was there anything unusual in a lieutenant-colonel of the line accepting an inferior majority in the Guards, when a field-marshal was their colonel, and the commissioned officers of other regiments were taken from their rank and file.

★★★★★★

This was particularly the case in 1746, when no less than twenty-six privates of the Life Guards were commissioned as lieutenants or ensigns in other regiments, many of them on American stations. It is believed that the famous geographer Thomas Hutchins, the historian of Bouquet's expedition, on this occasion received his first commission as ensign in the King's South Carolina Independent Company. *Hist. Rec., of the Life Guards.* These records of the British Army, which have been more than once referred to, were commenced twenty years since by command of William IV., and are intended to comprise a particular history of every regiment. The few volumes hitherto published are as elegant as useful; and it is to be regretted that so laudable an enterprise should progress so slowly.

★★★★★★

The recruiting standard of the regiment, it is true, was extraordinarily high: to be even a private in its ranks was not a privilege open to every subject of the crown, no matter how well he might by nature be qualified. No papist, no Scot or Irishman, no "vagabond," was suffered to be enlisted even as a private into this proud body; and the popular satire of the day shows what vulgar consequence was attributed to its non-commissioned officers.

★★★★★★

Witness the case of poor Dick Ivy, in Smollett's inimitable tale; the poet whom not "disappointment, nor even damnation," could drive to despair. And yet he could not make his quarters good in the milk-woman's cellar in Petty France, but "was dislodged and driven upstairs into the kennel by a corporal in the Second Regiment of Foot-Guards."

★★★★★★

One may form an idea of its arrogance when we find in the orderly-book of the Coldstreams a command to its men to behave civilly towards and not to laugh at or make game of the other troops, at a review by the king on the 26th of October, 1745. (II. MacKinnon.) Originally raised by Monk from the *élite* of Hesilrige's and Fenwick's parliamentary regiments, it took its name from its quarters at Coldstream, whence Monk marched it on New Year's day, 1660, "to restore the monarchy and give peace to his distracted country." At the Restoration it was specially exempted by Parliament from the universal disbandment of the army and was retained as a Guard by King Charles; and ever since that period it has continued to deserve and to enjoy a distinguished share of royal favour and public regard.

★★★★★★

It is believed that the only occasions upon which any considerable portion of this regiment was ever forced to ground its arms or surrender its colours wore at Ostend, in 1745, and at Yorktown, in 1781: on this last occasion the Guards either had no regimental flag, or it was secreted and never delivered.

★★★★★★

It would be an interesting task to trace the means by which a man destitute of all influence of family connection or prestige of great wealth—a mere Irish soldier of fortune, as by some he is termed—should have obtained and continued to retain through a long series of years such a desirable position. It may have been indeed that he purchased his promotions; but the cost of such a step was always enormous, and it is not likely that he should have had sufficient resources at his command.

★★★★★★

In 1720, the king fixed the price of a Lieutenant-Colonelcy in the Coldstreams at £5000; a Major's commission cost £8600; a Captain's £2400; a Captain-Lieutenant's £1500; a Lieutenant's £900; an Ensign's £450. In 1766, these rates were about doubled; and at present the Lieutenant-Colonelcy is worth £9000,

and an Ensigncy £1200. (I. MacKinnon.) The purchaser, however, must pass a previous examination to prove his competency,
and the money, it is believed, goes to the retiring officer.

★★★★★★

It is to his merit and actual services that we are inclined to attribute
his success. At the period of his appointment, a large portion of the
Second Foot-Guards were with Marlborough in Flanders; and it is not
improbable that thither the young soldier was sent to learn the first
rudiments of the art of war. In March, 1713, the regiment was recalled
to London, and on September 18th of the next year, Braddock's company was one of those which on his arrival received the first Elector
of Hanover who reigned over England. In 1719, a part of the regiment
took share in the Vigo expedition, and in 1742, its first battalion was
sent to the Low Countries, and Braddock undoubtedly among them.

At Dettingen, on the 16th of June, 1743, the Second Guards, commanded by the second Duke of Marlborough, behaved gloriously under the very eyes of the King and the Duke of Cumberland. At the
famous Battle of Fontenoy, fought on the 11th of May, 1745, between
Marshal Saxe, with Louis XV. and the Grand *Dauphin* by his side, and
the English and Dutch Allies, whose Captain-General was Cumberland, the Coldstreams again won great honour, losing in killed and
wounded two hundred and forty men.

Everyone knows what terrible slaughter took place on that memorable defeat, when the Irish Brigade fiercely swept away the thinned
ranks of the British, and gratified, for the first time since the fall of
James the Second, the feelings of triumphant revenge. But amid all the
carnage and confusion, the English Guards gained scarce less praise by
their cool retreat than by their furious charges, sullenly moving off
like a lion who, undismayed and almost disposed to turn again, grimly
recedes into the darkness from the watch-fire of the hunters.

★★★★★★

Perhaps history does not afford a more striking instance of undaunted courage, joined with the perfection of discipline, than
was displayed by the Guards on this memorable day. They were
ordered to attack the French Guards and the Swiss; who, in
perfect confidence, awaited the onset. The English advanced,
composed and steady as though on parade. As they drew near,
their officers, armed with nothing but a light rattan, raised their
hats to their adversaries, who politely returned the salute.

"Gentlemen of the French Guards," cried Captain Lord Charles

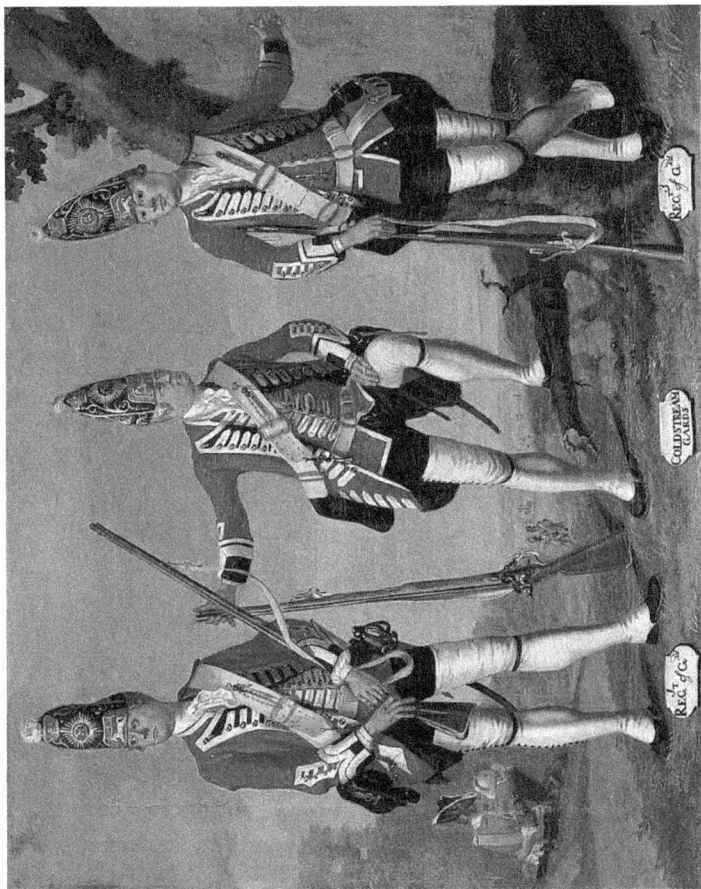

1st and 3rd Regiments of Foot Guards and Coldstream Guards

Hay, "fire, if you please."

"Pardon, *Monsieur!*" replied they; "the French Guards never fire first: pray fire yourselves!"

The order was given, and the French ranks were mowed down as ripe grain falls beneath the sickle. The English behaved throughout the conflict with the same steadiness; their officers in the heat of the fight with their canes turning the men's muskets to the right or the left as they seemed to require. (*Voltaire: Précis du Siècle de Louis XV.*, c. xv.) After nearly fifty years' service in such a regiment, no wonder that Braddock had formed exalted ideas of discipline.

★★★★★★

It was for his share in this day's bloody work, we may presume, that Braddock received, on the 27th of May, 1745, his promotion to be First-Major of his regiment, (XV. *Gent. Mag.* 333; I. II. MacKinnon), and on the 21st of the next November, to be its Lieutenant-Colonel. (XV. *Gent. Mag.*, 668; II. MacKinnon.) In the summer of 1745, he was with the Second in garrison at Ostend, whence in July he repaired to England to acquaint the Lords of the Regency with its condition, and thus probably escaped being present at its surrender on the 12th of August. (I, MacKinnon.) When Cumberland pursued Prince Charles's army from England in the winter of 1745-6, we know that Braddock was actively employed under his command, (I. MacKinnon), and probably shared in the butcherly glories of Culloden.

In September, 1746, he commanded the battalions of the First and Second Guards which were embarked upon the secret expedition of Lestock and Sinclair against Quiberon and L'Orient; and in May, 1747, at the head of the second battalion of the Coldstreams, was ordered to Flanders, where the Allies, under the Prince of Orange, were ineffectually striving to raise the siege of Bergen-op-Zoom. He was quartered in the autumn at Bois-le-Duc; in the winter near Breda; and in July, 1748, after marching to Ruremonde and encamping at Grave, was cantoned at Eyndhoven, where Cumberland had fixed his headquarters. Peace having been declared in January, 1749, the Coldstreams were once again stationed at London. As every company in this regiment has its own standard, it may be noted here that Braddock's ensign bore a star within a garter, with the union in the colour's *dexter*-corner; this device had first been adopted by Charles II. The badge was red. (I. MacKinnon.)

It is presumed that Lieutenant-Colonel Braddock continued attached to the Coldstreams until 1753; making a total of forty-three years' service in that regiment. If we suppose his age when he was made ensign to have been about fifteen years, we may conclude him to have been at least sixty years of age and upwards when he was killed in America. But, notwithstanding his appointment as brigadier-general on the 23rd of April, 1746, he was now, through debt or other causes, compelled to seek a temporary exile from England; and on the 17th of February, 1753, was nominated to the colonelcy of the Four-teenth Regiment of Foot, then stationed at Gibraltar. (XXIII. *Gent. Mag.*, 53. II. Mackinnon.) Anxious to lose no time at home, he has-tened to join his post, and set out at once to the Mediterranean; where his stay, though but temporary, was long enough to win the affections of a garrison rarely conspicuous for aught but violence and sedition.

★★★★★★

Walpole erroneously asserts (III. *Corresp.*) that he had been Governor of Gibraltar; "where, with all his brutality, he made himself adored, and where scarce any governor was endured before." But this is so far from being true, that it does not appear that between 1749 and 1753 he ever officially even acted as commandant in the governor's absence (Drinkwater's *Gibraltar*). He surely was never governor: martinet as he was, however, it is well to note this evidence of his popularity with his men.

★★★★★★

During his absence, nevertheless, he was not forgotten by his pa-tron and chief. On the 29th of March, 1754, he was gazetted a major-general, (XXIV. *Gent. Mag.*, 191); and, on the 24th of the ensuing September, was appointed to the command of the troops to be sent to Virginia, and *Generalissimo* of all His Majesty's troops on the North American Continent. (XXIV. *Gent. Mag.*, 530.)

These are meagre details, it must be confessed; and nothing can be unacceptable that will tend to clothe their dry skeleton with even the semblance of vitality. It may not, then, be amiss to refer to a tradi-tion (albeit, like most traditions, it be entitled to little credence) which insinuates that the secret of Braddock's advancement is, that he was a bold beggar—a sturdy tramp, so to speak—who, with an untiring per-tinacity that would not take No! for an answer, was forever dunning the authorities for renewed means of obtaining money and distinction.

To purchase at once relief from his importunities, and to promote the interests of the service, according to the same unreliable authority, he was selected for a distant command, the duties of which he was con-

105

fidently esteemed capable of perfectly fulfilling, while its emoluments would be something prodigious. Thus, it will be noticed, the foul finger of scandal has soiled alike the refutations of the adverse chiefs Braddock and Duquesne; two characters opposite as the poles in life but destined in their memories to an undying and indissoluble fraternity.

Such were the antecedents of the leader to whose hands the control of an expedition of such vital importance to the welfare of Great Britain and of America was committed. In the royal councils, the question had been thoroughly considered in all its bearings, and the most proper and feasible method of seizing the French forts and resuming possession of the wilderness they controlled was freely discussed.

One voice—which we may well believe to have been that of the sagacious Halifax—earnestly opposed the whole notion of relying upon British regulars to accomplish these desired ends: well aware of the nature of the contest that would ensue, he was for employing, at the government's expense, a provincial force, which should be raised upon the spot, among men familiar with the Indian warfare and the Indian country. Had this plan been adopted, and a sufficient number of regular troops added to preserve discipline and to garrison the posts to be acquired, there can be little question of its having met with perfect success.

CHAPTER 6

The British Army

The standing army of Great Britain was at that time singularly small, and still further reductions were in contemplation: in fact, when Braddock sailed, he left but three regiments in England; and so jealous was Newcastle lest Cumberland should have the filling up of commissions, that, in the very face of the coming storm, he would consent to no more being raised. (Walpole's *Mem. Geo. II.*) The rest of the army was scattered all over the world; and since the regular force was so incapable of enduring a heavy drain, one would have thought the idea of employing irregulars would have been highly acceptable.

The king, likewise, had four Independent Companies quartered at New York, three in South Carolina, and one at Providence. (*Historical Memoirs of the late Duke of Cumberland.*) These were not ranked with the regular line but were retained in America at the expense of Great Britain; and their services might have been most advantageously availed of in this crisis. The chief difficulty would have been the relative precedency of colonial and royal commissions; but even this might have been easily surmounted by making every officer receive his rank from the crown through the medium of a provincial authority; and the instances of Stanwix, Johnson, and Bouquet show what popularity might have attended the appointment of a commander not chosen from the regular ranks.

Meritorious as was this plan, it was utterly incomprehensible to the Duke of Cumberland, whose judgment was justly supreme in the cabinet on questions touching the art military. He was a person of fair capacity, of a thorough education in the German school of war—that school of discipline whose exponent was the great Frederick of Prussia—and was of the first rank in the service. He had heard a great deal, ten years before, of the value of irregulars: he had seen a whole empire trembling at the feet of a mere handful of undisciplined mountaineers; its armies blasted, its councils panic-struck, its rulers ripe for flight. With a ready wit he had taught his grenadiers to face and to foil this impetuous foe, and to turn the very secret of their success into failure and ruin.

He naturally now thought that the barbarians of America were to be encountered as successfully in 1755 as those of Scotland in 1745: and through his intervention, no other resolution was adopted by the ministry than that of placing their chief trust in a regular force. To Cumberland properly belongs all the responsibility of the conception and organisation of the executive portion of this enterprise, and the nomination of its leader. (I. Walp. *Mem. Geo. II.*; *Mems. of Cumberland.*) And conceding the question of the expediency of his policy, and considering the lights the duke seems to have possessed of the character of the war and the nature of the services expected from Braddock, it is not fair to say that the selection of the commander was an unwise choice. An enthusiast in the art of war, in which at an early age he had distinguished himself, the duke exercised, or endeavoured to exercise, an impartial regard to merit in his appointments; and we are particularly told, in regard to this one, that General Braddock's "courage and military discipline had recommended him as of ability for so great a trust." (I. Entick.)

★★★★★★

Smollett (*Adv. of an Atom*), says that Braddock was "an obscure officer, without conduct or experience, whom Cumberland selected for this service; not that he supposed him possessed of superior merit, but because no officer of distinction cared to engage in such a disagreeable expedition." He further intimates, too, an invincible aversion on the part of the duke and his royal father to the employment of Indian allies as scouts. But it is the satirist, not the historian, who speaks: the whole volume is one continued tirade against every person in power during the Seven Years' War, from Pitt and Mansfield to Frederick of Prussia and the Empress-Queen.

★★★★★★

The scheme which Braddock was to carry into effect was a very comprehensive one; and embraced nothing less than the complete restoration of English power upon the American Continent. (See Appendix 1.) As early as September, 1754, it was decided that two regiments of foot, the Forty-fourth, Colonel Sir Peter Halket, and the Forty-Eighth, Colonel Thomas Dunbar, then stationed in Ireland, should form the stamina of the proposed expedition. These were at once to be sent to the colonies, where, having effected the objects immediately in view, they were to remain three years, to put the country and its people in a suitable posture of future defence. (*Penn. Gaz.*, No. 1365.) It was intended that each of these regiments should embark five hundred strong, and that they should be recruited in America to a complement of seven hundred.

Two other regiments of one thousand men each, to be commanded respectively by Sir William Pepperell and William Shirley, Esq., the Governor of the province of Massachusetts-Bay, were likewise to be raised at the king's cost in America, and abundant stores of artillery, provisions, clothing, etc., were provided. In addition to these forces, which would at most make up but about thirty-five hundred men, the King's Independent Companies in America were to be under Braddock's command; and Royal Instructions had been sent to the different Governors, demanding not only the aid of the colonial troops, but the services of as many Indians as could be enlisted.

What with regulars, militia, and savages, it was hoped that England would thus be able to bring from twelve to fifteen thousand men into the field. With these a simultaneous movement was if possible to be made against Forts Du Quesne, Niagara, and Crown Point; while Colonel Lawrence, who was stationed in Nova Scotia, was instructed to capture Beau-Sejour; all these places being, according to British views, unlawfully occupied by France. An English fleet, hovering on the coast, was to intercept all military supplies from the French, and thus prevent their adding any fresh strength to the posts in question.

On the 14th of November, His Majesty opened Parliament with a

William Shirley

speech which, after the usual self-congratulatory remarks on the pa-cific relations still existing, announced his intention of improving the present advantages of a general peace to promote the commerce and protect the colonies in America. Parliament understood these words as they were meant, and straightway voted £4,000,000 for supplies; £1,000,000 of which was to increase the army and navy. The French representative, M. de Mirepoix, was not blind to this policy; but the object of his court was to stave off open hostilities, until it was thor-oughly prepared for the conflict: and accordingly the duke kept couri-ers flying from London to Paris, and from Paris to London, while he vowed and protested his master's intentions to be utterly pacific. But both countries persevered, notwithstanding their mutual diplomatic tergiversations, in steadily arming for the fray.

In the meantime, the preparations for the campaign were carried on with vigour and activity. It was settled that the 44th and 48th regiments should continue on the Irish establishment despite their transportation to America; thus, saddling its equivalent of the charges of the war on the sister kingdom, which, not being represented in the British parliament, was not called on to vote supplies. But their ranks being thinner than even in time of peace was customary, it was found necessary to recruit them by considerable drafts from other regiments, particularly from such as were then on duty in Ireland, unless sta-tioned at Dublin. A regiment of ten companies should have counted seven hundred men at its musters: it was believed that these would have mounted up to five hundred each, leaving the additional two hundred to be engaged in America; but the result showed a greater failure even than this.

To supply this deficiency, prompt steps were taken. On October 29th, 1754, one hundred men were drafted from Lord Bury's regiment (the 20th) at Bristol, and as many more from Colonel Buckland's at Salisbury, who were at once ordered to Cork, whither Major-General Bligh had already repaired from Dublin to superintend the proceed-ings for embarkation. (*Penn. Gazette*, No. 1360, No. 1362.) Early in the same month. Sir Peter Halket had picked up a few volunteers in London, and a sergeant and corporal of each company in the artillery were despatched to beat up recruits through the country. (*Penn. Gaz.*, No 1362.)

In Ireland, four sergeants, four corporals, five drums and sixty-five privates of Lieutenant-General Bragg's regiment (the 28th), and the same number from that of Colonel Pole (the 10th), at Limerick, were

PART OF LAKE ONTARIO

PLAN OF FORT NIAGARA,
with its ENVIRON.
Explanation.

A. The Fort.............. E. The Burying Place
B. The Dock & Harbour.. F. The Approaches
C. Two Lime Kilns....... G. The First Battery
D. The Brick Kiln....... H. The Second Battery
                          I. The Third Battery

Scale
100 Fathoms to an Inch

THE

RIVER

drafted to Cork: and in the beginning of November drafts were also made from Lieutenant-General Anstruther's regiment (the 26th), and from the second battalion of the Royals, at Galway. (*Penn. Gaz.,* No 1367.) So odious was their destined service, however, that every effort of the officers could not restrain desertion. Many of the new drafts or enlistments, too, consisted of the worst class of men, who, had they not been in the army, would probably have been in Bridewell; and this did not tend to elevate the personal standard of the two regiments.

The preparations in the way of military stores, ordnance, etc., were also conducted upon an extensive scale. Till the close of October, the workmen at the Tower were busily employed in making artillery and ammunition wagons and putting up cartridges for the expedition. Tents for eight thousand men, with marquees, drums, arms, accoutrements, &c., &c., as well as great quantities of ammunition, were shipped in the Thames for Cork. (*Penn. Gaz.,* No 1360.) Thither were also sent on the 9th of November twelve carriages with chests containing six hundred stand of arms from Dublin Castle. A number of army officers upon half-pay were recalled into service; and on the 19th of October, orders were issued to the artillery for a captain, four sergeants. and sixty bombardiers and matrosses, (artillery soldiers of a rank inferior to the bombardier or gunner) to hold themselves in readiness to embark at Woolwich for Virginia, (VI. *Penn. Col. Rec,* 303); upon the 28th, Mr. Montresor was gazetted as Chief Engineer, and James Pitcher, Esq., was named Commissary of the Musters. (II. *Penn. Gaz.,* No. 1360, No. 1369.)

Several additional surgeons were also provided; and James Napier, Esq., Master Surgeon of the Hospitals in Flanders during the preceding war, was appointed Director of the Hospitals belonging to the forces on the American expedition. (On the 15th of October, Sir John St. Clair, Lieutenant-Colonel of Offarrell's regiment of foot (the 22nd), had already been gazetted as Deputy Quarter-Master-General for all the forces in America, to rank as a colonel; who, with very little delay, hastened to Virginia to acquaint himself with the scene of his future duties.

Indeed, an unwonted energy reems at this time to have inspired the ministry. Not only were six thousand troops provided for the defence of the colonies at the cost of the crown, with an ample provision of the proper munitions of war (II. *Penn. Archives,* 293); but liberal supplies of money or its equivalent were granted to different provinces. To Virginia, for instance, were sent £10,000 in cash, with authority

48TH REGIMENT OF FOOT

to draw for as much more; and Pennsylvania, for purposes of war, was furnished with six hundred firelocks (or muskets), with bayonets, cartouche-boxes, &c., three tons of musket-balls, fifteen barrels of gunpowder, and five thousand flints. (II. *Penn. Archives*, 300.)

But all this unwonted display of vigour by a cabinet with whom ignorance and imbecility were the only stars that lighted the western horizon, was, *more suo*, destined to a rapid decline. During the ensuing three months exertion flagged, and nothing but delay and doubting appears to have characterized its proceedings. Upon the Sunday evening preceding the 12th of November, Braddock himself had arrived from France (on his route, we may suppose, from Gibraltar), at his house in Arlington Street, London; and on the same evening waited upon the king and the captain-general. The latter had arrived but at 9 a. m, of that same day, and had barely taken possession of his winter apartments. (*Penn. Gaz.*, No. 1362.)

During his brief stay in the metropolis, Braddock had long and repeated interviews with the duke, in which he received full and careful directions for his conduct; all of which, however, will be found repeated in the formal Letter of Instructions printed in the Appendix. On the Saturday before the 30th of November, he left Arlington Street for Portsmouth; whence he embarked for Cork on the *Centurion*, Commodore Keppel, to hasten and superintend the departure of the troops.

★★★★★★

The Hon. Augustus, second son of William Anne Keppel, 2nd Earl of Albemarle, was born April 2nd, 1725. He entered the navy as a midshipman at an early date and received his first wound at the capture of Paita. He met with rapid promotion, and at Goree and in the battle off Belleisle distinguished himself for good conduct. In 1762, he was a commodore in the fleet sent out under Sir George Pocock to the Havannah. In consequence of grave charges brought against him by Sir Hugh Palliser, he was court-martialled for his conduct in the sea-fight near Ushant on the 27th of June, 1778; but was most honourably acquitted, while his accuser became the object of general opprobrium. So strong was the sympathy with Keppel, that Parliament went to the unusual length of voting him its thanks. He had already (1763) been appointed Groom of the Bedchamber to the King; an office which he vacated in 1766. In 1782, he was made First Lord of the Admiralty; and in April of the same year, advanced to the peerage

114

under the title of Viscount Keppel of Elvedon, in the County of Suffolk. He died in 1786, when his title became extinct.

★★★★★★

But, with all his imperious energy and impatience of delay, it was not until the 14th of January, 1755, that his object was effected. The transport-ships from England came in irregularly and slowly. On the 19th of November, the *Seahorse*, man-of-war, had arrived there for this service; and on the 21st, the *Prince Frederick* transport. Burton master, of five hundred tons, of and from London, with stores, &c., made its appearance at Cork to take in troops. (*Penn. Gaz.*, No. 1368.) The *Centurion* followed close after, with most of the remaining transports and stores; and orders were at once issued for the men and baggage to be put on board. Still, there was a wearisome delay. Some transports, absolutely necessary to carry a portion of the expedition, which had duly sailed from England, were not yet arrived at the River Lee. A violent storm in the beginning of December had ravaged the coasts of Britain, and one vessel, with eight officers and sixty men on board, was lost off Falmouth. (III. Walp. *Corresp.*) The same gale had forced the *Severn*, Captain Rawlings, to put into Dartmouth, and the *Molly*, Captain Curling, to take refuge in Torbay.

CHAPTER 7

The Hour and the Man

Determined to wait no longer upon the tardy movements of the transports, Braddock, with his staff and a small part of the troops, returned to England in the *Centurion* and the sloop-of-war *Cruizer*, and on the 21st of December sailed from the Downs for Virginia; leaving the main body of the fleet to follow at their earliest speed. On the 20th of February, 1755, Commodore Keppel's little squadron, consisting of his own vessel, the famous *Centurion*, the *Norwich*, Captain the Hon. Mr. Barrington, and the *Syren*, Captain Proby, cast anchor in Hampton Roads.

★★★★★★

Not even the *Victory*, where Nelson died, was a more famous and favourite ship among British sailors than the old *Centurion*. In 1740, it was as her captain that Anson led his little squadron on their venturous voyage to "put a girdle round about the earth." In 1749, we find Keppel in command. In 1755, when he hoisted his broad pennant as commodore of the Virginia fleet, William Mantell, Esq., was his captain. Towards the end of July, the *Centurion*, along with the *Nightingale* and the *Syren*, Captain Proby, sailed from Hampton Roads northwardly; and on the 4th of September, she was with Boscawen's fleet (*Penn. Gaz.*, Nos. 1389, 1393).

Though rated as of 400 men and 60 guns, she mounted now but 54. In 1759, she covered Wolfe's landing at Quebec; and it is a little odd, that at the moment the two future circumnavigators, Cook and Bougainville, armed on opposite sides, were present with the ship whose fame rested on its having performed the same feat. When she at last was broken up, her figurehead—a lion, so exquisitely carved in wood as to suggest the workmanship of Gibbons himself—was preserved to delight the eyes of the Greenwich pensioners. It is still preserved at their Hospital. The Hon. Samuel Barrington, captain of the *Norwich*, was the 5th son of John, first Viscount Barrington. He was born in 1729, and died an admiral of the white, and lieutenant-general of the marines, 6th August, 1800. His second-lieutenant on this Virginia voyage was the celebrated Adam Duncan of Lundie, who had sailed with Keppel in the *Centurion* as a midshipman since 1749. The commodore, recognising his merit, made a special point of obtaining his promotion on this occasion. In later years, the great victory of Camperdown, which gave Duncan a peerage, testified to the wisdom of Keppel's judgment.

★★★★★★

On board the *Norwich* were the general, Captain Robert Orme, one of his *aides*, and Mr. William Shirley, his military secretary; and the arrival of the transports was daily, if not hourly, expected. But the first intelligence that reached the commodore's ears was a report that two French men-of-war had lately been seen hovering along the coast; and, fearful lest they should insult the coming fleet, the *Norwich* and *Syren* were at once ordered to sea again to look out for the enemy. (*Penn. Gaz.*, No. 1368.)

Braddock's long-expected arrival was hailed with a lively joy by the inhabitants of the colonies of Maryland, Virginia, and Pennsylvania; who certainly contemplated with enthusiasm the prospective discomfiture of the French; at the same time, perhaps, experiencing a secret satisfaction that the cost of the undertaking should mainly fall upon the mother country. Be that as it may, the expressions of popular pleasure on the occasion were neither circumscribed nor scanty; and to such gratulatory strains as these were the cisatlantic muses compelled to tune their unwonted lyres, (*Penn. Gaz.*, No. 1360):

Breathe, breathe, ye winds; rise, rise, ye gentle gales;
Swell the ship's canvass, and expand her sails!
Ye sea-green Nymphs, the royal vessel deign
To guide propitious o'er the liquid main:
Freighted with wealth, for noble ends designed,
(So willed great George, and so the Fates inclined.)
The ponderous Cannon o'er the surges sleep;
The flaming Muskets swim the raging deep;
The murd'rous Swords, conceal'd in scabbards, sail,
And pointed Bayonets partake the gale:
Ah! swiftly waft her to the longing shore;
In safety land her, and we ask no more!

Under convoy of two men–of–war, thirteen transports and three ordnance store-ships had left the Cove of Cork on the 14th of January, 1755; having on the last day taken on board £14,000 in specie. ((*Penn. Gaz.*, No. 1371.) The names of this little fleet were as follows:

TRANSPORTS.

Anna, Captain Nevin;	Hallifax, Captain Terry;
Terrible, Captain Wright;	Fame, Captain Judd;
Osgood, Captain Crookshanks;	London, Captain Brown;
Concord, Captain Boynton;	Prince Frederick, Captain Burton;
Industry, Captain Miller;	Isabel and Mary, Captain Hall;
Fishburn, Captain William Tipple;	Molly, Captain John Curling;
Severn, Captain Jehosaphat Rawlings.	

ORDNANCE STORE-SHIPS.

Whiting, Captain Johnson;	Nowall, Captain Montgomery;
Nelly.	

Parting company on the voyage, two transports, the *Fishburn* and the *Osgood*, each with one hundred men and officers on board, were on the 2nd of March the first to arrive at Hampton. (*Penn. Gaz.*, No. 1370.) The general's original notion seems to have been to await here the presence of all the troops, cantoning them as they came in according to a plan of Sir John St. Clair's. But perceiving the objections to this arrangement, he left orders with the commodore at the port for each transport, as it should arrive, to take on board fresh provisions for the men, and to proceed at once up the Chesapeake to Alexandria or Belhaven (as it was indifferently styled) on the Potomac; while he himself hastened to Williamsburg to obtain an interview with Governor Dinwiddie.

It would seem that there may have been some foundation for the rumour, that after conquering the French Braddock was to remain in this country as Governor of New York: but it was never alluded to in his intercourse with the colonies, (VI *Col. Rec.*) for the delays and difficulties of his undertaking began already to be foreshadowed, and his mind was more than sufficiently occupied with what he had in hand. The transports came in slowly: it was not until the middle of March that the Severn arrived with the last company of the 48th regiments Fortunately, despite their long and stormy passage, the health of the troops had continued good; but one man dying on the way. They were debarked at or hard by Alexandria, where they were for the present quartered. St. Clair had arranged an absurd plan for cantoning them in small divisions all over the country, which the general very wisely at once ignored. (Braddock's Despatches, in II. *Olden Time*; II. Sparks' *Washington*; II. *Penn. Arch.*, 286.)

The sword was now drawn; it but remained to cast away the scabbard. In London, the wits of the court with profane levity cited Scripture for their purpose and pretended to find in the inspirations of Ezekiel (cli. xxxv., 1-10), an assured prediction of the success of their arms in relation to the Ohio territories and Acadia. Punning on the words Mount Seir, Lord Chesterfield thus announced the prospective ruin of the French:

> Moreover, the word of the Lord came unto me, saying. Son of man, set thy face against Mount Seir and prophesy against it, and say unto it. Thus, saith the Lord God; Behold, Mount Seir, I am against thee, and I will stretch out my hand against thee, and I will make thee most desolate. . . . Because thou hast said. These two nations and these two countries shall be mine, and we will possess it.

Meanwhile, the pious Fontaine, secluded with his little flock in the western wilds of Virginia, lamented the turbulent times that had frustrated an expedition on the eve of departure for the exploration of the remotest sources of the Red River and the hardly-known Missouri, and the discovery of a water communication, through the heart of the continent, with the Pacific Ocean. (III. Walp. *Corr.*; Maury's *Huguenot Fam.*)

Upon the 10th of March, shortly after his arrival, the general had forwarded letters to the governors of the different colonies to meet him in council at Annapolis in Maryland, early in April, and urging on them the establishment of a common fund to promote the common end of the protection of the English frontiers. (VI. *Col. Rec.*) With the assistance of Sir John St. Clair, he next busied himself in organising the basis and plan of the coming campaign. This officer had arrived in America about the 10th of January, 1755, in the ship-of-war *Gibraltar*, Captain Spry; and since had found active employment in acquainting himself with the nature and scene of his future duties. Having procured from the Governors of Pennsylvania and Virginia, and from other sources, all the maps and information that were obtainable respecting the country through which the expedition was to pass, he proceeded in company with Governor Sharpe of Maryland upon a tour of inspection to Will's Creek.

The fort here was garrisoned by Rutherford's and Clarke's Independent Companies of Foot, which, being ordered thither from New York by Governor Dinwiddie, had arrived in Hampton Roads in H. M. S. *Centaur*, Captain Dudley Digges, on the 8th of June, 1754. (These were the troops so anxiously looked for by Washington at Fort Necessity, in July, 1754.)

On the 1st of September these troops were marched to Will's Creek, where they were joined by Captain Demerie's Independent Company from South Carolina; and on the 12th commenced erecting the works. On the 26th of January, 1755, Sir John and Governor Sharpe found the gallant fellows had built a sufficient fort, with several large magazines, and barracks for all the expected army. The latter were arranged in the manner of a fortified camp, flanking and flanked by the fort: ten four-pounders and some swivels constituted all their artillery.

This post was called Fort Cumberland, in honour of the captain-general. A company from Maryland had arrived there about the end of November 1754 and remained through the winter quartered in huts they built for themselves. Later in the season the Virginia troops made their appearance. On his return. Sir John descended Will's Creek and the Potomac two hundred miles in an open canoe, till he reached Annapolis; whence he repaired to Williamsburg to await the general's advent. He had inspected the Great Falls of the Potomac, and had no doubt that, by the aid of gunpowder, the rocks in the channel at that point might be removed to an extent sufficient to permit the passage of the flat-bottomed boats or *batteaux* in which the stores, etc., were to be transported to Fort Cumberland; and he employed a number of men upon that river to prepare the vessels.

He also laid out a camp for the army at Watkin's Ferry, although no use was ever after made of it. (VI. *Col. Rec.*; *Penn. Gaz.*, Nos. 1372,

1365, 1364.) It was very unfortunate that Sir John had not with him an engineer or two to whom a portion of these duties might have been entrusted, leaving him leisure to occupy himself in other quarters where his presence was not less needed. Thus, the four hundred men who were to fill up the ranks of the 44th and 48th regiments to seven hundred each, were looked for by the Ministry to come from Pennsylvania.

★★★★★★

In October, 1754, Sir Thomas Robinson advised the Governor of Pennsylvania of the king's wish that he should have at least 3000 men enlisted from whom to fill up the ranks of the 44th and 48th regiments, as well as of Shirley's and Pepperell's. The mandate, however, had no legal force, and was never in the least degree complied with. See VI. *Col. Rec.*

★★★★★★

This expectation was never fulfilled: so late as June 9th, 1755, we find Braddock writing to the governor of that province, entreating him to use his efforts for this end, and offering a bounty of £3 sterling for each man. (VI. *Col. Rec.*) The same colony was also relied upon to cut a road from a point on the Susquehannah, below the junction of the Juniata, to the Turkey Foot or forks of the Youghiogeny, by which flour and other stores might pass from Philadelphia to the army. This road Sir John advised to be made along the ridges of the hills, so as to avoid the washing of the floods; and, in fact, made every suggestion for its plan that experience could prefer to his mind. The busy trade which to their shame the northern colonies at that particular period carried on with the French also arrested his attention; and on all these various topics, as well as in regard to a commissary whom he had sent to purchase a hundred wagon-loads of flour, he addressed the Governor of Pennsylvania. (VI. *Col. Rec.*)

★★★★★★

When the prospect of a war between the two countries was imminent, and the French in Canada were anxious to lay in a store of provisions, the commercial colonies of New York, Rhode Island, and Massachusetts hastened to supply them. Within three months of the first battle, no less than forty English vessels lay at one time in the harbour of Louisbourg. It is proper to say that Pennsylvania was not otherwise engaged in this traffic than in selling flour to the merchants of other colonies, who pursued it until stopped by the stringent enactments of their own legislatures.

★★★★★★

Mr. Morris was anxious to do everything that St. Clair could ask, but his power was limited by the adjournment of his Assembly. Until it should vote supplies, he could raise no recruits nor cut any road; until it should declare the supplying of the French colonies with provisions illegal, he could not punish the offence. But such powers as he was vested with he freely used in this crisis. Pending the meeting of the Assembly, who were at once summoned to come together in Philadelphia, the governor appointed commissioners to survey the country and report on the most proper route for the desired road (VI. *Col. Rec.*); and in consequence of a letter from Commodore Keppel, informing him that, by virtue of the king's command, he should in future seize all ships carrying provisions and stores to the French from Pennsylvania, he also issued his warrant to all the collectors and port-officers within his jurisdiction, forbidding them to suffer any vessel to pass outwards respecting whose destination there could be the least doubt. (VI. *Col. Rec.*, 819, 323.) By these means, much was effected towards promoting the wished-for end.

It was in the course of this correspondence with Sir John that the general first came into connection with Mr. Morris, to whom he had brought introductory letters from Lord Halifax and Thomas Penn, the Proprietary. On the 14th of January, Dinwiddie wrote to Morris to ascertain if six hundred thousand pounds of flour and a quantity of salted beef could be procured in Pennsylvania for the use of the expedition; promising to pay for it himself should that province refuse. After some hesitation, fourteen thousand bushels of wheat were voted to be delivered, in the shape of flour, immediately upon the arrival of the troops at the mouth of Conecocheague Creek; a large stream which flows to the Potomac through what is now Franklin County in Pennsylvania: this being a larger quantity than was asked, and entirely at the cost of Pennsylvania. (VI. *Col. Rec*, 297; II. *Penn. Arch.*, 253. This flour was bought with part of the £5000 presently to be spoken of.)

Sir John having become involved in this negotiation, Morris's reply was submitted to Braddock, who had just then arrived; and it elicited from the general a communication couched in no very gentle terms. After bitterly inveighing against the conduct of a legislature which, in full view of the king's goodness in sending a large force to rescue their country from the hands of the enemy, had done not a thing to subsist the troops or to facilitate their progress to the Ohio, he employs the following significant threat in relation to billeting his men for their winter-quarters:

> My commission empowers me to settle the winter as I shall think most proper. You may assure your Assembly I shall have regard to the different behaviour of the several colonies, and shall regulate their quarters accordingly, and that I will repair, by unpleasant methods, what for the character and honour of the Assemblies I should be much happier to see cheerfully supplied. (Braddock's Letter of 28th Feb., 1755. VI. *Col. Rec.*)

As not only all of the general's correspondence, but many historical accounts of these transactions, abound in violent aspersions of the patriotism of Pennsylvania on this occasion, it may be as well to give here an impartial statement of the facts of the case. It seems the emission of provincial paper money or bills had many years before attracted the attention of the Crown. A legalised currency of notes that soon became ragged and defaced, and for the redemption of which no assured fund was provided, was certainly calculated to injure the trader at a distance as well as the holder at home; and consequently, in 1740, instructions were forwarded to Governor Thomas, of Pennsylvania, that he should in future pass no law for creating paper money which did not contain a clause suspending its operation until it was confirmed by the king.

The object of these regulations was to prevent any sudden emission of a fictitious currency, to be redeemed by posterity; and Sir Dudley Ryder, the most eminent counsel of his time, having been consulted on the question, had formally advised Mr. Hamilton (Mr. Morris's predecessor) that he and every other governor was fully bound by, and could not honourably nor safely violate them.

This was one cause of discontent between the Assembly and the governor; for the colony was not able to endure, or even to pay a very heavy direct tax; and the only mode in vogue of raising a large sum to meet an emergency was by an emission of bills. These the Crown was anxious to have redeemed in not more than five years, while the Assembly naturally preferred a longer day. Owing to the insuperable difficulty of any agreement upon a system of taxation in which the proprietary's unseated lands should pay their share with the rest of the province, the Assembly were now driven to a course which they perhaps hoped would place their governor absolutely and finally in a false position. They resolved to issue £40,000 in paper money (£20,000 of which should be for purposes of defence), to be redeemed in twelve years; carefully excluding from the bill any clause of suspension.

They hoped that the crisis would induce Mr. Morris to pass it into a law, and probably did not believe that any harm would come to him for so doing. But if he refused it, they would be in a position to charge him with the interruption of their efforts to serve the king. Of course, the governor could not assent to such an act with the written opinion before him of the man who at that very moment was Chief Justice of England; and so, he informed the Assembly. Warm bickerings at once broke out between them. The governor laid all the consequence of the French invasion at the doors of the legislature; and the legislature, in return, not only refused to modify their bill, but even insinuated that there was no invasion at all; that whether the territory on which Fort Du Quesne was erected belonged to the English or the French crown, it apparently was not within the limits of Pennsylvania. And since the king, said they, who certainly was the best judge of the limits of his own dominions, had already directed his attention to this question, they declined taking any share in the business; more especially as there was no war existing, in their eyes, between England and France. Such was the satisfaction which they gave to the requirements of Sir Thomas Robinson. (VI. *Col. Rec.*; XXV. *Gent. Mag.*, 230, 243.)

★★★★★★

There had been a general though a ridiculously absurd suspicion in Virginia, as well as Pennsylvania, that the story of French encroachments, &c., in the West was all a bugbear, gotten up by the Ohio Company in order to procure its occupation by the British, and so facilitate its own settlement. Thus Washington, who was interested in that concern, wrote, in 1757, to Lord Loudoun:

"It was not ascertained until too late that the French were on the Ohio; or rather, that we could be persuaded they came there with a design to invade His Majesty's dominions. Nay, after I was sent out in December, 1753, and brought undoubted testimony, even from themselves, of their avowed design, it was yet thought a fiction, and a scheme to promote the interest of a private company, even by some who had a concern in the government."—II. Sparks' *Washington.*

★★★★★★

Finding, however, that Mr. Morris was immovable, the Assembly resolved to borrow £5000 on its own credit, which was placed in the hands of a committee to be applied in defending the colony; and then suddenly adjourned without the governor's approbation.

It is so much the fashion in this generation to regard every ante-revolutionary dispute between a governor and his assembly as a struggle between tyrannical oppression and popular rights, that it is with some diffidence an opinion is here ventured, that in this instance the legislature of Pennsylvania were altogether in the wrong. Setting aside all question of expediency or policy, their object plainly was to force the governor to infringe the constitution. Failing this, they blindly persisted in a conduct which eventually drenched their borders in the blood of their own sons and raised a spirit which in less than ten years tarnished the honour of the province, trampled on its laws, and threatened its integrity.

★★★★★★

Allusion is here made to the Paxton riots, when a murderous array of frontiers-men marched on Philadelphia, threatening to repeat there the crimes they had already been guilty of at Lancaster. These shocking scenes would never have occurred, had the Ohio Indians been enlisted in time in the English interest.

★★★★★★

But it must be added that their errors were of the head, not of the heart; the tenor of their whole conduct compels the belief that they were honest and patriotic in their intentions, though sometimes very short-sighted. The censure which they received, often descending to sheer abuse, only tended, by a confidence of its injustice, to confirm them in the path they had adopted; and was quite as unmerited as that which their partisans liberally lavished on the governor. The real secret of the trouble consisted in the refusal of the Penns to be taxed. Every effort of the province to circumvent or break down this odious and unjust distinction was as violent as it was vain, until public opinion compelled its abolition.

At this very moment, when their government had refused to agree on any plan by which a provincial force could be raised in Pennsylvania to operate under Braddock against Fort Du Quesne, the men of Pennsylvania were enlisting by hundreds under the banners of Shirley and Pepperell, or carrying their services to Virginia or New York. In 1758, when affairs were better managed, the province raised 2700 troops for Forbes's army. But then, public matters on both sides of the Atlantic had taken a vastly different turn. In England, a Pitt had released the nation from the ministerial incubus by which it was oppressed; in Pennsylvania, the provincial levies were placed in every

124

BRADDOCK'S ARMY SURPRISED ON THE RIVER OHIO

proper respect upon a level with the regulars; and a community, which for three-quarters of a century had existed without a militia law had at last (Nov. 1755), been prevailed upon to consent to a measure, which at least put it in the power of those who wished to learn how to defend their country. (Sparks' *Wash.*; XXVI. *Gent. Mag.*, 83;VI. *C. R.*)

Unfortunately for himself, it was Braddock who was destined to reap this untoward harvest of popular discontent. Incapable of comprehending its origin, it was enough for him to know that it actually existed, and that, by soft words or wrathful, he could do very little with the legislature of Pennsylvania; or, indeed, with that of any other colony. His temper naturally led him to take at once the most unkind, and frequently unfounded, views of their conduct. He wrote to Mr. Fox, the Secretary of War:

> Pennsylvania will do nothing and furnisheth the French with whatever they have occasion for.

And again, he writes to Lord Halifax and to Sir Thomas Robinson, one of the Secretaries of State:

> I am very sorry that I am obliged to say that the inhabitants of these colonies in general have shown much negligence for His Majesty's service and their own interests. Nevertheless, they have not all equally deserved this censure; and particularly this province where I am (Virginia), ought not to be put in comparison with its neighbours, and may seem not to have merited these reproaches. . . . . I cannot sufficiently express my indignation against the provinces of Pennsylvania and Maryland, whose interest being alike concerned in the event of this expedition, and much more so than any other on this continent, refuse to contribute anything towards the project; and what they propose is made upon no other terms than such as are altogether contrary to the king's prerogatives and to the instructions he has sent their governors. . . . . I cannot but take the liberty to represent to you the necessity of laying a tax upon all His Majesty's dominions in America, agreeably to the result of council, for reimbursing the great sums that must be advanced for the service and interest of the colonies in this important crisis. (II. *Olden Time.*)

★★★★★★

Before blaming *in toto coelo* the rash judgment that dictated these intemperate counsels, it will be well to recollect that others besides Braddock (whether justly or not), were incensed

CAPTAIN ROBERT ORME

beyond bounds by the conduct of Pennsylvania: "A people," said Washington, "who ought rather to be chastised for their insensibility to danger, and disregard of their sovereign's expectations." I. Sparks' *Wash.* The suggestion of taxing America by Britain is perhaps one of the earliest on record.

★★★★★★

In what he insinuates respecting their connection with the French, Braddock was utterly wrong: in his allegations of a niggardly disposition on the part of the provincial Assemblies, he was perhaps not wholly incorrect. Virginia indeed had granted £20,000, Pennsylvania £5000, and North Carolina £8000 towards the common cause; and even Maryland seems to have voted £6000—all, however, in their respective currencies, which were much less than sterling. (XXV. *Gent. Mag.*, 308; II. *Olden Time.*) All of these sums were expended under their own directions. The contribution of South Carolina, amounting to £5714 5s. 8½d. sterling, was all the American money that ever reached Braddock's hands. As for the funds raised north of the Delaware, they were very properly applied to ends more immediately local. The main cost of the expedition was compulsorily borne by Great Britain.

It is not surprising, then, that the general lost his equanimity in contemplating not only the unexpected deficiency in that supply of money which he had been taught to expect from the colonies, but also the first examples of that miserable, equivocating system of shuffling delay and petty economy which too often characterised their action. Thus, all the provisions that Dinwiddie was to have supplied were discovered, at the eleventh hour, to be not forthcoming; and new and hurried arrangements had to be entered into at a moment when everything of the sort should have been finally concluded. As the particulars of this transaction will be found at large in the ensuing text, however, it need not be further alluded to here. But with all the explosions of his temper, there were many instances in which the general manifested a spirit as wise as it was discriminating, doing equal honour to his head and his heart.

Of these, was the manner in which he secured the services of Washington. The reader need hardly be reminded that in consequence of the king's order of November 12th, 1754, denying all precedence of rank to the colonial military in comparison with the bearers of commissions signed by himself or his American *generalissimo*, Washington, with a soldier's just feeling, had declined accepting any position in the troops raised by Virginia; and had, in fact, almost abandoned (with

128

what reluctance may be conceived), every idea of serving his country in the field. No man could more perfectly appreciate the motives of such conduct than Braddock; and few could more delicately, while tacitly acknowledging their propriety, have fulfilled his duty of bringing to his sovereign's service such valuable aid. On the 2nd of March, he caused this letter to be addressed to Major Washington:—

> Williamsburg, 2 March, 1755.
> Sir:—The general having been informed that you expressed some desire to make the campaign, but that you declined it upon some disagreeableness that you thought might arise from the regulations of command, has ordered me to acquaint you that he will be very glad of your company in his family, by which all inconveniences of that kind will be obviated.
> I shall think myself very happy to form an acquaintance with a person so universally esteemed, and shall use every opportunity of assuring you how much I am, Sir, your most obedient servant,
> Robert Orme, *Aide-de-Camp*

Washington's reply was couched in terms that evince clearly his gratification at this compliment. He had already addressed a congratulatory letter to the general on his safe arrival in this country; and he now ingenuously confesses that the laudable desire he possessed to serve, with his best abilities, his king and country, was not a little biased by what he calls selfish considerations, he continues:

> To explain, sir, I wish earnestly to obtain some knowledge in the military profession; and believing a more favourable opportunity cannot offer than to serve under a gentleman of General Braddock's abilities and experience, it does, you may reasonably suppose, not a little influence my choice.

But domestic cares for a space prevented him from repairing to his post; and it was not until two months from this that he reported himself to the General at Frederick Town, in Maryland; his appointment, being proclaimed to the army on the 10th of May, 1755. In all this unavoidable delay, he had been treated with the greatest consideration; Captain Orme informing him that:

> The general orders me to give you his compliments, and to assure you his wishes are to make it agreeable to yourself and consistent with your affairs; and, therefore, he desires you will so settle your business at home as to join him at Will's Creek, if

more convenient to you; and whenever you find it necessary to return, he begs you will look upon yourself as entirely master, and judge what is necessary to be done. (II. Sparks' Washington.)

Indeed, throughout the campaign, the general's appreciation of this illustrious man goes far to soften the common impression of his brutality and haughtiness. Washington and Franklin were perhaps the only two natives of America whom he distinguished with an unstinted measure of approbation; and it certainly argues no common character to have perceived in their dawning the future meridian brightness of these glorious minds. Washington never hesitated to express his convictions in opposition to Braddock's:

> From frequent breaches of contract, the general has lost all patience; and, for want of that temper and moderation which should be used by a man of sense upon these occasions, will, I fear, represent us in a light we little deserve; for, instead of blaming the individuals, as he ought, he charges all his disappointments to the public supineness, and looks upon the country, I believe, as void of honour and honesty. We have frequent disputes on this head, which are maintained with warmth on both sides—especially on his, as he is incapable of arguing without it, or giving up any point he asserts, be it ever so incompatible with reason or common sense. (Letter to W. Fairfax. II. Sp. *Wash.*)

While all will agree with Mr. Sparks that the general had but too good grounds for complaint, it is pleasant to see how anxious he was to render justice to even American merit, and to favour his Virginia *aide-de-camp's* desires for promotion in the regular army of his sovereign. Governor Dinwiddie, after the general's death, wrote home to Sir Thomas Robinson, the Secretary of State, his convictions that Braddock, had he survived, would have warmly recommended Washington to royal favour. And he afterwards repeated the same thing to the Earl of Loudoun when that incapable nobleman came to America to succeed Shirley in the chief command; strongly urging Washington's promotion in the regular establishment.

> General Braddock had so high an esteem for his merit that he made him one of his *aides-de-camp*; and if he had survived, I believe he would have provided handsomely for him in the regulars, (part of Dinwiddie's words.)

And Washington himself says very strongly to Lord Loudoun:

With regard to myself, I cannot forbear adding that, had General Braddock survived his unfortunate defeat, I should have met with preferment agreeable to my wishes. I had his promise to that effect; and I believe that gentleman was too sincere and generous to make unmeaning offers where no favours were asked. General Shirley was not unkind in his promises, but he has gone to England. (II. Sparks' *Washington*.)

These facts put a very different face upon a connection, honourable to both parties, which Lord Orford so falsely alludes to in his summing up of the Fort Necessity affair, when he says:

This brave braggart learned to blush for his rodomontade, and *desiring to serve General Braddock as aide-de-camp*, acquitted himself nobly! (I. Walp. *Mem. Geo. II.*)

The insinuation that Washington sought for the post was, under the circumstances, as ungenerous as untrue.

Owing to a delay in Shirley's progress, the congress of the governors of five colonies met, on the 14th of April, at Alexandria, instead of Annapolis, where Braddock had expected them; when the plans for the summer's operations were fully developed and explained. This having been done, Mr. Morris laid before the meeting the report of his road commissioners; who, in their portion of the embryo work, had succeeded beyond expectation. The document in question, moreover, presented a very characteristic specimen of the feelings with which those officers on whom the responsibility of failure would have to rest, had come to look upon the conduct of Pennsylvania. Sir John St. Clair had visited the commissioners with his warmest indignation, storming "like a Lyon Rampant," on account of the expedition having been so retarded by the delay of the road and the failure of the province to furnish provisions. (Shippen MSS., Vol. I.)

★★★★★★

He threatened them "that instead of marching to the Ohio, he would in nine days march his army into Cumberland County (Penn.) to cut the roads, press horses, wagons, &c.; that he would not suffer a soldier to handle an axe, but by fire and sword, oblige the inhabitants to do it, and take away every man that refused to the Ohio, as he had, yesterday, some of the Virginians; that he would kill all kind of cattle and carry away the horses, burn the houses, &c.; and that if the French defeated them by the delays of this province he would with his sword drawn pass through the province and treat the inhabitants as a parcel of traitors to his master; that he would tomorrow write to England by a man-of-war; shake Mr. Penn's proprietaryship; and represent Pennsylvania as a disaffected province: that he would not stop to impress our Assembly; his hands were not tyed, and that we should find: ordering us to take these precautions and instantly publish them to our governor and Assembly, telling us he did not value anything they did or resolved, seeing they were dilatory and retarded the march of the troops, and —— an —— (as he phrased it) on this occasion; and told us to go to the general, if we pleased, who would give us ten bad words for one that he had given. . . . . He would do our duty himself and never trust to us; but we should dearly pay for it. To every sentence he solemnly swore and desired we might believe him to be in earnest." The Shippen MSS. (consisting of the original papers, &c., of Edward and Joseph Shippen, Col. James Burd, and other members of a family that during the last century occupied a most distinguished position in Pennsylvania) are in the library of the Hist. Soc. of Penn. They contain a store of valuable information respecting the early history of the State, and an interesting correspondence with many of the chief characters in America.

★★★★★★

It was not difficult to present this transaction in its true light to the general, from whom St. Clair received a warm and severe reprimand for his officious violence. (II *Penn. Arch.*, 317.) The road, in the meanwhile, went on slowly enough. The Assembly, being sensible of the great advantage it would be to the province to have a direct communication with Fort Du Quesne, in time consented to its being made, and even projected another to Will's Creek; but the governor, ascertaining that they were not disposed to expend a sum sufficient to half carry through both of these designs, contrived that the latter road should be abandoned in favour of that to the forks of Youghiogeny, which was of the most pressing importance. (*Penn. Gaz.*, No. 1397.)

But even the cost of this alone gave great offence, as it stood the province in £3000, while they were willing to spend but £800. As there were but about one hundred men employed, its progress was very tardy. Provisions were not regularly supplied them. The laborers, too, were kept in constant alarm of the enemy; no guard was allowed them by the province; and it was not until the end of June that the general detached from his own army Captain Hogg, with fifty men, for their protection. Advertisements, in English and German, for more workmen were vainly dispersed through the country.

So great was the necessity of opening a communication by which provisions could be sent to the army from Pennsylvania, that Braddock at first declared he would not advance beyond the place where it was to encounter his own route, till it was made. "The general—the officers—the whole army place their account upon this road," wrote Richard Peters, the Secretary of the Province to the Commissioners. Finally, however, on the 17th of July, after they had once or twice been attacked by Indians and most of the party half frightened out of their senses, the chief commissioner, Mr. James Burd, received from Colonel Innes, at Fort Cumberland, notice of the general's defeat, and orders to retire without delay. Mr. Burd executed this movement with coolness and sagacity, leaving nothing behind him that he could possibly bring away, and indeed meriting by his conduct the praise which he subsequently received. It has been thought best thus to dispose, at one view, of the full history of this provincial road as connected with the campaign of 1755 (Shippen MSS. *passim*; II. *Penn. Arch.*; VI. *Col. Rec.*) it is now necessary to return to the Congress of Alexandria.

What had ever induced the Ministry to select Virginia, instead of Pennsylvania, as the spot from which the expedition was to march, cannot be discovered; but the choice was a most unfortunate one. The former province could afford neither forage, provisions, wagons, nor cattle; in all of which the latter abounded. To be sure, the land carriage between the heads of navigation in the Potomac and the branches of the Ohio was less than a hundred miles; but this was a convenience of which Braddock could not avail himself. And it was computed at the time that had he landed at Philadelphia his march would have been shortened by six weeks, and £40,000 would have been saved in the cost of the expedition. Carlisle would have made an infinitely better frontier station than Will's Creek, being far more accessible from Philadelphia than Fort Cumberland was from Alexandria, and through a more productive and cultivated country: the distance from Fort Du Quesne was, however, much greater.

This view is sufficiently proved from the fact that Forbes, in 1758, after full deliberation, judged it wiser to cut a new road through this province than to follow the path already opened by Braddock. The only motive, then, for the unhappy directions with which he was saddled must be believed to have been one publicly suggested in London at the time; namely, that to gratify a political favourite with a commission of 2½ *per cent*, on the funds sent to that country, Virginia was fixed upon for the debarkation of the troops. (Lewis Evans's *Second Essay*; XXV. *Gent. Mag.*, 378; 388. Hanbury was probably the person alluded to.) The moment the general began to investigate the preparations made here for his subsistence, he perceived their utter deficiency. The twenty-five hundred horses, two hundred and fifty wagons, and eleven hundred beeves which were promised him from Maryland and Virginia, were not forthcoming: twenty wagons and two hundred horses were all that could be produced; and the provisions furnished by Maryland were on inspection discovered to be utterly worthless. Such disappointments as these were sufficient to inflame even a placable temper; and in the general failure, his wrath blindly vented itself upon the people of that province which abounded in all that he desired, yet from which he had received nothing.

Fortunately, Governor Shirley had insisted upon Franklin's accompanying him to the Congress at Annapolis, where he remained after its adjournment to establish a post-route between Will's Creek and Philadelphia. He found the leading officers of the army imbued with a fixed detestation of Pennsylvania, alleging that the province had refused them wagons, horses, and food itself at any price; had denied them a road from the camp to their back-settlements; and was even in secret correspondence with the French. Franklin could only reply that the Assembly had, before their arrival, granted £5000 to support the king's troops; that it was understood Virginia and Maryland were to furnish the wagons, etc., and that Pennsylvania did not know that more were wanted; and that a committee was at that very time surveying the ground to lay out a road. He added that it was a pity the expedition had not landed in Pennsylvania, where every farmer had his wagon.

Catching at the hope held out in this conversation, Braddock at once asked him if he thought it possible still to procure horses and teams for the expedition in Pennsylvania; and if so, would he, at the general's cost, undertake to obtain a supply? To each part of this proposition Franklin cheerfully assented, and at once set about carrying the idea into execution in a manner not unworthy of his astute and usual worldly wisdom. (II. *Olden Time*; I. & VII Sparks' *Franklin*; II. *Penn. Archives*.) He caused a handbill to be printed and widely distributed through an extensive part of Pennsylvania, then comprehended but in three counties; in which, after an advertisement stating the terms upon which his natural son William Franklin or himself were desirous of hiring for the General fifteen hundred saddle or pack-horses, and one hundred and fifty wagons, each with a team of four horses, was published the following letter:—

To the inhabitants of the Counties of Lancaster, York, and Cumberland.

Friends and Countrymen:

Being occasionally at the camp at Frederic a few days since, I found the general and officers of the army extreamly exasper-ated, on account of their not being supply'd with horses and carriages, which had been expected from this province as most able to furnish them; but through the dissentions between our governor and Assembly, money had not been provided nor any steps taken for that purpose.

It was proposed to send an armed force immediately into these counties, to seize as many of the best carriages and horses as should be wanted and compel as many persons into the service as should be necessary to drive and take care of them.

I apprehended that the progress of a body of soldiers thro' these counties on such an occasion, especially considering the tem-per they are in, and their resentment against us, would be at-tended with many and great inconveniences to the inhabitants; and therefore, more willingly undertook the trouble of trying first what might be done by fair and equitable means.

The people of these back counties have lately complained to the Assembly that a sufficient currency was wanting: you have now an opportunity of receiving and dividing among you a very considerable sum; for if the service of this expedition should continue (as it's more than probable it will), for 120 days, the hire of these wagons and horses will amount to upwards of *thirty thousand pounds*, which will be paid you in silver and gold of the king's money.

The service will be light and easy, for the army will scarce march above 12 miles per day, and the wagons and baggage horses, as they carry those things that are absolutely necessary to the welfare of the army, must march with the army and no faster, and are, for the army's sake, always placed where they can be most secure, whether on march or in camp.

If you really are, as I believe you are, good and loyal subjects of His Majesty, you may now do a most acceptable service, and make it easy to yourselves; for three or four such as cannot separately spare from the Business of their plantations a wagon and four horses and a driver, may do it together, one furnishing the wagon, another one or two horses, and another the driver, and divide the pay proportionably between you. But if you do not this service to your King and Country voluntarily, when such good pay and reasonable terms are offered you, your loyalty will be strongly suspected. The king's business must be done; so many brave troops, come so far for your defence, must not stand idle through your backwardness to do what may reasonably be expected from you; wagons and horses must be had; violent measures will probably be used; and you will be to seek for a recompense where you can find it, and your case perhaps be little pitied or regarded.

I have no particular interest in this affair; as (except the satisfaction of endeavouring to do good and prevent mischief), I shall have only my labour for my pains. If this method of obtaining the wagons and horses is not like to succeed, I am obliged to send word to the general in fourteen days, and I suppose Sir John St. Clair, the hussar, with a body of soldiers, will immediately enter the province, of which I shall be sorry to hear, because

I am, very sincerely and truly,
Your friend and well-wisher,

B. Franklin.

Nothing could have better answered its purpose. St. Clair had actually, it is believed, served in a hussar regiment abroad; and usually wore a hussar uniform on duty in America. Of a violent, impetuous temper, he had on more than one occasion threatened to dragoon the lukewarm inhabitants into activity; and his character and profession forcibly recalling to the German farmers, who in great numbers occupied the back counties, the scenes they had witnessed at home, were artfully introduced by Franklin, and must have excited much amusement among Sir John's friends in camp. As for the English colonists, it was enough for them to be reminded that such things as a *Press* of private means for the benefit of the State still existed.

★★★★★★

I can but honour Franklin for ye last clause of his advertisement.—(W. Shirley to Morris. II. *Penn. Arch.*)

Gov. Morris was instructed by the Crown to aid the army in impressing wagons, etc., if necessary: and we find his warrant for that purpose issued to the Sheriff of Philadelphia, in September, 1755. (*Penn. Arch.* 432.) And see VI. *Col. Rec.*

★★★★★★

In a fortnight's space, the one hundred and fifty wagons and teams and two hundred and fifty-nine pack-horses were on their way to camp. In his letters to his government, the general expressed great satisfaction at Franklin's conduct in this business, which he characterized as "almost the first instance of integrity, address, and ability that he had met with in all these provinces," It is a pity it should be necessary to comment upon the difficulty which this matter afterwards brought upon its undertaker. Had Braddock lived, there would undoubtedly have arisen no trouble; but his death left his contractor involved in a debt of over £20,000, for which the owners of the property did not cease to importune him.

Governor Shirley, it is true, relieved him of the greater part of this responsibility, with warm expressions of sensibility of his public services in "engaging those wagons without which General Braddock could not have proceeded;" but he left a portion of the accounts to be settled by Lord Loudoun, who, according to his usual habits, utterly neglected doing anything in the premises; and it is believed the patriotic postmaster was never wholly repaid. He very usefully employed Braddock's new-born partiality, however, in procuring the release of bought servants enlisted into the army, whose time belonged to their masters. (VII. Sparks' *Franklin*.)

★★★★★★

See also Bouquet's testimony to his services on this occasion; (*Franklin*). As for the Earl of Loudoun, nothing could be juster than the comparison of his lordship to the figure of St. George over the door of a country inn, always on horseback, yet never going on!

★★★★★★

Returning from the congress of Alexandria, each governor sought his respective province, fondly imagining, perhaps, that the work was done and the fall of the French near at hand. This, at least, was the sentiment of the populace, who welcomed the prospect with noisy gratulation.

★★★★★★

Thus Shirley, passing through New York, was encountered by a turnout of the militia and a display of enthusiastic gentry, with whom he drank loyal healths and success to the king's arms; while "the doors, windows, balconies, and tops of the houses, being particularly decorated with red cloaks, &c., added," says the old chronicler, "no small beauty to the fame and diversion of the time." *Penn. Gaz.*, No. 1376.

★★★★★★

In the meanwhile, the general busied himself in getting the troops and stores advanced to Fort Cumberland, whence his march through a hostile wilderness, if not an enemy's country, was fairly to begin, and in concerting, with the different authorities, various measures of public convenience. Having fixed upon Winchester, Virginia, as the place to which his letters should be sent, he procured expresses to be laid by Pennsylvania and Maryland to that town. (*Penn. Gaz.*, No. 1377. The mail-rider started from Philadelphia every Thursday morning after the 15th of May, 1755.) Another object to which he devoted much attention was the obtaining of Indians to accompany his army. There is no point on which his conduct has been more misunderstood than this; he has always been looked upon as despising and refusing the services of the savages, and as actually repulsing their proffered aid: let us see what are the facts of the case.

Immediately upon the general's arrival in Virginia, he had spoken with Governor Dinwiddie in regard to this matter, and was given to understand that a large force of Catawba and Cherokee Indians, under the influence of his messengers, would presently arrive at Winchester, where they were to meet the Six Nations in council. The Catawbas alone would amount to one hundred and twenty warriors; and hopes of a considerable addition to this number might be based upon the management of the other tribes. The appointed time came, however, and brought with it no Indians. It would certainly seem that Dinwiddie was very much to blame in his whole conduct of this business.

Other men, no better qualified than himself to judge, put no reliance whatever upon the Southern Indians promised him by Mr. Gist; and there can be no excuse for his utter neglect to send messengers with presents to the Ohio savages, which should have been his first care on receiving the funds from Great Britain. Taught by injurious experience, however, to depend no more upon the promises of colonial undertakers, Braddock, so soon as he began to suspect Dinwiddie's arrangements would fail him, addressed himself to the Governor of Pennsylvania.

In his letter (April 15th, 1755), he states that he is told of a number of savages living within that province who formerly dwelt on the Ohio, who therefore were doubtless well acquainted with that region. Sensible of the value of such auxiliaries, he begged Mr. Morris to persuade their warriors to join his camp, and to advise him with what treatment he ought to greet them; desiring, too, that they should be informed he was on his way to remove the French, and to restore the country they occupied to its Indian proprietors, whose undisturbed enjoyment of it he was determined to protect. A week after, the governor ordered George Croghan (who, with Conrad Weiser, had the virtual management of the colony's intercourse with the savages), to send belts of *wampum* to all the lake tribes, the Delawares, the Shawanoes, the Wyandottes, Twightwees (or Miamis), and Piankeshaws, inviting them to join the English without delay. As a matter of course, it was now too late for such messages to produce any good effect; and no good effect was produced.

But in his immediate neighbourhood at Aughquick, Croghan managed to collect a small party of Iroquois, whom he led to the camp. These were chiefly the same who had been with Washington at Fort Necessity and had retired with him to Virginia. After remaining there some time, they repaired to Aughquick, in Pennsylvania; where they and their families (homeless, now, since their places on the Ohio were under the control of the French, whose blood they had shed) were supported during the winter of 1754-5 by that province. There were other Indians of the Six Nations who had in like manner left the Ohio, who, as well as these, were maintained by the public; the whole amounting to about three hundred souls. In April, 1755, however, the Assembly resolved to do nothing more for them; and, left to their own resources, the majority soon dispersed or went back to the French.

On the night of the 30th of April, Croghan received the governor's letter; on the 2nd of May, he set out for Fort Cumberland, with his remaining Indians, to the number of about thirty or forty men and sixty women and children; it being impossible for the warriors to leave their families behind them with no means of support. When the general arrived at Will's Creek on the 10th of May, he found these people awaiting him; and, after the usual negotiations, they formally took up the hatchet against the French, and agreed to follow his fortunes. These were the hundred Indians of whom Franklin speaks:

Who might have been of great use to his army as guides or

139

scouts, if he had treated them kindly; but he slighted or neglected them, and they gradually left him.

It is now a well-ascertained fact that forty or fifty, at the very most,
were all the fighting men who joined Braddock; the lesser number,
perhaps, being nearest the mark. Of these, but eight actually remained
with him to the close; and for permitting the rest to leave him, Braddock is much to be blamed. Captain Orme, it is true, says that they
departed, with a promise to return, under a pretence of placing their
families in safety upon the Susquehannah; but their manager, Mr.
Croghan, clearly explains this business. Colonel Innes, the Governor
of Fort Cumberland, did not wish to have the destitute families of
these people on his hands during the general's absence, and he accordingly persuaded him that he had best intimate to the warriors the
propriety of taking them somewhere else.

There thus being no provision for the entertainment of their children and wives whilst they were on the war-path, a majority of the
savages were compelled to return to their late abode in Pennsylvania;
the general retaining eight of them as scouts—a number which Innes
assured him would be perfectly sufficient. At the same time, he seems
to have laboured under the misunderstanding that the remainder of
the warriors would rejoin him on his march; which was far from being the case, albeit they were so anxious for war as to hang on to his
array till he reached Dunbar's camp.

★★★★★★

II. *Penn. Arch.*; VI. *Col. Rec.*; II. *Olden Time*; I. Sparks' *Franklin*.
Full details of the conduct and position of the Indians who
withdrew from the Ohio to Pennsylvania may be found in II.
P.A., VI. *C. R.*,

★★★★★★

Certainly, there is no reason to believe that Braddock was not desirous of the services of the savages, though perhaps he was not sufficiently versed in their nature to always employ the properest measures of securing them. Another reason he had for wishing the Indian
women at once removed from the neighbourhood of the troops, was
the licentiousness their presence introduced into the camp. An eye-
witness (Peters, the Secretary of Pennsylvania,) particularly states,
that besides other causes of discontent at not being more frequently
consulted with by the general, there were constant and high quarrels
among the Indians on account of the amours of the royal officers with

their squaws and the *largesses* the latter received.

These gentlemen "were so scandalously fond" of their swarthy lovers, that an order was issued forbidding their admission into camp. And that Braddock's general deportment on the march was not courteous and polite, may readily be conceded. Such was the impression it produced, that the Indians with him sent belts to their Susquehannah friends, warning them to keep away from the army, lest they should be mistaken for allies of the French.

★★★★★★

It is said that Braddock gave great offence to his Indians by forbidding them to take scalps, when, in fact, he published a reward of £5 to every soldier is well as Indian of his command for each scalp of an enemy. The sole authority for the story appears to have been John Shiekalamy, father of Logan, whose speech is celebrated by Mr. Jefferson; an influential but discontented Delaware, who, early in July, 1755, reported this tale among his kindred, and shortly after took up arms for the French. *Penn. Gaz.*, No. 1385.

★★★★★★

Thus, in the next month after his defeat we find them asserting to Mr. Morris that it was all caused by the pride and ignorance of that great general who came from England. Scarroyaddy their chief quoth:

He is now dead, but he was a bad man when he was alive; he looked upon us as dogs and would never hear anything that was said to him. We often endeavoured to advise him and to tell him of the danger he was in with his soldiers; but he never appeared pleased with us; and that was the reason that a great many of our warriors left him and would not be under his command. (VI. *C. R.*; II. *P. A.*)

The reader has here three distinct versions of the secret of this savage exodus from the tents of the English: namely, Scarroyaddy's, Croghan's, and Braddock's own—from which he may select such a reason as best suits him. It is not difficult, however, to reconcile and to combine them all.

★★★★★★

This chieftain, who played so active a part in Braddock's campaign, was an Oneida Indian, and one of the mixed band of various tribes of the Six Nations who lived, in 1754, near the Ohio. These people were used to choose from their number a ruler; and such for a time was Thanacharisson, the Half-King, who died at Aughquick in October, 1754, leaving his family very destitute. (VI. *Col. Rec*; II. *Penn. Arch.*) In the Washington papers he is known by the name of Monacatootha, and it is well to note here that the two appellations apply to the same individual. (II. *P.A.*).

As early as 1748, however, and almost universally in Pennsylvania, he was called Scarroyaddy, or perhaps more correctly, Skirooniatta. (II. *P.A.*; VI. *C. R.*) In the winter of 1754-5, he was sent by his people to Onondaga, to obtain the views of the confederates on the expected troubles and was about this time selected to succeed the Half-King. His services under Braddock were fully acknowledged at Philadelphia in August, 1755: "You fought under General Braddock," said Gov. Morris, "and behaved with spirit and valour during the engagement. We should be wanting to ourselves not to make you our hearty acknowledgments for your fidelity and assistance. We see you consider yourselves as our flesh and blood, and fight for us as if we were of your own kindred." (VI. *C. R.*) He ever continued a staunch ally to the English.

In Sept. 1755, he headed a war-party from Shamokin against the French (VI. *C. R.*), and indeed the records of the period abound in evidences of his usefulness, being constantly employed in the quest of intelligence upon various missions, or the pursuit of the foe. In the last object, he must have been tolerably successful. In the *Gent. Mag.* for Sept. 1756 (Vol. XXVI., 414), is a facsimile of his hieroglyphical memoirs, drawn by himself; by which it appears he had theretofore slain with his own hands no less than seven, and captured eleven warriors; and had been present in thirty-one combats, the majority of which were doubtless of a very trifling nature.

On his breast was tattooed a figure of a tomahawk, and that of a bow and arrow on each cheek. It will be seen how unluckily his son was killed during Braddock's march. In Dec. 1754, he had a wife and seven children with him at Aughquick (II. *P.A.*), so there was still left him a numerous posterity. It only remains to add that he was not free from the inevitable failing of his race, and on occasion would, as Burns has it, be "fou for weeks thegither." (VII. *C. R.*)

★★★★★★

142

With a single exception, these were all the Indians whom the general had any opportunity to secure. Between the 20th and the 27th of April, shortly after he had left Fort Cumberland, a few Delawares presented themselves to him, doubtless with no other view than to ascertain what terms they could obtain from him, and what were his chances of success. Whatever conclusion they came to, they never reappeared. The fact is, that the Indians were now in a state of high excitement and of bewildering doubt. There were of course among them predilections for one side or the other; but their wise men, whether of the French or the English faction, were not unwilling to stand neuter and lot the two European nations "fight it out themselves, and the more they destroy one another the better."

But, if they were to be involved in the dispute, their anxiety was to discover which would be the winning side; and this was probably the errand of the Delawares. So little trouble had, however, been taken at the proper time by the provinces to convince them of their desire for their services, that the conclusion arrived at by those who were really well disposed towards the English was to endeavour to remain neutral. Thus, the Delawares and Shawanoes living at Kittaning, under Shingas and King Beaver and Captain Jacob, as well as those at Log's-Town, although both places were near to Fort Du Quesne, steadily resisted all the blandishments of the French to join with them against their enemy; until in April or May, 1755, a party of Canadian Indians visiting their towns, persuaded them to the measure. Of the war-party which was at once sent forth, it is not unlikely the Delawares who came to Braddock formed a part. (VI. *C. R.*; II. *P.A.*)

That this should have been the state of relations between the English and the savages, was a fact as censurable as unfortunate; but it was the inexcusable fault of none else than the authorities of the neighbouring colonies, who utterly neglected to give them a single opportunity of selling their assistance, after their own national customs, and casting in their lot with the British. They looked for a belt to be sent them, and a supply of presents, ere they should engage in the war. The whole burthen and responsibility of doing what should long before his arrival have been done by Dinwiddie or Morris being thus cast upon a general who knew absolutely nothing about the matter, it is no wonder it turned out a bungling failure.

★★★★★★

"Certainly," says Mr. Secretary Peters, on the 12th May, 1755, "some general meeting was necessary and expected by the

143

Indians, that both they and we might see what number were for and what against the French encroachments; and in case it should have appeared a majority was on the side of the French, then it might have been prudent to have tried to bring the Indians over to a general neutrality—and it is the opinion of Mr. Weiser, our Indian interpreter, and my own, that this could have been effected, and would have saved the general an immense trouble, and the Crown an heavy expense." (II. *P.A.*)

Nor was this fact unperceived at the camp. On the 21st of May, Mr. W. Shirley thus writes: "I am not greatly acquainted myself with Indian affairs, though enough to see that better measures with regard to 'em might and ought to have been taken; at least to the southward. . . .Upon our arrival at this fort, we found Indian affairs so ignorantly conducted by Col. Innes, to whom they were committed, that novices as we were, we have taken 'em into our management." (II *P.A.*)

★★★★★★

Even while at Will's Creek, the army was ill supplied with provisions; and what they had being chiefly salted, were far from acceptable or even wholesome to men just released from a long and tedious sea-voyage, where fresh food was out of the question. The tables of the officers themselves were scantily and meagrely furnished: very little fresh meat, and that generally half-spoiled, was to be found upon their boards; and butter (in a limited quantity), at the general's alone. The men and the inferior officers were actually in want of almost the necessaries of life.

Franklin, in his autobiographical sketch, mentions that at Frederictown, while supping with Colonel Dunbar, that gentleman expressed a strong concern for the condition of his subalterns, whose purses, never very deep, were now utterly drained by the exorbitant prices exacted for every sort of domestic stores needed for a long march through the wilderness.

On Franklin's return to Philadelphia, he interested the Assembly's Committee to apply a small portion of the £5000 in their hands to procuring camp-supplies for these gentlemen; and accordingly by a special detachment of horses from Lancaster a present of as many parcels was sent to twenty subalterns of the 48th regiment; each parcel, according to his own inventory, containing the following articles:—

6 lbs. loaf sugar.	1 Gloucester cheese.
6 " Muscovado do.	1 keg containing 20 lbs. good butter.
1 " green tea.	2 doz. old Madeira wine.
1 " Bohea do.	2 gallons Jamaica spirits.
6 " ground coffee.	1 bottle flour of mustard.
6 " chocolate.	2 well-cured hams.
½ chest best white biscuit.	½ doz. dried tongues.
½ lb. pepper.	6 lbs. rice.
1 quart white vinegar.	6 " raisins.

This little act of attention upon the then postmaster's part (the details of which may well be repeated here), was very kindly acknowledged by the recipients, and led the way for other and more substantial provision for the support of the army. (VI. *Col. Rec.*; I. Sp. *Fr.*)

★★★★★★

"Colonel Dunbar writes in his letter of May the 13th concerning the present of refreshments and carriage horses sent up for the subalterns: 'I am desired by all the gentlemen who the committee have been so good as to think of in so genteel a manner, to return them their hearty thanks;' and again, on the 21st of May—'Your kind present is now all arrived, and shall be equally divided tomorrow between Sir Peter Halket's subalterns and mine, which I apprehend will be agreeable to the Committee's intent. This I have made known to the officers of both regiments, who unanimously desire me to return the generous benefactors their most hearty thanks, to which be pleased to add mine, &c.;'" and Sir Peter Halket, in his of the 23rd of May, says, "The officers of my regiment are most sensible of the favours conferred on the subalterns by your Assembly, who have made them so well-timed and handsome a present. At their request and desire, I return their thanks, and to the acknowledgments of the officers beg leave to add mine, which you, I hope, will do me the favour for the whole to offer to the Assembly, and to assure them that we shall on every occasion do them the justice due for so seasonable and well-judged an act of generosity.—*Assemby's Address*, 29th Sept. 1755.

★★★★★★

The three lower counties upon Delaware (which now constitute the State of Delaware), although intimately allied with Pennsylvania and subjected to the same proprietaries and governor, at this period formed a distinct government from their more powerful sister. Whether it was that its inhabitants were less opinionated than those of his other colony or not, Mr. Morris seems to have possessed more influence over them than he could bring to bear in Philadelphia; and he stirred them up to forwarding to the camp a present of fifty fat oxen and one hundred sheep for the use of the army, as well as the following provisions for the general's own use:—

Twelve Hams.	Four kegs of Sturgeon.
Eight Cheeses.	One keg of Herrings.
Twenty-four flasks of Oil.	Two chests of Lemons.
Ten loaves of Sugar.	Two kegs of Spirits.
One cask of Raisins.	A cask of Vinegar.
A box of Spice and Currants.	A barrel of Potatoes.
A box of Pickles and Mustard.	Three tubs of Butter.
Eight kegs of Biscuit.	

But it was not until late in the season that these welcome donations were despatched (VI. *Col. Rec.*; *Penn. Gaz.*, No. 1380); and in the meantime, the progress of the expedition was fatally delayed at Will's Creek for the want of stores. Not less time than a month or six weeks, at the most moderate computation, were thus consumed in awaiting the fulfilment of contracts for forage and food, which Braddock was obliged to make himself, in default of the proper and timely action of the colonies. It will be observed in season how dearly this shameful conduct was repaid; for, setting aside the loss to the crown of the whole cost of his undertaking, there is no doubt that a fortnight's earlier arrival on the Ohio would have given victory to his arms and peace to the borders of Pennsylvania, Virginia, and Maryland. In lieu of this, and in consequence of their own blind perversity, a desolating and ruinous war steeped for years their land in blood and cost them eventually ten times as much as would originally have ensured their perfect security.

No longer relying at all upon the faith of colonial assemblies or colonial contractors, the general, in the beginning of May, set about procuring, on his own responsibility, as representing the Crown, the stores necessary for his march to Fort Du Quesne. On the 10th of May Captain Leslie, who had been appointed Assistant to Sir John St. Clair, was sent into Pennsylvania to purchase forage; and on the 24th, Mr. Morris was empowered to make further contracts for flour and cattle, or in default of any other provision, even salt fish, to support the troops after July, when their present magazines would become exhausted.

Through the zealous cooperation of that energetic governor, this business was fortunately carried through satisfactorily; else, to use Braddock's own language, he should inevitably have starved: for it was not until the stores procured by Captain Leslie reached Fort Cumberland that the army was able to move. Three precious months had already been consumed upon the two hundred miles that separated this place from Annapolis; and above one hundred and fifty yet remained to be overcome ere the host should reach the bourne of its desires. (VI. *Col. Rec.*)

CHAPTER 8

The French Prepare

It is proper now to glance at the conduct of the ministry of France in this conjuncture, and to observe what preparations they had made to repel the advances of the English and to preserve their own encroachments. Although both governments had long persisted in positive declarations of their amicable intentions, neither was weak enough to place the least reliance upon assurances so thoroughly contradicted by the facts of their own conduct. Through its agents in France, England was never left uninformed of the extensive armaments that power was busily fitting out for its American possessions; while everything relative to Braddock's and Boscawen's instructions was known to the Cabinet of Versailles long before it was communicated to the public at home. One Florence Hennessey, an Irish physician, settled at London, was the spy employed. What were his sources of information is a mystery that has never been fathomed; but he assuredly had often access to the confidential secrets of the ministry, and was in possession of every detail of their foreign policy.

Detected at last, he was convicted of high treason and sentenced to its doom; but, after several reprieves, was finally pardoned by George III. at the intercession of, and as a personal favour to, the French King. But being thus apprised in abundant season of the designs of Great Britain, their opponents hastened to take the precautions which were so necessary in the then condition of their own colonies; and ships and men were at once set in train for Quebec.

The original force of 5000 militia, 600 Indians, and 400 regulars, which, in the year 1753, had been raised in New France for the occupation of the Ohio, (VI. *Col. Rec.*) almost exhausted the strength of that province, and, its object being accomplished, was now entirely dissolved. Small but sufficient garrisons were maintained in the posts thus erected, and probably little alteration was made in their strength until the troubles of 1754.

In February of that year, a very considerable number of French

147

troops arrived in the Mississippi, some of whom were doubtless sent up to their western stations; while the Governor of Louisiana left no stone unturned to engage every savage within his influence in the general plan against the English. (*Penn. Gaz.*, No. 1367; II. *Garneau*; VI. *Col. Rec.*) When M. de Contrecoeur first came upon Trent, in April, 1754, he probably had not more than from 750 to 1000 men with him; but his whole command had not yet arrived. By July, he was certainly strong enough to detach from 600 to 800 Indians, under M. de Villiers, against Fort Necessity; and at this period, he probably had under him all the 2000 men which were designed for him by his superiors. (II. *Garneau*;VI. *Col. Rec.*)

But when that victory was gained, and not an enemy remained within a hundred miles and more of his position, most of his troops were dismissed, and the fort remained, on the 25th of July, 1754, garrisoned by but 400 men, 200 of whom were workmen. M. de Merrier, the engineer by whom the works were planned, had on that day departed with about 1000 men. For this, and for other information concerning the condition of the fort, we are indebted to the indefatigable patriotism of Captain Robert Stobo, of Frey's regiment; who, having been one of the hostages surrendered by Washington at Fort Necessity a few weeks before, was now confined a prisoner within its walls. Watching his opportunity, he made the opposite plan of Fort Du Quesne and forwarded it, as well as two letters describing its weaknesses, to his countrymen, by the hands of a friendly Indian.

★★★★★★

In a former note, reference to Mr. Lyman C. Draper's notices of Stobo and Van Braam (I. *Olden Time*) was unfortunately omitted. The curious reader may consult them with advantage. A copy of Stobo's drawing was probably made in the provinces before Braddock's departure, since we find an engraved plan of Fort Du Quesne published and for sale at London in August, 1755, immediately on the tidings of Braddock's misadventure. (XXV. *Gents Mag.*, 383.) It has vainly been sought to procure a copy of this engraving.

★★★★★★

But a much fuller account is afforded in the *Journal* of one John M'Kinney, who, in February, 1756, was captured by the Indians and carried first thither and afterwards to Canada; whence he in a few months made his escape and returned, through Connecticut, to Pennsylvania. From a collation of these two narratives a tolerably clear idea of the nature and position of this slight but famous fortification may be formed.

Fort Du Quesne was situated on the east side of the Monongahela, on the tongue of land formed by the junction of that stream with the Alleghany. Though full of faults in its original construction, and small, it was built with immense labour, and it had "a great deal of very strong works collected into very little room," (II. *Garneau*; Bouquet in I. *O. T.*) By the doubtful evidences which we possess, its shape would seem to have been a parallelogram, its four sides facing very nearly to the points of the compass, but a bastion at each corner gave it a polygonal appearance.

Its longest sides were fifty yards; its shorter, forty. The position of these bastions (which were fewer in number in Stobo's time than in M'Kinney's, and probably so continued till the summer of 1755,) may be seen by reference to the engraved plan. These were made of very large squared logs, to the height of twelve feet, and compactly filled in with earth to the depth of eight; thus, leaving about four feet of ramparts to shelter the plateau. The sides of the fort nearest the rivers being comparatively protected by nature, were not furnished with bastions; but a strong stockade, twelve feet high, and made of logs a foot in diameter driven pilewise into the ground, extended from bastion to bastion and completely enclosed the area.

This stockade was ingeniously wattled crosswise with poles, after the fashion of basket-work, and loopholes, slanting downwards, were cut through them to enable the men to fire. At the distance of some four rods from these walls, as they may be called, a shallow ditch was dug completely environing them and protected by a second stockade, seven feet high, built in a manner similar to the first, and solidly embanked with earth. If we assume the proportions of Stobo's drawing to be correct, by a comparison of this work with the dimensions of the house marked "Soldiers' Barracks" on his plan, its extent will be found to be about seven hundred and seventy-five feet.

Two gates opened into the fort; the western from the water-side, and the eastern, about ten feet wide, from the land. Immediately between the eastern posterns was sunken a deep well, whose diameter was the width of the gateway, and over which a drawbridge was placed that at night, or in time of danger, was drawn up with chains and levers; and these actually formed the gate. Both portals were strongly framed of squared logs; but the eastern gate opened on hinges, and had a wicket cut in it for ordinary use. Within the fort, and hard by

FORT
DU QUESNE.
1754.
by Robert Stobo.

T. Sinclair's lith. Phila.

the eastern gate, were placed the magazine and kitchen; the former, twenty feet wide by forty long, and but five feet high, was built of heavy, hewed timber, deeply sunk into the ground to almost its full altitude, and its roof plastered with a coating of potter's clay nearly four feet in thickness.

By this means, it was comparatively secure from any missile save bombs or hot-shot thrown from the brow of the adjacent hills. It is to these precautions that we are indebted at this day for the solitary vestige of Old Fort Du Quesne that remains to us. Some workmen, in the summer of 1854—just about a century after Stobo wrote—being employed in making excavations for the Pennsylvania Railroad Company, brought to light this building, which alone, of all its comrades, had, from its peculiar formation, escaped as well the destroying hand of Time as the torch of its baffled creator, when, in 1758, he forever abandoned his beloved fortress and fled before the approach of Forbes. Leaves, dirt, and rubbish must soon have accumulated above its neglected roof.

The storms of winter came, and the freshets of the spring; and ere long not a human being had reason to believe that beneath his feet stood, intact almost as on the day it was built, the Old French Magazine.

★★★★★★

In 1776, a slight inequality of the ground, a few graves, and the traces of its fosse above denote the site of the fort: in 1831, a boatyard was placed on the very spot: and at this day not a vestige of old Fort Du Quesne is visible save the lately-exposed magazine. (V. & VIII. *Haz. Reg.*)

★★★★★★

Beside this, however, there were other buildings within the walls; heavy and substantial log-houses, such as the wants of the garrison might require. Two were store-houses or magazines; two others were barracks; a seventh was the commandant's residence; and lesser erections served for a guard-house and a prison. The backs of these were at but a yard's distance from the walls, which they aided greatly to strengthen; all the intervening space being filled in with earth. Their roofs, covered with boards sawed by hand upon the spot, were level at the eaves with the ramparts; nor were there any pickets or sharpened palisades crowning the walls. Had Braddock reached this place, it was St. Clair's proposition to erect a battery on the brow of the opposite hill, which perfectly commanded the fort, and thence, with hot shot, to set these buildings on fire, and so subdue the post.

All their artillery consisted of eight cannon; one-half of them three, and the remainder four-pounders; five of which were mounted on the north-western bastion defending the Powder-Magazine. When Stobo wrote, M. de Contrecoeur and a guard of five officers and forty men were all who lodged in the fort; bark cabins were erected around it for the rest of the garrison. Every preparation was made for their permanent comfort; and already kitchen-gardens upon the Alleghany and mills upon the Monongahela, and a vast cornfield, extending for a quarter of a mile up either stream, furnished promise of future subsistence. The woods all around had been cut down, and hardly a stump remained within musket-shot to shelter the approach of a foe. (VIII. Hazard's *Penn. Reg.*; Stobo's *Letters*; VI. *Col. Rec.*)

Although the Canadian militia returning to their homes left but a small garrison of regulars to hold the fort towards the end of the summer of 1754, yet, if any reliance may be placed upon the reports which reached the English provinces, there was still a plenty of aid within call; no less than 2200 fresh troops being sent thitherward from Quebec during that season; and on the 25th of September 300 Caghnawagas or French Indians and a convoy of provisions from Quebec arrived. (II. *PA.*)

★★★★★★

The Caghnawagas, according to Colden, were deserters from the Six Nations, who, settling in Canada under the auspices of that government, had, through continual accessions and their own natural increase, grown in time to become a powerful and warlike people.

★★★★★★

Five days before, when Lieutenant Lyon with a flag of truce from Virginia and a fruitless proposition to exchange La Force (the officer captured at Jumonville's defeat), for Captain Stobo, visited Du Quesne, he found but one hundred men in the fort. But despite their scanty numbers, they were pursuing a most dangerous policy towards English interests by assiduously tempting the Indians of the Six Nations in the vicinity to forswear their ancient alliances; and sending their Caghnawagas among the Shawanoes and other western tribes to bring them into the interests of Canada. A number of savages had frequented the post ever since the capture of Fort Necessity, and among these numerous and valuable presents were distributed.

Through the medium of the Delawares, or perhaps more directly from Quebec and France, through the intercession of the spy Hennessey, they were in November advised of the expected reinforcements from England; and not comprehending a six months' delay in the enterprise, the French had hastened at once to reinforce Fort Du Quesne with eight additional cannon, and a plenty of stores.

The garrison was also increased to 1100 men; and nearly 400 Indians, Adirondacks, Caghnawagas, and Ottawas, were sent thither from the confines of New France. The cost of maintaining such a force must have been enormous; and when the approach of winter, filling the ravines with snow, and making the mountains perfectly impassable, dissipated all apprehension of present disturbance, the great bulk of this army retraced its steps; and a garrison of perhaps not more than two hundred and fifty regular troops, under the veteran Contrecoeur, was left behind. ("An experienced and courageous soldier," says *Garneau*, II.)

About the same number were, however, stationed within call at Venango; and some allowance must be made for the neighbouring savages, most of whom would probably, though not certainly, have sided with the French. The only Indians they could at this time with positive assurance rely upon were they who occupied the thirty or forty bark cabins that had grown up about the fort, or they who had come from Canada, and of whom very few remained through the winter. In April, 1755, there were scarce two hundred men, French and Indians, to garrison the place; and had Braddock then been in a condition to have struck, his success would have been certain. (VI. *C. R.*; II. *P.A.*; *Penn. Gaz.*, Nos. 1379.) But by their scouting-parties, which were always ranging the mountains between the Ohio and the English settlements, they once more caught the alarm, and eagerly solicited reinforcements from Canada.

The Marquis de Duquesne, however, though anxious enough to preserve a maiden fortress the works which bore his name, could not be easily brought to believe that it was yet seriously threatened, and constantly treated with contempt the rumours that during the past winter had from time to time reached his ears; pronouncing all the menaces and preparations of the enemy a mere fanfaronade—"*un feu de paille*," ("a straw fire".) Thus, in the early spring of 1755, no steps had yet been taken in Canada for the relief of Fort Du Quesne. (II. *P. A.* And see Appendix.)

The conduct of the Court of St. James during this crisis was as little to be reconciled to a just notion of frankness and honourable dealing as that of its adversary. On the 15th of January—the very day after Braddock had sailed for Virginia—the Duc de Mirepoix proposed that each crown should prohibit all present hostilities, and that the matter of the Ohio territory should be left to an amicable adjustment; the destination and motive of the expedition which had just started being first pacifically explained. The ambassador could not at that very moment have been ignorant that his master was straining every nerve to throw such a force into Canada as would defy any attack; and they whom he addressed were well aware that he knew all this.

They, therefore, on the 22nd of the same month, furnished him with a Jesuitical reply, declaring that the only end of Braddock's mission was the defence and protection of the king's dominions in America, without any design to attack those of any other prince, or in any wise open the door to war; and that as to the Ohio country, the French must abandon and destroy all their settlements there, or, in other words, put matters in the condition they were in before the Treaty of Utrecht, before a friendly negotiation on that point could be thought of In order to gain time, the French dallied with these propositions, at first disputing, and then making a show of accepting them: but the English in turn increased their demands to the extent of all they could hope to gain by force of arms: demands to which it was impossible for aught save the *ultima ratio regum* should justify Louis in yielding. Diplomacy thus kept up a feint of peace, until the tidings of Boscawen's success reached Europe; when triumph on the one hand and rage and disappointment on the other rent in twain the veil which shadowed the effigy of war.

In April, 1754, the most formidable armament that the kingdom could produce was gathered in the harbour of Brest. Twenty-two vessels of war, bearing the flags of two admirals, were there assembled to receive the troops destined for America. Six regiments whose names were known on almost every battlefield of Europe, were there arrayed for embarkation; the regiments of Artois, of Burgundy, of Guienne, of Languedoc, and of Béarn, and the famous regiment *de la Reine*; comprising fully 3000 men destined to find, beyond the stormy sea, a painful exile or a bloody grave. With them embarked the German Baron Dieskau, the favoured pupil of Saxe, who was to command in chief the armies in America and the Marquis de Vaudreuil de Cavagnac, late Governor of Louisiana, and the second of his family to whom the government of Canada had been entrusted, who was to succeed M. de Duquesne.

★★★★★★

The high idea entertained of this officer's capacity may be seen in the rate at which the French paid his services. They gave him a salary of 12,000 *livres* as major-general; of 25,000 more as commander of the American expedition; and a retiring pension of 4000. *Penn. Gaz.,* No. 1385.

★★★★★★

Perverse gales for a time prevented the squadron from proceeding to sea; but at 8 o'clock on the morning of the 3rd of May the wind shifted to north-north-east, and the signal was at once given to weigh anchor and to set all sail. (I. Pouchot. M. Garneau fixes the date at the end of April; but Pouchot's journal of the voyage is so minute and interesting, that I prefer relying upon his statements.)

At half-past ten the voyage commenced. On the 7th of May the *Formidable*, the flag-ship of M. de Macnamara, who had hitherto accompanied the squadron, shortened sail, and with his particular command he presently returned to France. A gun from the *Entreprenant*, at whose mast-head floated the pennant of M. Dubois de la Mothe, called the attention of the majority of the vessels. Stretching; forward under a cloud of canvass, with a signal for the America-bound portion of the fleet to follow, the *Entreprenant* soon was lost beneath the verge to the anxious eyes not only of those who gazed from the receding galleries of the *Formidable*, but to the diligent espionage of half-a-dozen English frigates which had for weeks been lying in wait to watch the every movement of the French. But any information they could carry would reach England too late to be of service, since Admiral Boscawen had already, on the 27th of April, set sail from Plymouth with instructions which, it may be confidently asserted, though probably merely verbal, assured him that if he should be able to thwart, at any price, the arrival of the French at Canada, he would render a welcome service to his King and Country.

To this end he lay in wait for them among the misty vapours of the banks of Newfoundland: In it the same cloudy column that concealed the attack, furthered the escape. He captured, indeed, the *Alcide*, of 64 guns and 500 men, commanded by M. Hocquart, and the *Lis*, pierced for 64 guns, but armed *en flute* for the transportation of troops, commanded by M. de Lorgerie; and he came very near catching the *Entreprenant* itself. (The *Entreprenant* was finally destroyed by the English at the capture of Louisbourg, 1758. Mante.)

On board the ships captured, however, were Colonel de Rostaing (the second in command of the Canadian Army), and several other officers of distinction, and eight companies of the regiments of Languedoc and *la Reine*. It has been alleged that Boscawen acted dishonourably in this transaction, pretending peace with the French ships till at half-pistol range he opened his fire upon them with grape and cannister; but this does not seem credible. The conduct of his employers was much more censurable, who had assured M. de Mirepoix that the admiral's orders were not to act upon the offensive, and that whatever might fall out, England would not begin the war. Such a mendacious tale could hardly impose even upon that polite minister; and he rather vaguely replied "that the king his master would consider the first hostile gun fired at sea as a declaration of war."

Lord Orford says that Newcastle, having nobody left at home undeceived, had diligently applied himself to humbug the ambassador; and succeeded. At all events, one thing turned out exactly as Mirepoix had predicted—Boscawen's trivial success was the signal for open hostilities. "*Je ne pardonnerai pas les pirateries de cette insolente nation,*" ("I will not forgive the piracy of this insolent nation," exclaimed Louis XV.; and war was thenceforth inevitable. (Capt. Richard Howe, afterwards the celebrated Admiral Earl Howe, chiefly distinguished himself in this action.)

The safe arrival at Quebec of the rest of the fleet on the 19th of June and the succeeding days, increased the regular troops in Canada from 1000 to 3800 men. A militia of 8000 men was already in the field, or in garrison at the various forts. With all this numerous array, however, the Marquis de Duquesne was not at all aware of the dangers which environed the Ohio establishments, and left his government to his successor with the comfortable assurance that it was not possible for the English to traverse the Alleghanies in sufficient force to cause any uneasiness.

The experienced and courageous commander of Fort Du Quesne was thus left to rely upon his own strength and the aid derivable, in an emergency, from the contiguous posts and such Canadians and savages as were always, in greater or less numbers, near at hand. Fortunately for him, though it was probably done with no idea of its imminent danger, at least 950 men had been sent in April from Canada to recruit the line of fortifications between Lake Erie and the forks of the Ohio. (I. Pouchot; II. *Garneau*;VI. *Col. Rec*; Penn. Gaz., No. 1379.) And while every effort was made to obtain information of the intentions of their enemy, a strict watch was kept to prevent the betrayal of their own circumstances. One O'Conner, an English subaltern officer, was hanged as a spy at Quebec in the spring of 1755, and three others shared his fate; and on the 1st of May, two more British spies were executed. (*Penn. Gaz.,* Nos. 1394, 1396; XXV. *Gent. Mag.*, 332.)

★★★★★★

One of these inquisitive but unfortunate gentry had in his pocket a list of all the cannon cast at Quebec or imported thither since 1752, and of all the chief houses, the forts, magazines, &c., not only there, but on either side of the St. Lawrence to Montreal. Another was supplied with draughts of the batteries. These two were on the point of departure when they were suddenly arrested and hanged.

★★★★★★

CHAPTER 9

The British Movement

As little as possible has been said in this of the details of the march of the troops from their quarters in Alexandria to Will's Creek. But it may not be amiss to trace here, for the guidance of the reader, the exact line of route which they followed throughout the campaign. By St. Clair's advice, the army was to start from Alexandria in two divisions; one regiment and a portion of the stores to Winchester, Virginia, whence a new road was nearly completed to Fort Cumberland, and the other regiment, with the remainder, by way of Frederic, in Maryland. A portion of the stores were to be conveyed in part by water-carriage on the Potomac.

Accordingly, on the 8th and 9th of April, the provincials and six companies of the 44th, under Sir Peter Halket, set out for Winchester; Lieutenant-Colonel Gage and four companies remaining to escort the artillery. On the 18th of April, the 48th, under Colonel Dunbar, set out for Frederic, detaching a company to the Conococheague to expedite the transmission of the stores gathered there. Arriving at Frederic, however, it was found there was no road through Maryland to Will's Creek; and Dunbar accordingly was compelled, on the 1st of May, to cross the Potomac at the mouth of the Conococheague and strike the Winchester route. On the 5th, he crossed the Little Cacapon; and on the 8th, was again ferried over the Potomac to Maryland from a spot, hard by the mouth of Cacapon, which has since that day borne the name of the Ferry Fields.

Thence, along the river-side, through Shawanoe Old Town, the dwelling-place of the notorious Cresap, Dunbar passed through the

Narrows at the foot of Will's Mountain. (II. *Olden Time.*) At high noon on the 10th of May, while Halket's command was already encamped at their common destination, the 48th was startled by the passage of Braddock and his staff through their ranks, with a body-guard of light-horse galloping on either side of his travelling-chariot, in haste to reach Fort Cumberland. (He purchased this coach from Governor Sharpe and left it at Cumberland during the rest of the march. Orme's Letter to Sharpe. Sharpe's MS. *Corresp.* in Maryland Hist. Soc.)

The troops saluted, the drums rolled out the Grenadier's March, and the cortege passed by. An hour after, they heard the booming of the artillery which welcomed the general's arrival; and a little later, themselves encamped on the hillsides about that post. But in consequence of the difficulty of procuring teams, the artillery, &c., did not arrive until May the 20th.

The erection of Fort Cumberland and its strength have been already described. It stood upon the bank of Will's Creek, hard by its junction with the Potomac, on the site of the present town of Cumberland, and within what is now Alleghany County, Maryland. (Cumberland is now a thriving town with about 7000 inhabitants. It is 179 miles west by north from Baltimore.) Here had probably, in ancient days, been a Shawanoe village, and its Indian name, Cucucbetuc, is still preserved; and here, as we have seen, after a series of most distressing delays, Braddock at length succeeded in bringing together all his forces.

As nearly as can be ascertained, these consisted as follows: The 44th and 48th regiments, originally 1000 strong, were increased by the Maryland and Virginia Levies to 1400 men. Of the remaining levies, about one hundred were formed by the general into two companies of carpenters or pioneers, each composed of thirty men, two sergeants, two subalterns, and a captain. The duty of these was to open the road and make the necessary repairs to the wagons, &c., on the route; and a few of the most experienced of the others were received into a company of Guides, composed of a captain, two aids, and ten men. (II. *Olden Time.*) There was also a troop of provincial light horse which he had procured to be formed, and which hitherto had served as his body-guard; and a detachment of thirty sailors, with some half-dozen officers, furnished by Commodore Keppel to assist in rigging cordages, &c., should it be found necessary to build bridges on the way.

★★★★★★

The employment of seamen on this service seems to have caused a little natural surprise to those unacquainted with the circumstances of the case (II. *O.T.*); yet it was not a thing of unusual occurrence in America during this war. At Martinico and at Quebec they were employed to pull the guns. "An hundred or two of them, with ropes and pulleys, will do more than all your dray-horses in London." At Quebec, when Wolfe passed along the lines ere—

Fighting with the French
On the Heights of Abram,

—he found a number of jolly tars, who had been engaged in hauling up the cannon, meekly sliding into the ranks of his soldiery. As they were armed some with hangers, more with sticks, most not at all, he saw no advantage in permitting them to stay, and, despite their petitions, bade them retire. "God bless your honour!" they cried; "if we may not fight, at least let us stop and *see fair play between you and the French!*" Wolfe laughed at this droll request and thanked them and sent them to their ships. But they were not disposed, after all their toil, to go away without a share in the battle; and lurking about till it actually begun, they took an active part in its perils and glories. See XXV. *Gent. Mag.*130, 180.

★★★★★★

But the entire force which eventually marched from Fort Cumberland, as given by Captain Orme, consisted of 2037 men, out of a complement of 2100. To these must be added the Guides, the Lighthorse, and the seamen; in all not exceeding one hundred, which, with the staff and the eight Indians, who remained with the general unto the end, will make a total of about 2150 souls. The usual train of non-militants who always accompany an army was not wanting here—women, who could not fight; Indians who would not; and wagoners who cut loose their horses and fled, to a man, at the first onset.

Early in June, too, the well-known Captain Jack had repaired with his company to the camp and offered his services for the expedition. His merits as a guide and as an "Indian killer" were not unknown to Braddock, but the proffered services were coupled with some stipulations for freedom from the regular discipline of the army and were rejected. This singular man was once a frontier-settler. Returning to his cabin one evening after a long day's chase, he found it a heap of smoking ruins, and the blackened corpses of his murdered family smouldering in its embers. From that fatal hour, he vowed never but with life to forgive the race who had wrought his woe, and to his dying hour he was the most dreaded enemy the Indians knew.

In 1753, he held some commission under Governor Hamilton; and at this period, he was at the head of a party of bold woodsmen, clad, like himself, in Indian attire, and following very much the Indian mode of warfare. His home was in the Juniata country; but the celerity and extent of his movements caused his fame to reach from Fort Augusta to the Potomac. A mystery has always shrouded his personal history. His swarthy visage (darkened, perchance, by a tinge of baser blood) and destructive arm, however, live in the fireside legends of the West; and many a tale is told of the deeds of the Black Rifle—the Black Hunter—the Wild Hunter of the Juniata, or the Black Hunter of the Forest—under all of which sobriquets he was known. It was a misfortune for Braddock that he neglected to secure the services of such an auxiliary. (IV. & V. Haz. *Penn. Reg.*)

Being at last, if not thoroughly prepared, at least sufficiently so to warrant his undertaking the long and tedious journey that was before him, Braddock issued his orders for the army to leave Fort Cumberland. On the 30th of May, Sir John St. Clair, with Major Chapman, of the 44th, and 600 men, set out to clear a road to the Little Meadows on the Youghiogeny, thirty miles distant, where they were to erect a fortified camp. The army followed in three divisions: the first, under Halket, on the 7th of June; the next, under Gage, on the 8th; and the third, under Dunbar, on the 10th; Braddock delayed his own departure until the last man had marched; and the expedition was now fairly on its way to the Ohio. The opposite map will give the reader a perfect idea of its route, and in Captain Orme's text almost every detail of the march is minutely noted down.

★★★★★★

In 1847, Mr. T. C. Atkinson, of Cumberland, Maryland, being employed upon a railroad survey through this region, traced Braddock's route with great accuracy by means of the indications still remaining on the ground; and under his supervision, an excellent map was prepared by Mr. Middleton. This plan was subsequently engraved for the *Olden Time* (Vol. II.), where it appears with a very valuable explanatory paper by Mr. Atkinson. It is to the politeness of Mr. Craig that we are indebted for the original plate from which the impression that accompanies this volume is taken.

★★★★★★

160

Owing to the innumerable difficulties of its situation, the progress of the army was painfully slow; five miles being a good day's march, and even half this distance being sometimes barely accomplished. Roads were to be cut through the forests and over the steep mountains; streams were to be bridged, and morasses made passable. The number of wagons and pack-horses struggling through this untravelled land protracted the line to a most dangerous length, and all the difficulties predicted by Franklin were in a fair way to be realised.

★★★★★★

Entertaining some doubts of the result so confidently anticipated by the General, Franklin had remarked to him, "To be sure, sir, if you arrive well before Du Quesne with these fine troops, so well provided with artillery, the fort, though completely fortified and assisted with a very strong garrison, can probably make but a short resistance. The only danger I apprehend of obstruction to your march is from the ambuscades of the Indians; who, by constant practice, are dexterous in laying and executing them; and the slender line, near four miles long, which your army must make, may expose it to be attacked by surprise in its flanks, and to be cut, like a thread, into several pieces, which, from their distance, cannot come up in time to support each other." He smiled at Franklin's ignorance, and replied, "These savages may indeed be a formidable enemy to your raw American militia; but upon the king's regular and disciplined troops, sir, it is impossible they should make any impression." I. Sparks' *Franklin*.

★★★★★★

Accordingly, at the end of the first day's journey, it was resolved to considerably lighten their numbers and burthens. A part of the artillery and fifty men were sent back to Cumberland; fifty more, under Captain Hogg, were despatched as a covering party to the workmen on the Pennsylvania Road; and twenty-eight of the soldiers' wives were sent on their way to Philadelphia. So far as their names are any indication, they serve to show the Scottish complexion of the two regiments. (II. *P.A.*; VI. *C. R.*)

The officers, who even in the infantry always rode upon a march, returned to Will's Creek all but such luggage as was absolutely essential; and over a hundred of their superfluous horses were freely contributed to the public service; the general and his *aides* setting the example by giving twenty.

Braddock
A.D.

Road
Bradd

Allegheny R.
PITTSBURG
X Bute-field
Turtle Creek
Pittsburg
Greensburg Turnpike
Crooked Run
PENNSYLVANIA
Long R.
Sampson Mill
Sewickly C.
Mc Pleasant Turnpike
Peters C.
Noble Town
Jacobs C.
Indian C.
RIDGE
Youghiogheny R.
Bear Run
Monongahela R.
Stony Creek
Brownsville
National Road
Union T.
Lower Hill
Great M.
Meadows
Braddock
Briar Rt
VIRGINIA

k's Route

1755.

by Middleton

lock's Road

scale of miles

MARYLAND

VIRGINIA

Potomac R.

The route pursued by Braddock was in many respects an unwise one. It occasionally presented difficulties and how indifferently, even in the region immediately adjacent to Fort Cumberland, St. Clair had attended to its exploration. Much time and labour had already been exhausted on the road over Will's Mountain, which Major Chapman had surmounted, with considerable loss, on the 30th of May; and the service was finally indebted to a naval officer for the easy discovery of the valley path that leads around its base, subsequently adopted for the United States' National Road.

As it was, marching on a newly-opened track, Halket, who started three days before, had got no further on the night of the 10th than the men who left Will's Creek that morning; a distance of five miles. The truth is, that Sir John implicitly followed the path that Nemacolin, a Delaware Indian, had marked out or *blazed* for the Ohio Company some years before, and which, a very little widened, had served the transient purposes of that association, and of Washington's party in 1754. To be sure, with many windings, it led to the Ohio; yet a few intelligent scouts, sent out betimes, could not have failed to discover a shorter and a better course. But precautionary steps of this kind were not within the sphere of Braddock's comprehension.

In addition to every other reason of delay, a general sickness prevailed among the troops, caused by their long and continued confinement to a salt diet; from the effects of which, though few died, few escaped. During a later period of the march, even Washington's hardy constitution succumbed; and for many days he was severely, perhaps dangerously, unwell. Convalescent, at length, through the personal attention of the general, he was left on the road with a guard, to rejoin his post as soon as his strength would permit. Long ere these scenes occurred, however, an important change had been made in the constitution of affairs. The army had been ten days in reaching the Little Meadows, but twenty-four miles from Cumberland, passing, with a line sometimes four miles long, through numerous spots too well adapted for an ambush or a surprise not to arrest a soldier's eye.

Such were those dark forests of enormous white pines that shadow the region beyond the Great Savage Mountain. The loneliness and perfect monotony of such a scene are not readily to be described; it more resembles the utter stillness of the desert than anything beside. No bird chirps among the foliage or finds its food in these inhospitable boughs; no wild creature has its lair beneath its leafy gloom. Like the dark nave of some endless, dream-born cathedral, the tall columns rise before, behind, on every side, in uncounted and bewildering multiplicity, and are lost in the thick mantle that shuts out the light of heaven. The senses weary of the confusing prospect, and imagination paints a thousand horrid forms to people its recesses.

At every step the traveller half looks to find a bloody corse, or the blanched skeleton of some long-murdered man, lying across his pathway through these woods, so aptly named the *Shades of Death!* It was not until the 18th of June that the troops were beyond these inauspicious scenes; and Braddock, as, slowly descending the shaggy steep of Meadow Mountain—

He wound, with toilsome march, his long array,

—beheld his whole force in sight of the fortified camp erected by St. Clair at the Little Meadows. (II. Sp. *Wash.* Consult, also, Mr. Atkinson's paper in II. *O. T.*) Here a council of war was held, which is not noticed by Orme, and which consisted, as usual, of all the field-officers present. A further reduction of baggage was agreed upon, and a dozen more horses given to the service; among them, Washington's best charger, his luggage being retrenched to a single portmanteau, half-filled. Before the council met, Braddock also privately consulted him as to the propriety of pushing more rapidly forward with a light division; leaving the heavy troops, &c., to follow by easy marches.

This course Washington warmly approved, urging the present weakness of the garrison at Du Quesne, and the difficulty with which, during the dry season, any supplies could reach them from Venango by the Rivière aux Boeufs, whose waters were then at a very low stage. His rank did not permit him an opportunity of pressing these views at the council-board; but they were brought forward there by the general himself, and it was decided that St. Clair, with Gage and 400 men, should start on the 18th to open a road.

On the 19th, Braddock in person followed, with Halket (who acted as brigadier). Burton, and Sparks, and about 800 men, the elite of the army. Inasmuch as in the selection of the troops for this manoeuvre he made a point of choosing those he considered the best, without any reference to the wishes of his subordinates, this step gave great and lasting offence to Dunbar, Chapman, and the others left behind. (*Penn. Gaz.*, No. 1392.) He took with him four howitzers, four twelve-pounders, twelve cohorns, thirteen artillery-wagons, and seventeen of ammunition. The provisions were borne by pack-horses. His expectation was then to strike the fort by the 28th of June, at the furthest, ere the garrison should receive its reinforcements; five hundred regulars being reported to be at that moment on their way thither. Four artillery-officers, eighty-four wagons, and all the ordnance-stores and provisions which were not indispensable to the general's march, were left with Dunbar.

★★★★★★

II. Sp. *Wash.*; *Penn. Gaz.*, No. 1387; VI. C. R.; Sharpe (MS. *Corresp.*) says, "I think the general had with him 52 carriages; the artillery and 18 wagon-loads of ammunition included." This nearly tallies with the above statement; the 20 gun-carriages, 13 caissons, and 17 wagons, making just 50.

★★★★★★

From the Little Crossings, on the upper waters of Castleman's River (a tributary of the Youghiogeny), to the Great Crossings on those of the Youghiogeny itself, is but about seventeen miles; yet it was only on the 24th of June that the latter was passed. The advanced party under St. Clair was constantly engaged in cutting the road; but its progression was necessarily slow, and the rest of the army had to encamp at their heels and march within sound of their axes. Steep, rugged hills were to be clomb, to whose summits the artillery and baggage were with cruel labour drawn; headlong declivities to be descended, down which the cannon and wagons were lowered with blocks and tackle; or deep morasses to be threaded, where the troops sunk ankle or knee-deep in the clinging mire.

The road, too, was beset with outlying parties of the enemy, who constantly aimed at embarrassing their march. On one occasion, Scarroyaddy was even captured; and his treatment evidently shows that many of the savages in the service of the French were of his old acquaintance in Pennsylvania. (Captain Orme's *Journal*.) On another, three Mohawk Indians came into camp with intelligence from Du Quesne, for which they were well paid. But disgusted either by the general's indifference to their merits, or by the accounts of his demeanour which they received from their brethren in his ranks, they deserted during the night, and probably returned to the French, whence they came.

With them disappeared, too, one of the general's Indians, who had long manifested a disposition to slip off. During the march, he would constantly conceal himself upon the flanks; lying down flat behind a stump or a stone or creeping into a clump of tall grass. But he was as constantly routed out by the sergeants of the flanking parties, to whose surveillance he had been especially commended; men, trained in Ireland to find a hare squatting in her form beneath a cluster of fern, whose keen eyes, ever on the watch, never failed to discover the refuge of the would-be fugitive. But on the very next night after his flight, three Englishmen, straggling beyond the lines, were shot and scalped upon the very edge of the camp; in which affair he doubtless had a hand.

Not satisfied with the small temporal assistance which his province had afforded the expedition, Governor Morris by proclamation enjoined his people to unite with him in a solemn invocation upon Heaven to preserve and bless the royal arms; and the 19th of June was appointed as a season of public humiliation, of fasting, and of prayer. For that day, all servile labour was discontinued throughout the province: the sound of the mallet and the anvil was not heard; the fields were left untilled; the unfettered waters glided idly beneath the motionless wheel; and no smoky columns arose from the cold forge. An unwonted stillness prevailed over the land, save where from the house of prayer was uplifted the preacher's voice in supplication to Almighty God that:

> He would be pleased to avert the punishments due to their sins, favour them with a fruitful season, and give success to the measures which His Majesty, ever attentive to the good and welfare of his people, had concerted for the security and preservation of their just rights and commerce. (VI. *C. R.*)

While thus supernal succour was importuned, the arm of flesh was slowly advanced, and was even now on the borders. Until after it had forded Castleman's river, the course of the army was generally a very little north of west and lay entirely through Maryland. On the 21st of June, Braddock for the first time entered Pennsylvania. Traversing the high and watery glades of Somerset County and the precipitous region of Fayette, whose mountain-tops attain an altitude of 2500 feet above the sea, with valleys scooped between, 1000 feet below their summits, on the 30th of June he reached Stewart's Crossing on the Youghiogeny, about thirty-five miles from his destination. So far, the efforts of the hostile Indians were less a source of positive danger than of increasing annoyance. That indefatigable foe had by this time got into the rear of the army; their spies environed it on every side and watched its every motion. As one said to an English captive at Du Quesne:

Their scouts saw him every day from the mountains—that he was advancing in close columns through the woods—(this he indicated by placing a number of red sticks parallel to each other and pressed closely together)—and that the Indians would be able to shoot them down 'like one pigeon.'

But so strict was Braddock's police hitherto, that the English loss was very inconsiderable, consisting but of a wagoner, three bat-men, and a horse. Scattering in various directions, the savages threaded the woods in hopes of scalps and plunder. On the night of the 29th, they visited and fired into Dunbar's camp at the Little Meadows, which had been well fortified by St. Clair, and was entirely surrounded by an abattis. They also kept the workmen and convoys on the Pennsylvania road in such a state of alarm that in one day thirty deserted in a body, and the road was soon at a stand. (I. *O. T.*; VI. *C. R.*; *Penn. Gaz.*, Nos. 1386, 1387. A batman is an officer's servant. IX. Notes and Queries.)

It was on the evening of the 3rd of July at the camp at Jacob's or Salt Lick Creek, that Sir John St. Clair brought forward his proposition to halt here until Colonel Dunbar and the rest of the forces should come up.

★★★★★★

Probably a salt lick or spring on a branch of Jacob's Creek caused this double nomenclature, which has led to some little confusion; there being another stream called Indian Lick falling into the Youghiogeny. Orme styles it Salt Lick Creek; but Scull's large map (Lond. 1775), gives both titles.

★★★★★★

The continued remissness in furnishing supplies had compelled these troops to almost forego the use of fresh provisions, and they were afflicted as generally and even more fatally than those with Braddock by the disorders incident to such privations. Many had died; and many more, officers as well as men, were on the sick list. On the 2nd of July, however, Dunbar had moved forward from the Little Meadows; and his van was now not far from the Great Crossings, eleven days' march from Jacob's Creek. Considering this fact, and the disadvantages that would result from the delay, it was wisely resolved by Braddock's council to push forward. They conceived themselves to be (as in fact they were), amply strong enough to conquer the fort should they once sit down before it; and the absence of any organised opposition to their previous progress was well calculated to encourage the belief that, through the enemy's weakness, none would be attempted. Captain Orme afterwards wrote:

> Happy it was, that this disposition was made: otherwise the whole must either have starved or fallen into the hands of the enemy, as numbers would have been of no service to us, and our provision was all lost.

And had the general waited for Dunbar, it would have been most probably the middle of August ere he left Jacob's Creek. For so scanty in number were the miserable jades on which he depended, that this officer could only move one-half his wagons at a time. After one day's march, the poor beasts were sent back to bring up the remainder; and it was invariably two days' more ere the detachment could start from the spot of the first night's encampment. Washington said:

> Truly, there has been vile management in regard to horses. (VI. C. R.; II. Sp. *Wash.*)

★★★★★★

> Instead of proper draughthorses, all sorts of broken-down hacks, and spavined, wind-galled ponies, wore shamelessly palmed off upon the army by contractors who knew its condition was such that nothing could be rejected. Besides, there were (if not now, at least at a later period), scoundrels base enough to hang around Dunbar's camp, stealing every horse that was left to graze in the woods without a guard. Above three hundred were thus made away with. (VI. *C. R.*)

★★★★★★

To an army that looked longingly forward to a respite at Fort Du Quesne from the unwonted tasks to which it had been so long subjected, and to whom the exciting perils of the battle-shock offered far greater attractions than a supine existence in the wilderness, where no friend was to be encountered, no enemy to be met in open combat, the orders to advance were welcome tidings. Animated by the confidence of success, it moved onward, regardless of natural difficulties, with all that disciplined courage and tenacity of purpose which have ever characterized the Anglo-Saxon race, eager to behold at length the hostile hold, to tear down the hated banner that so insultingly waved over British soil:—

> *Tho' fens and floods possest the middle space,*
> *That unprovok'd they would have feared to pass;*

Nor fens nor floods can stop Britannia's bands
When her proud foe rang'd on their border stands.
(Addison; *The Campaign.*)

But the fatal halts which Braddock had already too often been obliged to make, proved in the end the cause of his ruin. It will presently be seen of what importance the saving of three days only would have been; for it was in those three days, the last of his march, that the whole plan of attacking and destroying his army was conceived, organised, and executed. The traditionary repugnance of M. de Contrecoeur and his red allies to the hazardous experiment would, in all probability, have prevented its adoption at any other moment, as effectually as it did any previous concerted opposition to the march of the English through passes so admirably fitted by nature for defence, that Braddock himself was amazed at their unoccupation. And, as it happened, every account he received but tended to confirm him in his security. On the 3rd of July, he had endeavoured to prevail on his few Indians to go out for intelligence; a thing he has always been blamed for neglecting, but which he had constantly solicited at their hands, and which they now declined as resolutely as before.

Perhaps it was a sense of their scanty numbers that induced this conduct; perhaps a natural reluctance to encounter their own brethren whom they knew to be with the French; but more probably, it was their extreme discontent with the manners of the general that closed their ears to all his suggestions.

On the 4th of July, however, he was more successful. Urged by bribes, and the promise of greater rewards, two Indians were persuaded to depart on a scouting expedition; and no sooner were they gone than Christopher Gist, the general's guide, was privately despatched on the same errand. On the 6th, both Indians and Gist rejoined the army, having penetrated undiscovered to within half a mile of the fort. Their reports were favourable and similar; they found the passes open, and no indications of a heavy force about the works, although there was evidence of outlying parties, and perhaps reinforcements, within a moderate distance. The Indians had even encountered a French officer shooting in the woods hard by Du Quesne, whom without hesitation they killed and scalped. Gist was less fortunate. He, in turn, had been set upon by two hostile savages, and had narrowly succeeded in escaping with his life. Welcome as was this promise of an undisturbed advance, the day was clouded by a fatal event that must have considerably disturbed even savage equanimity.

A number of French Indians had beset and scalped a few loiterers, and a general alarm was spread through the line. In the midst of the excitement, Braddock's Indians in advance were met by a party of his rangers, who, regardless of or blind to their signals of friendship, fired upon them, killing the son of Scarroyaddy, their chieftain. The general took what steps suggested themselves to his mind to prevent this misadventure impairing the regard of the dead lad's kindred, and, as it would appear, not without success.

Eager as was the army for the fray, it cannot be denied that at this moment there was much in it to weaken its efficacy. The soldiers complained bitterly of the severe and unusual labours which they were compelled to undergo. The quality of their food was not satisfactory, and the quantity was thought too small; nor was the time allotted them in camp always sufficient to properly dress their victuals. The same necessity which exacted this treatment deprived them also of the hitherto invariable allowance of spirits. They had nothing but water to drink, and that often bad and unwholesome. To add to their discomforts, the sagacious provincials were fully impressed with the dangers of a battle to be fought in the woods and against the savages upon the principles of European tactics; and by their constant predictions of calamity did not a little dishearten the regulars of the two regiments.

Nor were matters on a better footing in higher quarters. Disputes and jealousies were rife among the leaders; and by this time the general was not even on speaking terms with Halket and Dunbar. Braddock had already, however, conceived a plan to benefit such of the officers as he looked upon with favouring eyes. It was his intention, when Du Quesne should have been captured, to incorporate the provincials into a royal regiment, the command of which was to be bestowed upon Lieutenant-Colonel Burton of the 48th. His *aide-de-camp*. Captain Morris, was to have been the Lieutenant-Colonel of the new regiment, and Captain Dobson (the senior captain of the 48th), its major: while Orme was to succeed to Burton's position in the 48th. A number of other promotions would necessarily have followed these changes, in which it is not improbable Braddock would have taken occasion to fulfil his promise of providing for Washington. But his defeat and death scattered all these politic schemes to the winds. (Sharpe's MS. *Corr. Review of Military Operations in North America, &c.*)

We are now approaching the last dread scene of our tragic story, and events crowd thick and rapidly upon us. On the night of the

4th of July, the army halted at Thicketty Run, a petty branch of the Sewickly Creek, where, by some dismal fatality, it seems to have remained until the 6th, awaiting the return of its spies and the arrival of a supply of provisions from Dunbar's camp, under convoy of a captain and a hundred men. In the rear of this party, which appeared on the 6th, came Washington. Debilitated by his recent sickness, he was unable to endure on horseback the ordinary fatigues of such a road, and journeyed in a covered wagon; but it was not until the 8th that he rejoined the general.

It was perhaps to this unhappy delay of twenty-four hours that the destruction of the army is attributable; yet it was such as even a more provident leader than Braddock might well have been excused in making. By it he looked to gain intelligence of his foe and subsistence for himself; both objects of primary importance.

CHAPTER 10

The Fatal Crossing

It must be borne in mind that the English were now on the west side of the Monongahela, within the obtuse triangle formed by the forks of the Ohio at whose apex stood Fort Du Quesne; but a glance at the maps will show how far they had diverged from the direct line thither. As Mr. Sparks has well pointed out, (II. *Olden Time*), it must have been Braddock's original design to continue his march on the same shore, were it possible to have avoided the passage of the Narrows in so doing. His guides had rightly informed him that this was a spot where the road must be made upon a narrow, alluvial formation for some two miles along the bank of the stream, with the river on his left hand and the mountain-side upon his right; and that it would require much labour ere it could be made passable.

The perils of such a route were self-evident; therefore, abandoning all idea of pursuing it, he started on the morning of the 7th, and leaving the Indian track which he had followed so long, essayed to work his way across Turtle Creek some twelve miles above its confluence with the Monongahela: a step which, had it been carried out, would have ensured his success. He would then undoubtedly have sat down before the fort with little or no opposition on his way. But the fates were against him. On reaching the eastern branch of Turtle Creek, or rather what is now called Rush Creek, the road suddenly terminated in one of those headlong, precipitous descents so common along the edges of the water-courses of Alleghany County; practicable perhaps for footmen, or even sure-footed pack-horses, but utterly impassable to artillery and wagons.

A halt was at once commanded, and St. Clair sent forth with a suitable force to explore the country. He soon returned with the pleasing intelligence that he had hit upon the ridge which led directly to Fort Du Quesne. But after reflection upon the labour it would require to construct a road across the hill-environed head-waters of Turtle Creek, it was finally decided to quit that rugged region altogether, and to proceed directly to the Monongahela; and at a place where it makes a considerable bend to the north, to cross at the upper arm of the elbow, to follow the chord which would subtend the arc made by the river's curve, and to recross the stream at a point just below the opposite mouth of Turtle Creek.

Two excellent fords with easy banks afforded a strong inducement to pursue this plan: but had he persisted in the movement across Rush Creek, he would have marched through a country presenting comparatively few facilities for an ambuscade or covers for an enemy; whereas in twice crossing the Monongahela he exposed himself to the risk of encountering a determined opposition at either ford. The further and really more fatal hazard of running headlong against a natural entrenchment impregnable to the most determined efforts of one ignorant of its key, cannot be supposed to have entered into his calculations. Nor would the Narrows route have saved him from this danger, since, from the natural formation of the country, it must at the second ford have become identical with that Braddock actually pursued. Thus, in either case, there was no possibility on the Monongahela road of evading the spot where the enemy's ambush was eventually laid.

Having settled upon his course, on the 8th of July Braddock, following the valley of Long Run, marched south-westwardly eight miles towards the Monongahela; and pitched his camp for the night upon an inviting declivity between that stream and another rivulet called Crooked Run, some two miles from the river. He was now within two easy marches of the Ohio, to gain which he looked for no other opposition than what he might encounter in the morrow's fordings; and so far, as we can discover, there were in his ranks but two individuals at all diffident of success. William Shirley, the general's secretary, was out of all patience at the manner in which the expedition had been conducted; and was determined to go back to England the moment a campaign was brought to a close, of the success of which

BRADDOCK'S ARMY AT THE RIVER MONONGAHELA

he was more than doubtful. It is with a little surprise that we find reason to suppose the second in command was not free from similar forebodings.

As though gifted with that mysterious power of "second sight" which is attributed to the seers of his native land. Sir Peter Halket, whose sands of life had but twelve more hours to run, with a melancholy earnestness pressed that night upon the general the propriety of thoroughly examining every foot of ground between his present position and the fort, lest through this neglect he should peril his army's existence, and as it were plunge his head into the lion's jaws. The advice, as will be seen, was not altogether neglected; but its more important feature of beating the forest as hunters of the Highlands would drive their game was set aside by Braddock as unsuitable to the exigencies of his position. (I. Entick.)

With a sad presentiment of undefined evil, Halket withdrew. Did he in sooth possess the fatal power of peering into futurity, and exploring the secrets of unborn Time, what awful visions would have pressed upon his soul! Unconscious of their doom, around him slumbered hundreds of gallant men, sleeping their last sleep on an unbloody couch, nor heeding the tempest gathering fast above, which, overcoming like a summer's cloud, should pour destruction on their devoted heads. Through the long summer's day, the wearied army, anticipating aught rather than defeat, had marched steadily onward. The encircling woods shut out all prospect of the heavens save the serene blue sky directly overhead, bright with meridian splendour: but all around, beyond their narrow ken, a dark curtain hung like a pall upon the skirts of the horizon and driving clouds and gathering eagles boded the coming storm. Footsore and toilworn, the troops were now steeped in slumber; and in dreams that came from heaven through the ivory gates, they beheld themselves

——*arrived at last*
Unto the wished haven.

They saw their labours crowned with glory, their wanderings rounded with well-earned repose. But through the narrow passage that lay between them and their promised land rolled darkling the waters of an unseen stream, blacker than night, deeper than the grave: for on its shore, not death alone, but dishonour, and disgrace, and defeat, with welcoming hands, awaited their approach. Behind the western hills their sun had sunk for evermore, incarnadining in his parting rays the bright current of the Monongahela, overhung by stately groves bending to the waters their pensile boughs;

———*lucos, amoenae*
Quos et aquae subeunt et aurae.
———groves past
Which flow and gales.

To the prophetic vision of the Scottish *deuteroscopia*, these waters would have curdled with the clotted gore of the morrow's eve; the moaning trees would have sighed responsive to the sad wailings of the winds of night; and along the guilty shores would have flitted in griesly bands the bloody ghosts of the unburied slain.

In the meantime, with a commendable discretion, (the utmost, perhaps, that he was capable of) Braddock had concluded his arrangements for passing what he regarded as the only perilous place between his army and the fort, which he designed to reach early on the 10th. Had the proposition, started and abandoned by St. Clair, to push forward that very night a strong detachment to invest it before morning, been actually made to him, it is very probable he would have discountenanced it. As, in all human likelihood, it would have been crowned with success, it is as well for the general's reputation that the suggestion aborted.

What precautionary steps his education and capacity could suggest, were here taken by Braddock. Before three o'clock on the morning of the 9th, Gage was sent forth with a chosen band to secure both crossings of the river, and to hold the further shore of the second ford till the rest of the army should come up. At four, St. Clair, with a working-party, followed to make the roads. At six a. m., the general set out, and having advantageously posted about 400 men upon the adjacent heights, made, with all the wagons and baggage, the first crossing of the Monongahela.

Marching thence in order of battle towards the second ford, he received intelligence that Gage had occupied the shore according to orders, and that the route was clear. The only enemy he had seen was a score of savages, who fled without awaiting his approach. By eleven o'clock, the army reached the second ford; but it was not until after one that the declivities of the banks were made ready for the artillery and wagons, when the whole array, by a little before two o'clock, was safely passed over. Not doubting that from some point on the stream the enemy's scouts were observing his operations, Braddock was resolved to strongly impress them with the numbers and condition of his forces; and accordingly, the troops were ordered to appear as for a dress-parade.

In after life, Washington was accustomed to observe that he had never seen elsewhere so beautiful a sight as was exhibited during this passage of the Monongahela. Every man was attired in his best uniform; the burnished arms shone bright as silver in the glistening rays of the noonday sun, as, with colours waving proudly above their heads, and amid inspiring bursts of martial music, the steady files, with disciplined precision, and glittering in scarlet and gold, advanced to their position. (

★★★★★★

"My feelings were heightened by the warm and glowing narration of that day's events by Dr. Walker, who was an eye-witness. He pointed out the ford where the army crossed the Monongahela (below Turtle Creek 800 yards). A finer sight could not have been beheld; the shining barrels of the muskets, the excellent order of the men, the cleanliness of their apparel, the joy depicted on every face at being so near Fort Du Quesne—the highest object of their wishes. The music re-echoed through the mountains. How brilliant the morning; how melancholy the evening!"—Judge Yeates' Visit to Braddock's Field in 1776; VI. *Haz. Reg.*

★★★★★★

While the rear was yet on the other side, and the van was falling into its ordained course, the bulk of the army was drawn up in battle array on the western shore, hard by the spot where one Frazier, a German blacksmith in the interest of the English, had lately had his home. Two or three hundred yards above the spot where it now stood was the mouth of Turtle Creek (the Tulpewi Sipu of the Lenape), which, flowing in a southwestwardly course to the Monongahela that here has a north-westward direction, embraces, in an obtuse angle of about 125°, the very spot where the brunt of the battle was to be borne. The scene is familiar to tourists, being, as the crow flies, but eight miles from Pittsburg, and scarce twelve by the course of the river.

For three-quarters of a mile below the entrance of the creek, the Monongahela was unusually shallow; forming a gentle rapid or ripple, and easily fordable at almost any point. Its common level is from three to four hundred feet below that of the surrounding country; and along its upper banks, at the second crossing, stretches a fertile bottom

PLAN of the Field of Battle and Distribution of the Troops as they were on the march, at the time of the attack on the 9.th of July, 1755

PL.VI.

OHIO R.

FORT DU QUESNE

MONONGAHELA RIVER

REFERENCES.

I   French and Indians when discovered by the guides.

BRITISH TROOPS.

A.   Guides with 6 Light Horse.
B.   Van of the advanced party.
C.   Advanced party commanded by Lieu.t Col. Gage.
D.   The Working party comm.d by Sr. John St. Clair.
E.   2 Field Pieces, 6 pounders.
F.   Guard to Ditto.
G.   Tool Waggons.
H.   Flank Guard.
I.K.   Main Body of the Army.
    Light Horse.
K.   Sailors.
L.   Serg.t & 10 Grenadiers.
M.   Sub.n & 20 Men.
N.O.   12 Pounders.
    Comp.s of Grenadiers.
P.   Van Guard.
Q.   Train of Artillery.
R.   Rear Guard of the whole Army.
S.   A Hill.
V.   Ground where the principal part of the Battle was fought.

Turtle Creek

Part of the Narrows

Frazier's

N.B. The distance from Frazier's House to Fort Du Quesne is 7 computed miles.

of a rich pebbled mould, about a fourth of a mile in width, and twenty feet above low-water mark. At this time, it was covered by a fair, open walnut-wood, uncumbered with bush or undergrowth. (II. Sp. *Wash.*, 470. XVI. *Haz. Reg.*)

The ascent from the river, however, is rarely abrupt; but by a succession of gentle alluvial slopes or bottoms the steep hill-sides are approached, as though the waters had gradually subsided from their original glory to a narrow bed at the very bottom of the ancient channel. At this particular place, the rise of the first bottom does not exceed an angle of 3°. Above it again rises a second bottom of the same width and about fifty feet higher than the first, and gradually ascending until its further edge rests upon the bold, rocky face of the mountain-line, climbing at once some two hundred feet to the usual level of the region around.

★★★★★★

The frontispiece of this volume gives an exact view of the battle-ground at this day. It is taken from the opposite side of the Monongahela. The crossing is just above the upper part of the stream visible in the engraving. The house and grove in the centre of the piece occupy very nearly the precise spot where was fought the hottest part of the action.

★★★★★★

A firm clay, overlaid with mould, forms the soil of the second bottom, which was heavily and more densely timbered than the first; and the underwood began to appear more plentifully where the ground was less exposed to the action of the spring floods. In the bosom of the hill, several springs unite their sources to give birth to a petty rivulet that hurries down the steep to be lost in the river. Its cradle lies in the bed of a broad ravine, forty or fifty feet deep, that rises in the hill-side, and crossing the whole of the second bottom, debouches on the first, where the waters whose current it so far guides, trickle oozily down through a swampy bed.

Great trees grew within and along this chasm, and the usual smaller growth peculiar to such a situation; and a prodigious copse of wild grape-vines (not yet entirely gone) shrouded its termination upon the first bottom and shadowed the birth of the infant brook. About two hundred yards from the line of hills, and three hundred south of the ravine just described, commences another of a more singular nature; with its steep sides, almost exactly perpendicular, it perfectly resembles a ditch cut for purposes of defence. Rising near the middle of the second bottom, it runs westwardly to the upper edge of the first, with a depth at its head of four or five feet, increasing as it descends, and a width of eight or ten. A century ago, its channel was overhung and completely concealed by a luxurious thicket of pea-vines and trailers, of bramble-bushes and the Indian plum; its edges closely fringed with the thin, tall wood-grass of summer.

But even now, when the forests are gone and the plough long since passed over the scene, the ravine cannot be at all perceived until one is directly upon it; and hence arose the chief disasters of the day. Parallel with, and about one hundred and fifty yards north of, this second gulley, ran a third; a dry, open hollow, and rather thinly wooded; but which afforded a happy protection to the enemy from the English fire. Either of these ravines would have sheltered an army: the second—the most important, though not the largest—would of itself afford concealment to a thousand men. (A close personal examination of these localities during the summer of 1854, has confirmed in my mind the conclusion long since arrived at by Mr. Sparks.)

There is little reason to doubt that as Braddock drew near, M. de Contrecoeur was almost decided to abandon his position without striking a blow, and, withdrawing his men, as did his successor, in 1758, leave to the English a bloodless victory. He certainly was prepared to surrender on terms of honourable capitulation. A solitary gun was mounted upon a carriage, to enable the garrison to evacuate with the honours of war; it being a point of nice feeling with a defeated soldier that he should retire with drums beating a national march, his own colours flying, and a cannon loaded, with a lighted match. This deprives the proceeding of a compulsory air; and to procure this gratification, Contrecoeur made his arrangements. (Mante.)

The British Army was so overwhelming in strength, so well-appointed and disciplined, that he perhaps deemed any opposition to its advance would be not less fruitless than the defence of the works. However, this may be, he had as yet, on the 7th of July, announced no definite conclusion, though possibly his views were perceptible enough to his subordinates. On that day it was known that the enemy, whose numbers were greatly magnified, were at the head-waters of Turtle Creek. On the 8th, when his route was changed, M. de Beaujeu, a captain in the regulars, proposed to the commander that he might be permitted to go forth with a suitable band to prepare an ambuscade for the English on the banks of the Monongahela, and to dispute with them the passage of the second ford.

Gᴜɴ-ᴛᴏᴡɪɴɢ

If we may believe tradition, it was with undisguised reluctance that Contrecoeur complied with this request, and even then, it is said, refused to assign troops for the enterprise; bidding him call for volunteers as for a forlorn hope. To that summons the whole garrison responded. If this tale be true, Contrecoeur recanted his determination, and wisely preferred making him a regular detachment, conditioned on his success in obtaining the union of the Indians, who, to the number of nearly a thousand warriors, were gathered at the place. (XVI. *Haz. Penn. Reg.*, 100.) Accordingly, the savages were at once called to a council. These people, consisting of bands assembled from a dozen different nations, listened with unsuppressed discontent to the overtures of the Frenchman. Seated under the palisades that environed the fort, or standing in knots about the speaker, were gathered a motley but a ferocious crew.

Alienated from their ancient friends, here were Delawares from the Susquehannah, eager to speed the fatal stroke, and Shawanoes from Grave Creek and the Muskingum; scattered warriors of the Six Nations; Ojibwas and Pottawattamies from the far Michigan; Abenakis and Caughnawagas from Canada; Ottawas from Lake Superior, led on by the royal Pontiac, and Hurons from the falls of Montreal and the mission of Lorette, whose barbarous leader gloried in a name torn from the most famous pages of Christian story.

★★★★★★

"Went to Lorette, an English village about eight miles from Quebec. Saw the Indians at mass and heard them sing psalms tolerably well—a dance. Got well acquainted with Athanase, who was commander of the Indians who defeated General Braddock in 1755—a very sensible fellow." MS. *Journal of an English Gentleman on a Tour through Canada in* 1765; cited in Parkman.

★★★★★★

To these reluctant auditors Beaujeu stated his designs.

They said in reply:

"How, my father, are you so bent upon death that you would also sacrifice us? With our eight hundred men do you ask us to attack four thousand English? Truly, this is not the saying of a wise man. But we will lay up what we have heard, and tomorrow you shall know our thoughts."

On the morning of the 9th of July, the conference was repeated and the Indians announced their intention of refusing to join in the expedition. At this moment a runner—probably one of those dislodged by Gage in the early dawn—burst in upon the assembly and heralded the advent of the foe. Well versed in the peculiar characteristics of the savages, by whom he was much beloved, and full of tact and energy, Beaujeu took ready advantage of the excitement which these tidings occasioned.

"I," said he, "am determined to go out against the enemy. I am certain of victory. What! will you suffer your father to depart alone?"

Fired by his language and the reproach it conveyed, they at once resolved by acclamation to follow him to the fray. In a moment, the scene was alive with frantic enthusiasm. Barrels of bullets and flints, and casks of powder, were hastily rolled to the gates: their heads were knocked out, and every warrior left to supply himself at his own discretion. Then, painted for war and armed for the combat, the party moved rapidly away, in numbers nearly 900 strong, of whom 637 were Indians, 146 Canadians, and 72 regular troops.

★★★★★★

Another French account estimates the French and Canadians as 250, and the savages as 641: a third, at 233 whites and 600 Indians. See Appendix. The English rated their numbers from as high as 1500 regulars and 600 Canadians besides savages (XXV. *Gent. Mag.*, 379), to as low as 400 men, all told. (I. Sp. *Franklin*. Drake's *Indian Captivities*); and Washington himself could not have believed they exceeded 300. (II. Sp. *Wash.*).

★★★★★★

Subordinate to Beaujeu were MM. Dumas and De Ligneris, both captains in the regular army, four lieutenants, six ensigns, and twenty cadets.

★★★★★★

For his conduct on the 9th of July, M. Dumas was early in the subsequent year promoted to succeed M. de Contrecoeur in the command of Fort Du Quesne. Here he proved himself an active and vigilant officer, his war-parties ravaging Pennsylvania, and penetrating to within twenty leagues of its metropolis. A copy of instructions signed by him, on 23rd March, 1756, was found in the pocket of the Sieur Donville, who, being sent to surprise the English at Fort Cumberland, got the worst of it and lost his own scalp. This letter concludes in a spirit of humanity honourable to its writer. (II. *P.A.*) In the spring of 1759, the king created him a major-general and inspector of the troops of the marine, who seem to have constituted the bulk of the usual Canadian army. At the siege of Quebec and during the rest of the war he was actively employed.

In July, 1759, he commanded in the unlucky *coup des écoliers*, where 1500 men, partly composed of lads from the schools, in endeavouring to destroy Monckton's battery, became so bewildered in the darkness as to mistake friend for foe, and nearly destroyed each other. We may presume he fought not where Montcalm fell on the Heights of Abraham; since, after the surrender of the capital he held Jacques Cartier with 600 men by order of M. de Levis. And when that general besieged Murray in Quebec, in 1760, Dumas was in command of the lines from Jacques Cartier to Pointe-aux-Trembles. At last, the capitulation of Montreal gave Canada to the English, and Dumas passed with his comrades in arms to France.

Here I do not doubt he was visited by the same persecutions that waited alike on almost every man who had been in a Canadian public employ—on the peculating Bigot and the upright Vaudreuil. Ultimately, however, and after 1763, he was made a brigadier and appointed to the government of the Isles of France and of Bourbon. (I. Pouchot; II. *Garneau*; I. *O. T.*) Thus, much may be positively stated of Dumas. To the romantic story of his persecution by Contrecoeur we cannot attach implicit faith. It says that jealousy of his success induced Contrecoeur to send Dumas home on a charge of purloining the public stores; that he was tried and cashiered and retired in disgrace to Provence; that during the revolutionary war Washington informed Lafayette of these circumstances, whose influence speedily brought Dumas in triumph to Paris to receive the grade of a general officer. (XVI. *Haz. Reg.*; II. *O. T.*)

Since Pouchot deliberately insinuates (Vol. I.), that Dumas was inclined to such practices, we may conclude it not unlikely that on his return to France his conduct was severely scrutinised; but much of the rest of the anecdote is palpably false. It is believed by many that Alexandre Dumas, the famous novelist, is a son of this general; but this view is not confirmed by the *Mémoires* of the former. He says that his father, Thomas-Alexandre Davy de la Pailleterie, a general of the Republic, was born at St. Domingo in 1762, son of Marie-Alexandre-Antoine Davy, marquis de la Pailleterie (born 1710, died 1786), a colonel of artillery, and

Marie Tessette-Dumas of St. Domingo.

It is said this last was a quadroon. Independent of the impossibility of the general, and the improbability of the colonel, being the Dumas of Braddock's defeat, it is hardly likely that no reference to the fact, were it so, would be found in the highly-coloured pages of our auto-biographer. There was a Comte Mathieu Dumas, a French general who served with Rochambeau in America, but he certainly was not this man. Indeed, the name is so common in France that there may well have been several bearing it, occupying high ranks, in the army at the same time. Had we a series of the *Almanach Royale* to refer to, the point might be settled.

★★★★★★

Though his numbers were thus not so greatly inferior to Braddock's, it is not likely that Beaujeu calculated on doing more than giving the English a severe check, and perhaps delaying for a few days their advance. It is impossible that he should have contemplated the complete victory that was before him. (Pouchot is clear on this point.Vol. I.)

Chapter 11

The Jaws of the Trap

On the evening of the 8th of July, the ground had been carefully reconnoitred and the proper place for the action selected. The intention was to dispute as long as possible the passage of the second ford, and then to fall back upon the ravines. But long ere they reached the scene, the swell of military music, the crash of falling trees, apprised them that the foe had already crossed the river, and that his pioneers were advanced into the woodlands. Quickening their pace into a run, they managed to reach the broken ground just as the van of the English came in sight.

Braddock had turned from the first bottom to the second and mounting to its brow was about to pass around the head of the ravines to avoid the little morass caused by the water-course before described. His route did not lay parallel with the most dangerous defile, where the banks are so steep and the cover so perfect but passed its head at an angle of about 45°; thus, completely exposing his face and flanks from a point on the second bottom, at a hundred yards distance, to another within thirty, where he would turn the ravine. Of course, the further he advanced the nearer he would approach to its brink, till the whole should finally be left behind: thus, opening a line of two hundred

185

yards long, at an average distance of sixty, to the enemy's fire. Had he possessed the least knowledge of these defiles, he would undoubtedly have secured them in season, since nothing would have been easier than their occupation by Gage's advanced party. But not a man in his army had ever dreamed of their existence.

The arrangement of the march from the river's bank had been made as follows: The engineers and guides and six light-horsemen proceeded immediately before the advanced detachment under Gage, and the working-party under St. Clair, who had with them two brass six-pounders and as many tumbrils or tool-carts. On either flank, parties to the number of eight were thrown out to guard against surprises. At some distance behind Gage followed the line, preceded by the light-horse, four squads of whom also acted as extreme flankers at either end of the column.

Next came the seamen, followed by a subaltern with twenty grenadiers, a twelve-pounder and a company of grenadiers. Then the vanguard succeeded, and the wagon and artillery train, which began and ended with a twelve-pounder: and the rear-guard closed the whole. Numerous flanking-parties, however, protected each side; and six subalterns, each with twenty grenadiers, and ten sergeants, with ten men each, were detached for this purpose.

The greater part of Gage's command was actually advanced beyond the spot where the main battle was fought, and was just surmounting the second bottom, when Mr. Gordon, one of the engineers who were in front marking out the road, perceived the enemy bounding forward. Before them, with long leaps, came Beaujeu, the gaily-coloured fringes of his hunting-shirt and the silver gorget on his bosom at once bespeaking the chief. Comprehending in a glance the position he had attained, he suddenly halted and waved his hat above his head.

At this preconcerted signal, the savages dispersed to the right and left, throwing themselves flat upon the ground, and gliding behind rocks or trees or into the ravines. Had the earth yawned beneath their feet and reclosed above their heads, they could not have more instantaneously vanished. The French (some of whom, according to Garneau, were mounted; this is very improbable, however) held the centre of the semi-circular disposition so instantly assumed; and a tremendous fire was at once opened on the English. For a moment. Gage's troops paused aghast at the furious yells and strangeness of the onset. Rallying immediately, he returned their fire, and halted a moment till St. Clair's working-party came up, (Sharpe's MS. *Corresp.*); when he

BRADDOCK'S MARCH

bade his men advance at once upon the centre of the concentric line.

As he drew near, he was again greeted with a staggering discharge, and again his ranks were shaken. Then, in return, they opened a fire of grape and musketry, so tremendous as to sweep down every un-sheltered foe who was upon his feet, and to utterly fright the savages from their propriety. Beaujeu and a dozen more fell dead upon the spot, and the Indians already began to fly, their courage being unable to endure the unwonted tumult of such a portentous detonation. But reanimated by "the clamorous exhortations of Dumas and De Ligneris. and observing that the regulars and militia still preserved a firm front, they returned once more to their posts and resumed the combat.

For a time, the issue seemed doubtful, and the loud cries of "*Vive le Roi*" of the French were met by the charging cheers of the English. But precision of aim soon began to prevail over mere mechanical discipline. In vain the 44th continued their fire; in vain their officers, with waving swords, led them to the charge: hidden beneath great trees, or concealed below the level of the earth, the muzzles of their pieces resting on the brink of the ravine, and shooting with a secure and steady aim, the majority of the enemy rested secure and invisible to their gallant foemen.

★★★★★★

None of the English that were engaged saw more than 100, and many of the officers as well as men who were the whole time of its continuance in the heat of the action, will not assert that they saw an enemy. (Sharpe's MS. *Corresp.*)

★★★★★★

In the meantime, Braddock, whose extreme rear had not yet left the river's bank, hearing the uproar in advance, ordered Burton to press forward with the vanguard, and the rest of the line to halt; thus, leaving Halket with four hundred men to protect the baggage while eight hundred engaged the enemy. But just as Burton, under a galling fire, was forming his troops upon the ground, Gage's party gave way and precipitately endeavoured to fall into his rear; confusing men who were confused before. (*Penn. Gaz.* No. 1393.) The manoeuvre was unsuccessfully executed, and the two regiments became inextricably commingled. Vainly Braddock strove to separate the soldiers, huddling together like frightened sheep. Vainly the regimental colours were advanced in opposite directions as rallying-points.

The officers sought to collect their men together and lead them on in platoons. Nothing could avail. On every hand the officers, distinguished by their horses and their uniforms, were the constant mark of hostile rifles; and it was soon as impossible to find men to give orders as it was to have them obeyed. In a narrow road, twelve feet wide, shut up on either side and overpent by the primeval forest, were crowded together the panic-stricken wretches, hastily loading and reloading, and blindly discharging their guns in the air, as though they suspected their mysterious murderers were sheltered in the boughs above their heads; while all around, removed from sight, but making day hideous with their war-whoops and savage cries, lay ensconced a host insatiate for blood.

★★★★★★

The yell of the Indians is fresh on my ear, and the terrific sound will haunt me until the hour of my dissolution. I cannot describe the horrors of that scene. No pencil could do it, or no painter delineate it so as to convey to you with accuracy our unhappy situation. (Capt. Leslie's Letter, 30th July, 1755. V. *Haz. Reg.*)

★★★★★★

Foaming with rage and indignation, Braddock flew from rank to rank, with his own hands endeavouring to force his men into position. Four horses were shot under him, but mounting a fifth, he still strained every nerve to retrieve the ebbing fortunes of the day. His subordinates gallantly seconded his endeavours, throwing themselves from the saddle and advancing by platoons, in the idle hope that their men would follow: but only to rush upon their fate. The regular soldiery, deprived of their immediate commanders, and terrified at the incessant fall of their comrades, could not be brought to the charge; while the provincials, better skilled, sought in vain to cover themselves and to meet the foe upon equal terms: for to the urgent entreaties of Washington and Sir Peter Halket that the men might be permitted to leave the ranks and shelter themselves, the general turned a deaf ear. (VI. *Haz. Reg.*) Wherever he saw a man skulking behind a tree, he flew at once to the spot, and, with curses on his cowardice and blows with the flat of his sword, drove him back into the open road.

★★★★★★

The enemy kept behind trees and loggs of wood and cut down our troops as fast as they could advance. The soldiers then insisted much to be allowed to take to the trees, which the general denied and stormed much, calling them cowards, and even went so far as to strike them with his own sword for attempting

The shooting of General Braddock

the trees. (Burd to Morris; VL C. R.)

★★★★★★

Wherever the distracted artillerymen saw a smoke arise, thither did they direct their aim; and many of the flankers who had succeeded in obtaining the only position where they could be of any service, were thus shot down. Athwart the brow of the hill lay a large log, five feet in diameter, which Captain Waggoner, of the Virginia Levies, resolved to take possession of. With shouldered firelocks he marched a party of eighty men to the spot, losing but three on the way; and at once throwing themselves behind it, the remainder opened a hot fire upon the enemy. But no sooner were the flash and the report of their pieces perceived by the mob behind, than a general discharge was poured upon the little band, by which fifty were slain outright and the rest constrained to fly.

By this time, the afternoon was well advanced, and the whole English line surrounded. The ammunition began to fail, and the artillery to flag; the baggage was warmly attacked; and a runner was despatched to the fort with the tidings that by set of sun not an Englishman would be left alive upon the ground. Still, gathering counsel from despair, Braddock disdained to yield; still, strong in this point only of their discipline, his soldiers died by his side, palsied with fear, yet without one thought of craven flight.

At last, when every aide but Washington was struck down; when the lives of the vast majority of the officers had been sacrificed with a reckless intrepidity, a sublime self-devotion, that surpasses the power of language to express; when scarce a third part of the whole army remained unscathed, and these incapable of aught save remaining to die or till the word to retire was given; at last, Braddock abandoned all hope of victory; and, with a mien undaunted as in his proudest hour, ordered the drums to sound a retreat. The instant their faces were turned, the poor regulars lost every trace of the sustaining power of custom; and the retreat became a headlong flight. Washington says:

> Despite of all the efforts of the officers to the contrary, they ran, as sheep pursued by dogs, and it was impossible to rally them.

Beneath a large tree standing between the heads of the northernmost ravines, and while in the act of giving an order, Braddock received a mortal wound; the ball passing through his right arm into the lungs. Falling from his horse, he lay helpless on the ground, surrounded by the dead, abandoned by the living. Not one of his trans-

191

atlantic soldiery "who had served with the duke" could be prevailed upon to stay his headlong flight and aid to bear his general from the field. Orme thought to tempt them with a purse containing sixty guineas; but in such a moment even gold could not prevail upon a vulgar soul, and they rushed unheeding on.

Disgusted at such pusillanimity, and his heart big with despair, Braddock refused to be removed, and bade the faithful friends who lingered by his side to provide for their own safety. He declared his resolution of leaving his own body on the field: the scene that had witnessed his dishonour he desired should bury his shame. With manly affection, Orme disregarded his injunctions; and Captain Stewart, of Virginia (the commander of the Light-horse which were attached to the general's person), with another American officer, hastening to Orme's relief, his body was placed first in a tumbrel, and afterwards upon a fresh horse, and thus borne away. (III. Walp. *Corresp.*; II. *Garneau.*) Stewart seems to have cherished a sense of duty or of friendship towards his chief that did not permit him to desert him for a moment while life remained.

It was about five o'clock in the afternoon when the English abandoned the field. Pursued to the water's edge by about fifty savages, the regular troops cast from them guns, accoutrements, and even clothing, that they might run the faster. Many were overtaken and tomahawked here; but when they had once crossed the river, they were not followed. Soon turning from the chase, the glutted warriors made haste to their unhallowed and unparalleled harvest of scalps and plunder. The provincials, better acquainted with Indian warfare, were less disconcerted; and though their loss was as heavy, their behaviour was more composed. In full possession of his courage and military instincts, Braddock still essayed to procure an orderly and soldierlike retreat; but the demoralisation of the army now rendered this impossible.

With infinite difficulty, a hundred men, after running about half a mile, were persuaded to stop at a favourable spot where Braddock proposed to remain until Dunbar should arrive, to whose camp Washington was sent with suitable orders. It will thus be seen how far, was his indomitable soul, from succumbing in the discharge of his duties, beneath the unexpected burthen that had been laid upon him. By his directions Burton posted sentries here, and endeavoured to form a nucleus around which to gather the shattered remains of the troops, and where the wounded might be provided for. But all was idle. In an hour's time, almost every soldier had stolen away, leaving their officers

Braddock's Fall

deserted. These, making the best of their way off, were joined beyond the other ford by Gage, who had rallied some eighty men; and this was all that remained of that gallant army which scarce six hours before was by friend and foe alike deemed invincible.

The Retreat

With little interruption the march was continued through that night and the ensuing day, till at 10 p.m. on the 10th of July, they came to Gist's plantation; where early on the 11th some wagons and hospital-stores arrived from Dunbar for their relief. Despite the intensity of his agonies, Braddock still persisted in the exercise of his authority and the fulfilment of his duties. From Gist's he detailed a party to return towards the Monongahela with a supply of provisions to be left on the road for the benefit of stragglers yet behind, and Dunbar was commanded to send to him the only two remaining old companies of the 44th and 48th, with more wagons to bring off the wounded; and on Friday, the 11th of July, he arrived at Dunbar's camp. Through this and all the preceding day, men half-famished, without arms, and bewildered with terror, had been joining Dunbar; his camp was in the utmost confusion, and his soldiers were deserting without ceremony.

Braddock's strength was now fast ebbing away. Informed of the disorganised condition of the remaining troops, he abandoned all hope of a prosperous termination to the expedition. He saw that not only death, but utter defeat, was inevitable. But conscious of the odium the latter event would excite, he nobly resolved that the sole responsibility of the measure should rest with himself and consulted with no one upon the steps he pursued. He merely issued his orders and insisted that they were obeyed.

Thus, after destroying the stores to prevent them falling into the hands of the enemy (of whose pursuit he did not doubt), the march was to be resumed on Saturday, the 12th of July, towards Will's Creek. Ill-judged as these orders were, they met with but too ready acquiescence at the hands of Dunbar, whose advice was neither asked nor tendered on the occasion. Thus, the great mass of those stores which had been so painfully brought thither were destroyed. Of the artillery, but two six-pounders were preserved; the cohorns were broken or buried; and the shells bursted. One hundred and fifty wagons were burned; the powder-casks were staved in, and their contents, to the amount of 50,000 pounds, cast into a spring: and the provisions were

Braddock's Death

scattered abroad upon the ground or thrown into the water.

Nothing was saved beyond the actual necessities for a flying march; and when a party of the enemy some time afterward visited the scene, they completed the work of destruction. For this service—the only instance of alacrity that he displayed in the campaign—Dunbar must not be forgiven. It is not perfectly clear that Braddock, intelligently, ever gave the orders; but in any case, they were not fit for a British officer to give or to obey. Dunbar's duty was to have maintained here his position, or at the least not to have contemplated falling back beyond Will's Creek. That he had not horses to remove his stores, was, however, his after excuse. (Sharpe's MS. *Corresp.*;VI. *C. R.*; *Penn. Gaz.*, No. 1392.)

★★★★★★

The people nick-named this man "Dunbar the tardy." I. Watson's *Annals*, 100. What provisions belonging to the army remained in Morris's hands were afterwards applied to its uses or sold by him on its account. II. *P.A.*

★★★★★★

It was not until Sunday, July 13th, that all this was finished; and the army with its dying general proceeded to the Great Meadows, where the close was to transpire:

Last scene of all,
That ends this strange, eventful history.

Ever since the retreat commenced, Braddock had preserved a steadfast silence, unbroken save when he issued the necessary commands. That his wound was mortal he knew; but he also knew that his fame had received a not less fatal stab; that his military reputation, dearer than his own life to a veteran or those of a thousand others, was gone forever. These reflections embittered his dying hours; nor were there any means at hand of diverting the current of his thoughts or ministering to the comfort of his body: even the chaplain of the army was among the wounded.

He pronounced the warmest eulogiums upon the conduct of his officers (who indeed had merited all he could say of them) and seems to have entertained some compunctions at not having more scrupulously followed the advice of Washington, or perhaps at the loss of power to provide for that young soldier's interests as thoroughly as he would have done had he returned victorious. At all events, we find him singling out his Virginia *aide* as his nuncupative legatee, bequeath-

196

Braddock's Burial

ing to him his favourite charger and his body-servant Bishop, so well-known in after years as the faithful attendant of the patriot chief.

★★★★★★

So, says Mr. Custis, in his *Life of Martha Washington*. Howe (Hist. Coll. Virg., 184), recites the death in Augusta County, in Feb. 1844, of the slave Gilbert, aged 112 years, whom he represents to have been Washington's attendant not only at Braddock's but at Cornwallis's defeat; and Washington himself (II. Sparks), seems to refer to one John Alton as his servant on this occasion.

★★★★★★

The only allusions he made to the fate of the battle was to softly repeat once or twice to himself—"Who would have thought it?" Turning to Orme—"We shall better know how to deal with them another time;" were his parting words, A few moments later, and he breathed his last. (I. Sp. *Franklin*.)

Thus at about eight on the night of Sunday the 13th of July honourably died a brave old soldier, who, if wanting in temper and discretion, was certainly, according to the standard of the school in which he had been educated, an accomplished officer; and whose courage and honesty are not to be discussed. The uttermost penalty that humanity could exact, he paid for his errors: and if his misfortune brought death and woe upon his country, it was through no shrinking on his part from what he conceived to be his duty. He shared the lot of the humblest man who fell by his side.

So, terminated the bloody battle of the Monongahela; a scene of carnage which has been truly described as unexampled in the annals of modern warfare. Of the fourteen hundred and sixty souls, officers and privates, who went into the combat, four hundred and fifty-six were slain outright, and four hundred and twenty-one were wounded; making a total of eight hundred and seventy-seven men. Of eighty-nine commissioned officers, sixty-three were killed or wounded; not a solitary field-officer escaping unhurt. The summing up of the whole loss is given in the table overleaf.

The number of women and servants killed cannot be ascertained, since they are not entered on the roster of an army: certain it is, however, that but three of the latter were spared. As for the Pennsylvania wagoners, they escaped to a man. At the very first onset each driver cut loose his team, and selecting the best horse, fled with headlong precipitation. In fact, of the whole number which originally set forth, but two never returned to their homes; one of whom had died of dis-

RANK.	KILLED.	WOUNDED.	SAFE.
General	1		
Secretary	1		
Colonels and L.-Colonels	1	2	
Major		1	
Captains	7	7	7
Lieutenants	11	15	12
S. Lieutenants or Ensigns	3	5	6
Midshipmen	1		1
Chaplain		1	
Quarter-Master		1	
Surgeon's Mates	1	5	
Sergeants	17	20	21
Corporals and bombardiers	18	22	21
Gunners	6	8	4
Boatswain's Mates	1		1
Drummers	2	6	24
Matrosses and Privates	386	328	486
TOTAL	456	421	583

ease and the other been scalped on the march. The battle was fought on the afternoon of Wednesday, the 9th of July; yet such was their haste, that at 5 a.m. of Thursday their leader rushed into Dunbar's camp with the dismal tidings that the whole army was destroyed and himself the sole survivor! (*Penn. Gaz.*, Nos. 1381, 1392.)

The enemy's loss was very inconsiderable, being but three officers killed and two wounded; two cadets wounded; twenty-five soldiers and savages slain; and as many more badly hurt. Beside the artillery abandoned by the English to the victors, they lost everything they had with them save the clothes on their backs and the arms in their hands. ("Two 12-pounder cannon," says Burd, "six 4-pounders, four cohorns, and two Hortts, with all the shells, &c." VI. *C. R.* There is a discrepancy between this statement and that of the park which the general set forth with.)

One hundred oxen that had just been brought up; all the wagons, provisions, baggage, and stores; the military chest, containing £25,000 in specie; and the general's cabinet with his instructions and private papers fell into the enemy's power. These last were transmitted at once to Canada; and their contents soon made known by the French Government to every court in Europe, as eternal monuments of the perfidy of Britain. (I. Pouchot; VI. *C. R.*; Sharpe's MS. *Corresp.*; II. *O. T.*)

Whether we regard the cause, the conduct, or the consequences of this battle, the reflections it gives rise to are alike valuable and impressive. It brought together practically for the first time in our history the disciplined regular of Europe and the rifleman of America; and it taught the lesson to the latter that in his own forests he was the superior man. It was the beginning of a contest in whose revolving years the colonies became a school of arms, and a martial spirit of the people was fostered and trained till they had attained that confidence which naught but custom can afford.

Had Braddock been successful, the great province of Pennsylvania, and probably those of New Jersey, Maryland, and New York, freed from danger, would have continued in their original ignorance and aversion of military science. His failure left their frontiers open to the enemy, and the spirit of self-preservation soon compelled them to welcome the weapons from which they had once recoiled with loathing. It was there and then that Morgan and Mercer, Gates and Washington, first stood side by side in marshalled array; and in that day's dark torrent of blood was tempered the steel which was to sever the colonies from the parent-stem.

★★★★★★

Daniel Morgan was born in Pennsylvania and was serving as an overseer in Virginia shortly before Braddock's arrival. Though then a lawless, dissipated character, be was the possessor of a wagon and a team of horses, with which he engaged in the expedition. Being on an occasion behind time with his wagon, he was sharply reprimanded by an officer. He replied probably with insolence, and the officer drew his sword upon him. Morgan fell on him with his whip, knocked the weapon from his hand, and beat him severely. For this offence he was sentenced to receive 500 lashes, but fainting beneath the cat, 50 were remitted. According to his own story, his adversary subsequently perceived that the original fault was his own and made the *amende honorable* to the wagoner. In the battle, or on some occasion of the campaign, he was shot in the back of the neck, the ball passing through his mouth and teeth. It is a little odd that Morgan, who afterwards rose to the rank of general in the army of the Revolution was, under the command of Gates, one of the most active opponents of Burgoyne at Saratoga, in 1778. (Howe's *Hist. Coll. Virg.*) As for Dr. Hugh Mercer (the same that died so gloriously at Princeton, in 1777), he is constantly said to have been engaged in Braddock's campaign. He certainly

200

played an active part in Pennsylvania during the remainder of the war.

★★★★★★

A soldier of the revolution, himself a captive at Fort Du Quesne when Braddock was defeated, sagaciously observed:

> Had an enforced colonial obedience to the omnipotence of Parliament been attempted in 1754, instead of twenty years later, it would have been undoubtedly successful; for with the partial exception of the people of New England, the Americans were equally destitute of means of defence or skill to use them. (Drake.)

The power and policy of England gave them both; Bouquet and Amherst and Gage himself enured them to the hardy toils of battle; every regiment that was sent to America left skilful soldiers on its shores; and when the final struggle came, it was with the dagger itself had sharpened that the fatal blow was struck; and too late the mother-country realised the fate of Waller's eagle:—

> —*Which on the shaft that made him die,*
> *Espy'd a feather of his own*
> *Wherewith he wont to soar so high.*

But there are other and less satisfying lights in which we must for a moment behold this scene. Never was there an affray, proportionably to the numbers engaged, more awfully destructive of life. Not even at Waterloo, in all the flush and pride of youthful valour and filled with the recent memories of their distant homes, fell on their earliest battle-field a larger share of officers. What terrible tales the tidings of that day of carnage bore to those remote homesteads around which yet lingered the parting echoes of their farewell, cannot be traced here. The fond eyes still filled with the fading image of their youthful heroes, too soon to be dimmed with bitterest tears—the hands that dropped the half-twined chaplet of victorious laurel to prepare the cypress-wreath—the hearts whose high triumphal hopes were by one sudden stroke shaken with the throbbings of despair—all are passed away like the objects they lamented—gone

> *Où va la feuille de Rose*
> *Où va la feuille de Laurier.*
> (Where is the rose leaf)
> (Where is the bay leaf)

201

Early or late, the inevitable fate fell equally upon the peaceful home-dweller beyond the wide-spread fields of barren foam and the warrior upon the rugged banks of occidental streams: the mourned and the mourner have alike disappeared and been forgotten: and they who rest by the murmuring ripple of the Monongahela beneath the brown shades of an American forest, as quietly sleep in their confused and nameless graves as she who lies beneath the churchyard walls of England, above whose mouldered tomb sweep constant sounds of Christian bells.

Of the many melancholy passages of this most melancholy day, some not uninteresting incidents are still recollected. The preservation of Washington is an anecdote of popular currency. With two horses shot under him and four bullets through his coat, and a special mark for the enemy's rifles, not a single stroke told upon his person. In 1770, on the banks of the Great Kanhawa, an aged chief journeyed from his distant lodge to see once more the favourite of the Great Spirit against whom his own gun and those of his young men were fifteen years before so often turned in vain. Well might the eloquent Davies express at the time the public conviction that the signal manner in which Providence had hitherto watched over the heroic youth clearly presaged his future importance to his country. (II. Sp. *Wash.*)

Nor was the salvation of two other officers less worthy of remark, since the story displays the exercise of some of the noblest qualities that can inspire the heart of man to immortal deeds. When the retreat was sounded, Captain Treby of the 44th lay writhing on the ground, so desperately wounded as to be unable even to crawl beneath the shelter of the nearest bush. With death close following at their heels, the human herd rushed by regardless of his fate, when his situation arrested the attention of a gentleman volunteer named Farrel. Uncareful of the peril to which he exposed his safety by such an action, Farrel placed the helpless sufferer upon his own back, and in this wise bore him to such a distance from the field as to be able to procure further assistance and eventually place him beyond the reach of danger.

★★★★★★

Mante, 28; where it is said that in 1772 Mr. Farrel was a captain in the 62nd Foot. I take him, however, to be the same Thomas Farrel who, on March 15th, 1763, was appointed to a captaincy in the 65th Foot. (*Army Reg.* for 1765, p. 120.) In 1763, Captain John Treby still held his rank in the 44th. (*Army. Reg.* 1763, p. 98.) About the close of the century, we find "a Colonel Treby" apparently a man of fashion in Wiltshire. Chafin's *Cranbourne Chase*.

★★★★★★

And equally magnanimous was the enthusiastic bravery of the men of Captain John Conyngham's company. At the first fire his horse was shot down and he himself severely wounded. Falling beneath the animal's body, all his efforts to extricate himself would have been in vain had not his soldiers, "for the love they bore him," rushed to his relief; and while many of their number were shot dead in the attempt, succeeded finally in bearing him in triumph from the spot.

★★★★★★

Capt. Matthew Leslie's Letter of 30th of July, 1754.V. *Haz. Reg.*, where Conyngham's convalescence is indicated. In 1763 there was no one of this name in either the 44th or 48th regiment; but in 1765 a John Conynghame appears as Lieutenant-Colonel of the 29th Foot (date of commission, 13th Feb., 1762), and a John Conyngham as captain in the 7th Foot: (date of commission, 15th Oct. 1759.) *Army Reg.* 1765 pp. 60, 82.

★★★★★★

Such incidents as these are enough to brighten a thousand darker shades of character.

Among the most distinguished of the dead was Sir Peter Halket of Pitferran. Colonel of the 44th, and a gallant and sagacious soldier; whose two sons were fighting by his side when he fell. One of these, Lieutenant James Halket of his own regiment, hastened at the moment to his aid, and with open arms bent to raise the dying form. But pierced by an Indian bullet his body dropped heavily across his leader's corpse, and father and son lay in death together.

There is a generally accepted tradition that Braddock was murdered by one of his own men. Thomas Fausett, a subsequent resident of Fayette County, Pennsylvania, is not only commonly believed to have been the perpetrator of the deed, but actually, in later years, avowed the fact. Such an interesting incident—paralleled only by the case of Charles of Sweden—demands in this place a thorough investigation; and this more particularly since the tale, mendacious as we now believe it to be, has been fortified by such constant and positive assertion, and such popular currency, that even Mr. Sparks has not disdained to sanction its naked repetition.

★★★★★★

II. Sp. *Wash.* Of course, Mr. Sparks would not be justified in omitting a mere allusion to a matter so confidently asserted by our local historians. But the occurrence is pointed out here to show how widely error may be diffused.

★★★★★★

A careful summary of the evidence in this matter shall therefore be given; and the result will show what ridiculous forgeries may be foisted off upon the student under the name of History.

It must be premised that not one contemporaneous authority, either in public or in private, even breathed a suspicion of such a circumstance. Washington, who must have participated sooner or later in the secrets of the provincial troops, knew nothing of it. Neither Orme, with all his scorn of colonial morality, nor Sharpe, who hated Braddock, and with his confidential correspondents spared not his memory, once alludes to it. It is not hinted at in Governor Morris's letters, nor in those of Franklin; nor in any of the numerous American and European writings of the period that have been examined. The only original passage that can be at all wrested to bear on this point is to be found in the *Gentleman's Magazine* for August, 1755. In the first statement of the battle, abounding in pardonable but manifest inaccuracies, it contains this remark:

> It is, however, said that the slaughter among our officers was not made by the enemy; but as they ran several fugitives through the body to intimidate the rest when they were attempting in vain to rally them, some others, who expected the same fate, discharged their pieces at them; which, though loaded, they could not be brought to level at the French. (XXV. *Gent. Mag.*, 380.)

This assertion, though unsupported by contemporaneous or other respectable authority, possibly may be true. In 1854, while the writer visited the *locus in quo* in the hope of gaining some hitherto neglected circumstance of the expedition, he received a sufficient number of tales, it is true; but of which all, save two, were so absurdly false as not to merit even remembrance. An aged man who said that he had known Fausett declared that there were three brothers in the action, of whom one was slain by Braddock, and the other by the captain of Thomas Fausett's own company; and that in a like manner the death of both was avenged. The importance of this point will be presently seen. (At the time, I did not believe in the truth of a word of this story.)

Let us now take up Fausett's own assertions. In 1781, (twenty-six years after the defeat,) a subsequent writer in the National Intelligencer (believed to have been the late William Darby, Esq.) was cognisant of the common report in Fayette County that this man had killed the General. In 1791, he put the plain question to him: "Did you shoot General Braddock?" and the reply was prompt and explicit: "I did shoot him!"

As an apology, he added that for the preservation of the rest of the army, the instant removal of such an obstinate leader was inevitable. And this narrative is further confirmed by the testimony of the Hon. Andrew Stewart, of Uniontown, who often heard Fausett make the same avowal. It also appears that he was a man of unusual stature and of rude habits; dwelling alone in a mountain-cabin, earning a precarious subsistence by his rifle, and rarely herding with his kind but to get drunk. His usual account of the transaction was this: Joseph, his brother, in defiance of Braddock's injunctions, persisting in sheltering himself behind a tree, was finally cut down by his infuriated commander; on which Thomas, who from a little distance witnessed the whole, instantly levelled his gun and shot Braddock down. (Day's *Hist. Coll.* Penn.)

★★★★★★

Here occurs, too, another inconsistency. In 1794, says the writer in the *Intelligencer,* Fausett declared himself to be in his 70th year. In January, 1828, he died at the Laurel Hill, aged 114 years, says a clerical contributor to the Christian Advocate, who has done much to extend the belief of the truth of the tradition. It is not doubted that the reverend annotator believed all that he recited to have been a fact; but it is impossible for a man who was but 70 years old in 1794 to have attained 114 by 1828. The age of 97, as given by Hazard (I. *Penn. Reg.*), is patriarchal enough, and far more probable; but it is equally irreconcilable with Fausett's own statement.

★★★★★★

So much for Fausett's own story. It does not satisfactorily appear that Thomas Fausett had any other brother in the action than Joseph; therefore, it may be concluded there is either confusion or a positive falsehood in the various versions of the tradition lately cited. However, this may be, it is certain that Thomas Fausett was enlisted at Shippensburg, Pennsylvania, by Captain Poison, into Captain Cholmondeley's company of the 48th regiment; and that, deserting from the same subsequently to the battle, he was not retaken by the 1st of

September, 1755. (*Penn. Gaz.*, No. 1394.) And as Captain Cholmondeley was killed in the fight, it is not impossible that it was he who slew Joseph Fausett and was in turn murdered by his brother. But, in the face of all the negative testimony that has been adduced, it is useless to propose the confessions of an ignorant peasant, uttered in his cups twenty years after, as proof of the manner of death of the chief of the army. Yet, it may be urged, Fausett is not singular in his tale: it is supported by the assertion of other witnesses. This is very true: let us see what their assertions are worth.

The first and most important witness is William Butler; who served throughout the Seven Years' War, under Braddock in 1755, under Forbes in 1758, and under Wolfe in 1759. He states that in Braddock's expedition he was marched, with twenty-five hundred others, from the camp at Philadelphia, by way of Germantown and Reading, towards Du Quesne; that Dunbar, who had arrived at Baltimore, joined them on the route; and that Washington led four hundred riflemen:

> At the time of the action, he was just off duty, near Washington's tent. Near there he saw Generals Braddock, Forbes, and Grant talking, and Braddock calling out to Captain Green to clear the bushes ahead by opening a range with his artillery. Then Washington came out, put his two thumbs into the arm-pits of his vest, made a little circle, and came into their presence and said, 'General, be assured, if you even cut away the bushes, your enemy can make enough of them artificially to answer their purposes of shelter and concealment: it will not answer.'
> Braddock, upon hearing this, turning to his officers, said sneeringly, 'What think you of this from a young hand—a beardless boy?'
> He was a great user of snuff, which he carried loose in his pocket; of middle stature, and thick set.

He then goes on to the distinct declaration that the general was slain by:

> One Fawcett, brother of one whom Braddock had just killed in a passion: this last, who killed Braddock, was in the ranks as a non-commissioned officer: the former was a brave major, or colonel; by birth an Irishman. The soldier shot Braddock in the back; and this man, he said, he saw again in 1830, at or near Carlisle. (II. Watson's *Annals Phil.*)

Now, we are willing to admit that Butler, being in his 104th year when he put forth this story, may have mistaken its last date; since Fausett was dead and buried at the period when he said he was at Carlisle; but how shall we get over the remainder of his chapter of blunders? In the first place, Braddock's army was never at Philadelphia; he never saw that city in his life. Nor did Dunbar join him from, Baltimore, where he did not arrive, and probably never visited. There was no Captain Green in the army, nor any General Forbes, or Grant; nor was any such order given or conversation held. Washington had no command whatever in the army; he was merely attached to the staff; and the four hundred riflemen are more like Falstaff's men in green buckram than substantial beings of flesh and blood.

Nor were there any tents at all pitched "at the time of the action." The last had been struck six hours before. In short, poor old Butler had so lamentably jumbled together in his mind the two expeditions of Forbes and Braddock (if, indeed, he ever served with the latter), that in repeating the last rhodomontade that imagination or some gasconading gossip had served him with, he could not keep the twain separate. At his age, when an old soldier shoulders his crutch and fights his battles o'er again, he is too apt to repeat, as of his own memory, the last idle tale that has been put into his mouth. But we cannot be expected, after finding every other of his statements unfounded, to place any credence in the most absurd of all.

★★★★★★

Butler had another story, to the effect that he was sentinel before Braddock's tent one day when Washington approached. Instead of coming to the tent diagonally, as anyone else would have done, he came marching down in a decided and—according to Butler's representation of the performance—in an exaggerated military step, and perfectly straight line. When parallel with the tent, he suddenly faced about, marched to its door, and informed Braddock that unless he procured a greater number of Indians and threw them out as scouts, the army would certainly be cut to pieces. This advice Braddock disdainfully repulsed.

Now, setting aside the improbability of this dramatic tale, let us simply point out the fact that the sentries for the general's tent were taken exclusively from the two regiments. Therefore, Butler could not have been in the position he alleges. But the anecdote may be worthy of preservation, as showing a possible sentiment in the ranks that Braddock held Washington's advice as naught.

★★★★★★

The evidence of Billy Brown, a negro living at Frankford, Pennsylvania, taken in 1826, when he was ninety-three years old, is next adduced to confirm Fausett's story. But though he speaks with much hesitation and uncertainty as to the important fact, he gives us a sufficient number of other anecdotes to test the veracity of his recollections. He, too, is alleged to have been at the deaths of Braddock and Wolfe. Born in Africa and brought a slave to this country at an early age, he loved to tell his hearers of the elephants of his native land, so prodigious as to make "quite a fog with their breath!"

> He was present in that memorable fight as servant to Colonel Brown, of the Irish regiment, and was most of the time near the person of General Braddock. He said his character was obstinate and profane. He confirmed the idea that he was shot by an American because he had killed his brother. He said that none seemed to care for it: on the contrary, they thought Braddock had some sinister design; for no balls were aimed at him! He kept on foot and had all the time his hat bound across the top and under his chin with his white handkerchief. They suspected that the white emblem was a token of his understanding with the French. He told me, (continues the relator of this conversation), that Washington came up to him in the fight, and fell upon his knees to beseech him to allow him to use three hundred of his men in tree-fighting; and that the general cursed him, and said, 'I've a mind to run you through the body;' and swearing out, 'we'll sup today in Fort Du Quesne, or else in hell!' (I. & II. Watson's *Ann.*; Watson's MSS. in *Penn. Hist. Soc.*)

★★★★★★

It is not pleasant to thus doubt the genuineness of some of the stores garnered up by this worthy and laborious collector; but to ignore them entirely, or to admit them as true, would be equally repugnant to our convictions. It may be noted here, that as Braddock had no notion of reaching Du Quesne before the 11th, his alleged invocation was, to say the least, an oath of supererogation. It is odd that Ormsby puts the same expression into Forbes's mouth: "he would sleep the next night in the fort or in hell!" II. *O. T.*

208

★★★★★★

Now, there was no Colonel Brown in the army. A Colonel Burton, indeed, there was; and the negro may have confounded their names; though, since he continued to serve the same master for eight years, it seems a little strange that he should stumble so on this point. Nor did Braddock fight unaimed at or on foot. He was continually mounted and had four horses shot under him. The idea of putting Washington on his knees is too palpably false for comment.

The third and last account that remains to be examined is fathered by Daniel Adams, of Newburyport, Massachusetts, and may be shortly dealt with. In 1842, he proclaims what he had been told by one who had it from another, who was present at the occurrence:

> He stated that the principal officers had previously advised a retreat, which the general pertinaciously refused; that after nearly all the principal officers were shot down, he was approached by a captain to renew the advice, whom he forthwith shot down. Upon seeing this, a lieutenant, brother of the captain, immediately shot Braddock. Several of the soldiers saw the act but said nothing. Braddock wore a coat of mail in front, which turned balls in front; but he was shot in the back, and the ball was found stopped in front by the coat of mail. (II. Watson.)

CHAPTER 13

Conclusions

The reader is now in possession, *totidem verbis*, of all the evidence in the case; and may deduce his own conclusions. He will bear in mind the character and circumstances of the principal witness, and the inducements which a man who had deserted from his colours may find in a moment of intoxication to magnify his crime. Supposing he had killed his captain, it was a simple murder, calculated to excite disgust perhaps, but nothing further. But by substituting the commander's name, he became at once the pot-house hero; the cynosure of their neighbouring eyes to whom the slaughter of a British general was become to be regarded as a praiseworthy achievement.

He will likewise consider the credibility of the remaining witnesses, not one of whom could have known the fact of his own knowledge, since they unite in making poor Fausett a colonel, a major, or at least a captain, when he was but a private at sixpence *per diem*; and will notice the manifold errors with which dotage or ignorance had

209

embroidered the tissue of their memory. No two unite on the same facts. If there be any force in the good old law maxim—*Qui falsus in singulis, falsus est in omnibus* (Who is false in each of them, is a false one in all things)—he will not be long in coming to a conclusion; but if he should still hold to the Fausett story, we can only commend him to the pages of Mandeville or Pinto; if any "historian" since the days of Herodotus can pretend to appease such an appetite for the marvellous.

In considering the conduct of this battle, it is easy to perceive how readily victory might have been lured to perch upon an opposite banner. Had the American method of Indian-fighting been followed from the outset, the whole plan of the campaign must have been altered. But, pursuing the instructions under which he acted, there were several occasions when malicious fate would seem to have dashed the chalice from Braddock's lips. Thus, when he abandoned the design of passing to Fort Du Quesne by the headwaters of Turtle Creek, he lost a golden opportunity. And as it was, had his advanced party been but half an hour sooner in reaching the ravines, all might have been well. The invisibility of their foe was the chief feature in that contest which disconcerted the English.

An enemy sheltered by trees only could never have so surprised them; the dusky forms, flitting from cover to cover, would soon have familiarized their eyes with the tactics of the foe; and though perhaps with heavy loss, they would probably have got the better of their adversaries. Instead of this, while men were dropping by scores on every side, not more than half a dozen Indians were seen by the majority of the troops at any one time during the fight; and the fire appeared to issue from the very bowels of the earth itself. So ignorant were all of the existence of the ravines, that when convinced by subsequent reflection that some such shelter must have been, it was the belief of the survivors that the French had prepared elaborate and artful entrenchments here, in which the army was involved. (II. *P.A.*; VI. *C. R.*)

Nothing was more easy than, as the column approached a part of the defile hitherto undefended, for a hundred warriors to glide unperceived under the cover to the spot, and at their very feet to open an instantaneous and murderous fire upon the bewildered troops. In vain the artillery swept the scene. The harmless balls passed ten feet above the heads of the savages, who lay concealed beneath the surface of the earth. A more astute or experienced leader would have had out his rangers beating the forest on every side, peering into every thicket and tangled dell, and would never have been left unacquainted with the precise topography of such a dangerous spot.

Even after the slaughter had commenced, it would have been easy to have cleared the ravines, by bringing a field-piece to their mouths and with grape and cannister sweeping their channels from bottom to top, sending their naked inhabitants scattered and howling like wolves through the forest. Following this manoeuvre, a column of grenadiers at the bayonet's point and properly supported on the upper plains, would have completed the business. The Indian has not that moral courage—the child of discipline—which will enable him to stand a charge. He dreads the cold steel. And though the front ranks of the storming party would perhaps have fallen to a man, the very nature of the passage would have protected the remainder; and few of the enemy would have had an opportunity of giving more than one fire. But it is too plain why these methods were not pursued.

It is ever an invidious task to point out how a lost field might have been won; but it was reserved for another leader in the same war to give a practical exemplification of the stratagem which turned the Battle of Hastings, and of which Braddock might well have availed himself. Had he been as sagacious as Bouquet at Bloody Run, he would have exercised a manoeuvre so difficult and dangerous that nothing but the last necessity can justify its use; so ingenious that no Indians can ever hold out against it, if properly carried out.

So soon as the fortune of the day seemed perilous, had the rear-guard and wagons been quietly moved back to the river-side, and at least a portion of the pack-horses reconveyed across the stream, it would greatly have facilitated a retreat, without withdrawing any strength from the forces at the time engaged. This being done, the army might have countermarched in three divisions, as though re-tiring. The two wings should have proceeded in opposite diagonal directions towards the Monongahela, encouraging the enemy with an appearance of haste; while the centre slowly retraced its own steps, filling as it were in a perpendicular line upon the base of the triangle whose subtense was occupied by the rear-guard and whose sides were the courses of the wings.

The Indians would inevitably have pursued, though at first with caution; and beyond a doubt a number of lives, particularly of the centre, would have been sacrificed. But when both factions reached the open woods of the first bottom, and the savages beheld the water dotted with wagons and crossing horses, their exultation would have known no limit, and hatchet in hand they would rush on the flight.

Then would have been the moment to annihilate them. The rear-guard, widening its ranks to receive the thinned centre and to enable the artillery posted for the emergency to open on the foe, should attack him in front while the wings, in likewise facing about, fell upon his either flank. One discharge the troops might have poured in, and then given him the bayonet. The result would have been instant and inevitable. Enclosed between three crashing fires of grape and musketry, driven before three gleaming walls of steel, all converging to a common centre, the enemy would have been utterly and instantly crushed; and before that evening's sun was set.

Fort Du Quesne would have been in flames and abandoned. These are no idle speculations; and though a manoeuvre like this requires a steady obedience and abundant nerve, yet its efficacy has been amply tested. And surely no men were more capable of its execution than Braddock's soldiers, whose discipline was perfect until three hours of unceasing disaster had thrown their souls back into a chaotic confusion where self-preservation was the only surviving thought.

The die was cast, however, and the victory was with those who could only abuse it. In the exuberance of their joy, the Indians had not bestirred themselves to make prisoners. Scalps were the first object of their search; and not only from the dead, but from the throbbing temples of the yet living, the bloody trophy was torn, and weltering in his gore the wretch was left to die of his wounds, or, more horrid still, to, perish beneath the fangs of the wild creatures of the forest or the obscene beak of the bird of prey. Then the enraptured warriors turned to a harvest of spoil such as never before or since gladdened a savage eye.

What share of the booty fell to the French or Canadians, we know not; probably, however, they managed to secure the money and the more valuable stores, while the ignorant native was busy in stripping the gaudy clothing from the corpses on the plain, and, frantic with joy, parading in the scarlet sash, brilliant gorget, and gold-laced coat of a murdered officer. The artillery was claimed by the garrison as the spoil of Louis XV.; but such were the difficulty of transporting the pieces and the apprehension of Dunbar's vicinity, that the howitzers and twelve-pounders were spiked and dismounted and left on the field, and the shells bursted. The brass six-pounders only were taken to the fort, where that very night a division of the plunder was made.

★★★★★★

In March, 1756, the artillery (including the howitzers and mortars), captured here was sent to Niagara, and afterwards to Frontenac; and served the French a useful part in the war. In August, 1756, Montcalm opened his lines against Fort Ontario with a part of it. I. Pouchot; *Penn. Gaz.*, Nos. 1389, 1393; I. *Entick*; VI. *C. R.*

★★★★★★

Since nearly every Englishman with strength left to run had fled from the field, few but the wounded fell into the enemy's hands; and it not being their use to cumber themselves with infirm captives, these were speedily put to death. By an Indian report there were thirty prisoners, men and women, carried off by the Chesagechroanus. (VI. *C. R.* These may have been the Chaounaons or Shawanoes.)

But the evidence of William Johnson, a Pennsylvania resident during all this period at Venango, at Du Quesne, and among the Ohio Indians, is positive that there were but three of the English saved alive, and these women; one of whom was retained by the French commander at Venango, and the other two sent slaves to Canada. (VII. *C. R.*) A score of regulars, however, ignorant perchance of savage customs and not dreaming of other treatment than that of prisoners of war, being cut off from flight threw down their arms and surrendered.

A Virginian, too, was captured, (*Penn. Gaz.*, No. 1389); and these are the only English that so far as can be ascertained remained in life when the victors left the field; yet of even this little band one-half were tomahawked ere they reached the Ohio. A darker departure was reserved for their fellows.

During all that anxious day, James Smith, an American captive languishing within the walls of Fort Du Quesne, listened with careful ear for the roll of the English drums, or explored with seeking eye the forest paths whence he looked for the coming of his deliverers.

An hour before sunset the French and Indians returning to the fort halted within a mile's distance and announced their success by a joyful uproar, discharging all their pieces and giving the scalp-halloo. Instantly the great guns responded, and the hills around re-echoed to their roar. Pushing hastily on, the majority of the savages soon appeared, bloodstained and laden with scalps, and uncouthly arrayed in the spoils of the army. Tall grenadier's caps surmounted their painted faces, and the regimental colours trailed disgracefully at their heels. With less disordered pace the French succeeded, escorting a long train of pack-horses borne down with plunder.

Last of all, and while the parting light of day lingered on the beautiful bosom of the Ohio, appeared a small party who had dallied

213

behind to make the needful preparations for the crowning scene of horror. Before them, stripped perfectly naked, their faces blackened and their hands bound behind their backs, with reluctant steps were driven twelve British regulars on whom God's sun had shone for the last time. Delirious with excitement, their barbarous conquerors could hardly wait for the tardy night to consummate their unhallowed joy. A stake was at once sunk on the opposite bank of the Alleghany, whither the crew repaired; the prisoners lost in dumb sorrow at the surprising fate which they now began to comprehend.

Here one by one they were given to the most cruel and lingering of deaths. Bound to the post under the eyes of their remaining comrades and of the French garrison, who crowded the ramparts to behold the scene, they were slowly roasted alive. Coals from an adjacent fire were first applied to various parts of the victim's person. Sharp splinters of light dry pine wood were thrust into his flesh, and ignited to consume and crackle beneath the skin, causing the most exquisite tortures. His trunk was seared with red-hot gun-barrels; blazing brands were thrust into his mouth and nostrils; boiling whiskey was poured in flames down his throat, and deep gashes made in his body to receive burning coals.

His eye-balls were gradually consumed by the thrusts of pointed sticks or the application of a heated ramrod; and the warrior was prized the most highly who could furthest prolong sensibility in his prey, and extract a renewed cry of anguish from the wretch who had almost ceased to suffer: "his weary soul hanging upon his trembling lips—willing to take its leave, but not suffered to depart!" The last expedient was generally to scalp the poor creature, and on his bare, palpitating brain, flash gunpowder or throw a handful of live embers. Terrible as it may seem, the human frame will endure such torment for an hour or more ere vitality ceases; consequently, the horrors of this night endured till dawn, affording a scene unmatched by any other out of Pandemonium. The dark back-ground of the deep woods; the river flickering in the glare of a score of huge fires kindled on its shore; the shrieking soldier bound to the stake, and mingling his dolorous cries with those of his companions, foretasting their own woe; and, to complete the picture, a thousand savages, their naked ghastliness made more hideous by paint, yelling like famished wolves, and waving aloft red torches or dripping tomahawks blood-encrusted to the heft, as with maniac bounds they danced like lubber fiends around the prisoner.

"It seemed," said an eye-witness, "as if Hell had given a holiday and turned loose its inhabitants upon the upper world."

And, shame to tell, there on the opposite shore frowned the gloomy bastions of Fort Du Quesne, from whose ramparts, with the fair flag of France (never more sullied than on this occasion), heavily drooping above their heads, Contrecoeur and his brave garrison beheld unmoved to remonstrance the terrific spectacle. (Smith's Narrative, in *Drake*.)

★★★★★★

When we contrast the excesses permitted to the savages in this war by Frenchmen of all ranks, from Contrecoeur to St.Veran, with the conduct of the English leaders, humanity rejoices with national pride. Of 870 Indians in Amherst's army, 700 withdrew in one body at the capture of Fort Levi in 1760. They insisted on their right to massacre the captured Frenchmen; but Sir Jeffrey sternly warned them that the first blow struck in this design should be the signal for his falling on them with his whole army. Even victory was too dear a purchase to a man of honour at such a rate. (Mante.) But though no punishment in kind was inflicted by Amherst, the French Indians escaped not unscathed during the war. The destruction of Kittaning; the invasion of the Muskingum; the fall of Pontiac;—involved not only the loss of much life, but of national pride; and other scourges than the sword wasted their borders. Within a year the Abenakis, so active against Braddock, were visited with the smallpox, and nearly entirely extirpated. (II. *Garn*.)

★★★★★★

Return we now to the army and its dead general. On the morning of July 14th, he was buried, "decently but privately," in a spot purposely selected in the middle of the road; nor was care spared to close evenly the mouth of his grave, and to pass the troops and the train over the place, in order to efface any guide-marks by which sacrilegious and hostile hands might be enabled to disinter and insult his remains.

★★★★★★

Mr. Headley (XLIV. *Graham's Mag.*, 255), gives a picturesque sketch of Braddock's interment by torch-light, and adds that the services for the burial of the dead were read by Washington; but the *Journal* is distinct that he was buried the next morning. It is probable, however, that the services of the church were recited; and since the chaplain was wounded, it is not improbable that Washington, the only active member of his family, paid this sad duty to his chief.

★★★★★★

But this disgusting feat was reserved for other days and other men.

★★★★★★

Until the opening of the National Road, Braddock's was a thoroughfare between Baltimore and the Ohio. About 1823, while working on it, some laborers exposed his remains, still distinguishable by their "military trappings." "One and another took several of the most prominent bones, and the others were reinterred under the tree on the hill, near the National Road. Mr. Stewart of Uniontown (father of the Hon. Andrew Stewart), afterwards collected the scattered bones from the individuals who had taken them, and sent them, it is believed, to Peale's Museum in Philadelphia." Day's *Penn.* I have essayed without success to trace further particulars of this disgraceful tale.

★★★★★★

So soon as Braddock was beneath the sod, the march was resumed under Dunbar, who, with 300 wounded in his ranks, arrived at Fort Cumberland on Tuesday, July 22nd, at two in the afternoon. (VI. *C.R.*) By his position in the rear and the sluggishness of his motions, this officer had already acquired the unflattering sobriquet of "Dunbar the Tardy;" and his conduct now encountered the censure of his superiors, the disgust of his equals, and even the criticism of his inferiors. At headquarters, his retreat was estimated as more disastrous than the defeat itself. (II. *P.A.*)

★★★★★★

"What dishonour," writes Shirley, "is thereby reflected on the British Army! Mr. Dunbarr has ever been esteem'd an exceeding good officer, but nobody here can guess at ye reason of his retreat in the circumstances he was in, and some severe reflections are thrown out upon his conduct: Some would have him sent with 500 men to bring back what he bury'd with 1500."

★★★★★★

During all this time, there was no thought in the colonies but of Braddock's certain triumph. In Philadelphia the warmer spirits, eager to echo back the first jubilant shout from the western mountains, were already taking about subscription papers, and preparing to kindle the staid city with festal fires. But the cooler counsels of Franklin tempered their zeal.

★★★★★★

"I looked grave," he writes, "and said it would, I thought, be time enough to prepare the rejoicing when we knew we should have occasion to rejoice. They seemed surprised that I did not immediately comply with their proposal. 'Why, the d—1!" said one of them, "you surely don't suppose that the fort will not be taken?'

"'I don't know that it will not be taken; but I know that the events of war are subject to great uncertainty.'" I. Sp. *Fr.*

★★★★★★

Upon the adherents of the Assembly, in particular, the disastrous intelligence came with a double sting, when they reflected how it would sharpen the governor's invectives on their obstinacy and neglect. At first, they would not confide in a syllable of the intelligence; and men even insulted Mr. Morris in the public streets, "for giving out that General Braddock was defeated;" (VI. *C. R.*) nor, indeed, did he in turn omit any occasion of blaming this matter on his opponents.

On July 11th, Col. Innes at Cumberland received the first uncertain news, and hurried away expresses to the neighbouring provinces. Close at the heels of his flying posts came the runaway wagoners seeking their Pennsylvanian homes. Morris was in the interior at the moment, superintending the construction of the new road, and the transmission of supplies; and at Carlisle he satisfied himself of the miserable fact. The wagoners, examined under oath by him, in their confused accounts all united on the main point—that the army was annihilated.

To confirm all the rest, moreover, came an open letter from one of Braddock's messengers, sent from post to post, and spreading terror as it passed; for it was marked to be read as it went at every hostel on the road; "by Mr. Bingham at the Sign of the Whip, and from that to be told at the Indian Queen." On the 16th, the governor gave his Assembly a week's notice to meet him at Philadelphia and urged the instant organisation of such a force as should enable Dunbar to resume the offensive, ere yet the defenceless borders were overrun by the foe. (VI. *C. R.*) This too he warmly pressed on Shirley, to whom the chief command of all the king's American armies was now fallen. Meanwhile Dunbar announced his intention to abandon everything, and to put his troops, in the month of July, in winter quarters at Philadelphia.

Against this Morris remonstrated, and effectively pleaded to have at least a few men left in the posts west of the Susquehannah. Dunbar called a council, whose report shows conclusively what cowardly or stultified infatuation must have governed the destruction near the Meadows; since it appears that the troops being now half-naked and the munitions naught, the army had become more demoralised than ever. Leaving then a considerable part of his still remaining stores with the Virginia and Maryland troops at Fort Cumberland (of which place Col. Innes had been appointed governor), on the 2nd of August he started, 1200 strong, for Philadelphia. Much to Dinwiddie's indignation, who considered that these at least had been ordered by the king for the especial service of the Ohio campaign, he took with him too the three Independent Companies.

It may be noticed here that beside those who had recovered, and the small proportion that had succumbed after reaching it, there were still 300 of Braddock's army left at the fort wounded and unable to travel. (VI. *C. R.*; II. *P.A.*)

General Shirley's first orders (6th August) were that Dunbar should march the 44th and 48th, by Philadelphia and Jersey, direct to Albany; leaving the three Independent Companies at Cumberland. But by Morris's influence on the 12th he issued supplementary orders that those of the 6th should be followed only in case it were found impossible to carry out a renewed design against Du Quesne. The army was to be put in the best order possible, and, when united with the expected Pennsylvania, Maryland, and Virginia provincials, to fall on Du Quesne or Presqu' Isle. Failing success in this, he was to cover the English frontiers. (VI. *C. R.*)

This scheme was never undertaken. The Assembly and the governor still persevered in their opposite stand-grounds; and no troops were raised in Pennsylvania. The three colonies came into no concurrent measures; and, to crown all, Dunbar and his men had no notion to repeat the horrors of the 9th of July. (II. *P.A.*;VI. *C. R.*) In truth, he made a very reasonable explanation of the impropriety of reattacking the French, which was approved by every field-officer and the five oldest captains of his command. He pleaded the advanced season (it was now near the end of August) to begin provincial preparations; the fact that all his artillery was but four six-pounders, the balance being destroyed or strengthening the walls of the French Fort; and the destitution of the troops. There were not half enough tents, and all sorts of clothing and camp equipage was absolutely required. Defections, too, were incessant. By September, there were no less than one hundred and seventy-five deserters from his immediate command.

★★★★★★

See Gov. Morris's proclamation of 6th Sept., 1755 (*Penn. Gaz.*, No. 1394), where a guinea a head is offered for their capture. In the long list of names, it may be noticed that of the 74 deserters from the 44th, seventy-one were American recruits; three only having come with it from Ireland. So, of the 48th, whose 40 deserters consisted of forty-three enlistments and but three Irish drafts. The three Independents had fifty-five deserters. In the same journal (No. 1393) we find Capt. Adam Stephen advertising four deserters from his command at Cumberland.

★★★★★★

In short, as Morris wrote at the time to Shirley:

They are in a very bad order; the officers disagreeing with one another, and most of them having a contempt for the colonel that commands them, while the men are in a poor and ragged condition, and don't relish another campaign, as it is called.
I find, also, that the scheme is to loiter as much time and make as many difficulties as possible, that these troops may not move from this place (Philadelphia), or, if that cannot be done, then, that they may go no further than Albany this season. (VI. *C.R.*)

With a persistive aversion to the scene of danger, unusual, to say the least, in the history of British arms, the troops, with their backs ever to the distant foe, attempted nothing more. With all his faults, certainly Braddock could never have counselled such a course. Moving languidly through Shippensburg and Lancaster, the army, like a scotched snake, "dragged its slow length along," till at last, on August 29th, it reached Philadelphia and encamped on Society Hill; the city having refused to provide quarters. (VI. *C. R.*)

★★★★★★

Society Hill was mainly comprehended within Second and Front, and Union and Pine Streets; but its slopes probably extended to Fourth and to Cedar Streets. It was then a considerable elevation, mostly unoccupied and unenclosed, and used for public purposes by the citizens. Here was the provincial flag-staff, when, so early as 1730, the Assembly ordered the royal standard to be displayed on Sundays and holidays; and here Whitfield, with an eloquent vociferation, discovered to the rapt multitude that Tillotson was no "Christian believer."
A water-battery (perhaps the earliest fortification here) was erected beneath its bank by Franklin's famous "Association;"

and whenever a salute was to be fired, this hill was the chosen spot. The erection of the market-house in Second Street at last caused this district to be built up and the hill to be cut down and graded; and probably there are now comparatively few residents of Southwark who dream of its ancient elevation. Dunbar's troops were encamped on the west of Fourth, between Pine and Cedar Streets. I. *Watson.*

★★★★★★

Here, with tender solicitude, the suffering troops were cared for. The naked were clothed, the hungry fed, the sick and wounded hospitably treated. Churchman and Quaker united with characteristic zeal in the fulfilment of duties alike recommended by Religion and Loyalty. In fine, the troops had scarce been here three weeks ere the officers took occasion to testify their gratitude or their gallantry by a ball to the ladies; which was given in the State House on Monday, the 22nd of September. (I. *Watson.*)

★★★★★★

When, during the revolution, each other religious society in Philadelphia had given to the Whigs the use of a church for their quarters or hospitals, the late Col. Biddle (father of Thomas Biddle, Esq.,) was deputed to select a Quaker meeting-house for the like purpose. Col. Biddle was himself a Friend, though, in girding on the sword and becoming a man of war, he had greatly scandalised his brethren. He could therefore say to his ancient associates, "We only ask you to treat the Continentals as you did Braddock's soldiers after their defeat: give them a flannel jacket apiece and an apple-pie dinner!"

★★★★★★

On October 1st, fifteen hundred strong, the army marched for New York and Albany by Perth Amboy. (*Penn. Gaz.*, Nos. 1397, 1399.)

Dunbar's pusillanimous retreat before no foe (for their own accounts show that the enemy, fearful of his advance, scampered as quickly back to Du Quesne lest he should fall on them, as he, dreading their attack, did from the Great Meadow), if dictated by a cold valour, was surely not executed in sound discretion.

★★★★★★

Thomas Dunbar had been Lieutenant-Colonel of the 18th (Royal Irish) Foot; and, 29th April, 1752, was named Colonel of the 4Sth. In Nov. 1755, his regiment was given to another; he being sent into honourable retiracy as Lieutenant-Governor of the city and garrison of Gibraltar, with a salary of £730, which post he filled so late as 1765. Though he was never again actively, or even independently, employed, he was made a major-general Jan. 18th, 1758; and a Lieutenant-General December 18th, 1760. He was dead before 1778.

★★★★★★

In every quarter the colonies for whose protection he was sent were disconcerted by his conduct. All who could, fled to the closer settlements; and by early autumn, the borders were ravaged with fire and sword. (II. *P.A.*) The history of the steps that ensued in defence of the middle provinces; of the savage and desolating war that laid their confines in ruins, and swept, almost unopposed, over the greater part of Pennsylvania; or of the subsequent career of Dunbar's soldiery, now withdrawn from this portion of the stage, do not come within the compass of our story. A brief glance at the fate of Fort Du Quesne subsequent to the battle must conclude the narrative.

Immediately on their victory, many of the French troops seem to have been sent to the more northern posts; whence, probably, they had, for this urgency, been withdrawn. The greater number of the Indians, too, were speedily dispersed; seeking their homes ere yet the fresh lustre of victory began to dim. Nor did they all part from their allies on friendly terms. The Ottawas, who are said to have been five hundred strong in the battle, already provoked by the conduct of the French on the field, now fell into hot dispute with them in the division of the spoil

Casting scornfully back the hatchet they had received from Contrecoeur, they vowed henceforward to ally themselves with his enemies. As they left the fort, and under the very eye of its garrison, they encountered two Frenchmen, whom they unhesitatingly killed and scalped. This done, they disappeared in the forest gloom. (VI. *C. R. Penn. Gaz.*, No. 1403.) The troops, hastening to Frontenac, uncertain if it had not already fallen before Braddock's arms, on the 1st of August encountered other savage bands, gay in the spoils they had stripped from the slain; who, by the waters of Erie, gave them the first advices of the rout of the Monongahela. (I. Pouchot.)

For several months longer M. de Contrecoeur continued in command at Fort Du Quesne. It does not appear that he was considered to possess all the requisite talents for the maintenance of his difficult and precarious position; but it was not until after Montcalm's arrival in May, 1756, and his conference with Vaudreuil at Montreal, that he was superseded by the more energetic Dumas. In anticipation of the nine thousand men which the English were expected to bring to bear upon this post and Niagara, thirty-five hundred Canadians and savages were at this time posted along the lines from Lake Erie, by the Ohio, to the Illinois; but the fall of Oswego, and the disarrangement of the English plans, prevented, for a season, the threatened attack. The expense to France of its Ohio defences during the year 1756 did not fall far short of three millions of *francs*. (I. Pouchot; II. Garneau.)

Meanwhile, the English, though they effected nothing, were not idle. Instantly on Dunbar's retreat, Dinwiddie proposed to Pennsylvania and Maryland to unite with his government in building a fort at the Great Crossing or the Meadow in the ensuing October. His notion was to furnish it with six guns from Cumberland, and, burning the woods for a mile about to prevent covert for an enemy, to garrison it during the winter of 1755-6 with eight hundred men. (VI. *C. R.*) Unfortunately, this plan fell through. Had it been adopted, it would have been a mighty protection to the English settlements. For two years, the French position on the Ohio was as a floodgate to open ruin and woe upon the adjacent colonies; and though its destruction was ever a main object, yet opinions differed as to the wisdom of attacking it directly or through its connections on the Lakes.

In December, 1755, Shirley held a council at New York; where the plans of the ensuing campaign, including the reduction of all the Ohio establishments, were resolved on; but, as has just been noticed, they were not destined to any result. In the early autumn of 1757, (or perhaps sooner,) M. de Ligneris relieved Dumas in his command; and about the same time, reinforcements were furnished from Canada to the number of four hundred men. (VII. *C. R.*; II. Garneau.)

In the summer of 1758, however, Brigadier-General John Forbes had undertaken its reduction. With three hundred and fifty men of the Royal Americans, twelve hundred of Montgomery's Highlanders, and sixteen hundred Virginia and twenty-seven hundred Pennsylvania provincials (making a total of fifty-eight hundred and fifty men, beside one thousand wagoners), he set out from Philadelphia. At Raystown, he halted and sent forward Bouquet, with two thousand men, to occupy the Loyalhanna.

Conceiving himself able to its capture, this officer imprudently detached Major Grant, with eight hundred men, to make the necessary observations; but the party was surprised and dreadfully cut up by M. Aubry, with seven or eight hundred Frenchmen and an unknown number of savages. Following up their victory, they soon advanced against Bouquet himself, who was entrenched in a position to which, in honour of a favourite general, was given the title of Fort Ligonier. It was with difficulty that they were repulsed. At this juncture, Forbes was almost tempted to abandon the enterprise; but the good news he presently received persuaded him to resume his route.

Their triumph at Grant's Hill had wrought the ruin of the foe. The Ottawas, Ojibwas, Pottawattamies, and Wyandots gathered thither, since July, from the distant lakes, believing that the English were now entirely discomfited, had returned to their deserted families and homes. The troops from Detroit and the Illinois had likewise retired; and the utmost strength of De Ligneris, who was still in command, did not exceed five hundred men. English emissaries, too, among the neighbouring Indians, and the conciliating gifts and promises of the Quakers, had not been working in vain.

The Ohio tribes were inclined to a peace. No persuasion could tempt them to come to the relief of the French; and as the overwhelming army of Forbes drew near, De Ligneris, after firing the buildings, and destroying the stores and all that he could of the works, retired with the garrison to Fort Machault, on Lake Erie, embarking his artillery for the Illinois, and, without a blow, abandoned the long-desired and dearly-bought prize to the English. On the 25th of November, 1758, the standard of Great Britain was unopposedly displayed upon the dismantled fortress. (Garneau; Smith's *Narr.*; Mante.)

During the 24th, Forbes had encamped at Turtle Creek, twelve miles' distance from the Ohio, where his council advised him that the provisions and forage were so nearly exhausted as to render a retreat a question of grave propriety. With a furious oath he spurned their monitions, resolved to carry the fort the next day, or to leave his body beneath its walls; and orders were issued for an early march. That very evening his scouts reported that in the distance they had discovered the smoke of a wide conflagration; and at midnight the camp was startled by the dull, heavy sound of a remote explosion; and it was rightly conjectured that the enemy, with purpose or by accident, had destroyed their magazine. Encouraged by this view, the army pushed eagerly on; the provincials in their fringed hunting-shirts and modest uniform leading the way. (Wm. Butler—before cited, says it was green turned up with buff. II. Watson.)

Next, with solid tread and disciplined array, came the Royal Americans, their dark scarlet coats faced with blue, and their drums beating a lively march. In a litter in their midst reclined the wasted form of their dying old general, known among the savages for his indomitable obstinacy by the title of the Head of Iron, Last of all, in a long and picturesque line, followed the 77th Highlanders in kilts and belted plaids, the "petticoat warriors" of Indian sarcasm.

★★★★★★

Nothing could surpass the horror of the Highlanders at the barbarous customs of Indian battle, or their rage at the well-comprehended insults which were offered to themselves. At Grant's defeat, a flying Scot reported the fate of his comrades. "They were a' beaten," he said, "and he had seen Donald M'Donald up to his hunkers in mud, and a' the skeen aff his head!" (Howe's *Virg.*)

★★★★★★

Apprehensive of an ambush, the troops moved on in wary step; for Forbes alone was aware of the rumoured evacuation, and he was too cautious to be thrown off his guard by placing implicit reliance on its truth. As they approached the fort the route fell into a long, open racepath, where the savage was wont to pass his prisoners through the ordeal of the gauntlet; and here a dismal prospect met their eyes. On either side a long row of naked stakes were planted in the ground, on each of which grinned in decaying ghastliness the severed head of a Highlander killed or captured under Grant; while beneath was insultingly displayed the wretch's kilt. Disgusted and provoked at the scene, the Americans quickened their pace and hastened on. The next moment the 77th came suddenly upon the ground.

One who was present among the advanced provincials relates, that the first intimation given by the Scots of their discovery of the insulted remains of their butchered brothers, was a subdued, threatening murmur, like the angry buzzing of a swarm of bees. Rapidly swelling in violence, it increased to a fierce, continuous, low shriek of rage and grief, that none who listened to would willingly hear again. In this moment, officers as well as men seem to have abandoned every sentiment but of quick and bloody vengeance, and, inspired by a common fury, cast all discipline to the winds.

Their muskets were dashed upon the ground, and bursting from the ranks, the infuriated Gael, with brandished claymore, rushed madly forth with hope to find an enemy on whom to accomplish retribution. Startled at the sudden sound of swiftly-tramping feet, the amazed provincial looked round to see the headlong torrent sweep by, burthening the air with imprecations, and foaming, said he, "like mad boars engaged in battle." When we consider the provocation that had so excited their noble rage, it is almost a matter of regret that of all the cruel band there remained not one behind. The fort was in flames, and the last boat of the flying Frenchmen was disappearing in the evening mist that hung around Smoky Island. The coronach sung by the waters of fair Loch Lomond or in the gloomy pass of Glencoe was not yet to awake a responsive sorrow in the breast of the widows of the foe. (I. & II. *O. T.*)

★★★★★★

It is sad to relate that after Grant's defeat M. de Ligneris was so base as to deliver up five of the prisoners to be burned at the stake on the parade-ground of the fort by his confederate savages. The remainder were tomahawked in cold blood. What countless scenes of like barbarity were enacted here during the war cannot be computed. The narrative would defile a full page in History: but happily, for human nature, the memory of these infamies lies buried with their perpetrators.

★★★★★★

Since 1755 a smaller work had been added to the fortifications of Du Quesne; built about two hundred yards distant from the first, so as to more effectually command the Alleghany, by which their connection with Canada was preserved. The scientific Bouquet pays a suitable testimony to their strength. But now they were a heap of smoking ruins, and the stacks of thirty chimneys alone remained to point out the place of the houses. The enemy had departed in such haste as to leave unsprung the mine which was to explode the magazine of Du Quesne; and here the victors gathered the only *spolia opima* of the expedition; sixteen barrels of powder and ball and "a cartload of scalping-knives." A tenable post was speedily erected from the ruins of the old, to which was now given the name of Fort Pitt; and leaving two hundred men to garrison it through the winter, Forbes soon wended his way back to Philadelphia, where he died early in March, 1759. His body rests in the chancel of Christ Church in that city. (I. *O. T.*)

Before marching from Fort Pitt, however, Forbes took care to perform a sacred duty. It was well known that the unburied bones of Braddock's army lay bleaching on the ground, and he was resolved to pay this last, late tribute to their memory. Himself not only a Scot but a native of Halket's own shire, his affectionate zeal was prompted by the presence of a son and brother. The then Sir Peter Halket, a major of the 42nd, had come to America and accompanied Forbes for no other end than to ascertain, with what certainty he might, the fate of his father. A lingering hope haunted his soul that his kindred might not have been slain outright and were possibly even yet captives among the foe. Accordingly, with other officers of the Highland regiment. Sir Peter set forth with a company of Pennsylvania Rifles under Captain West, an elder brother of Benjamin West the painter. With him as guides went a few Indians from the neighbourhood, who had fought for the French on that fatal day.

> Captain West and his companions proceeded through the woods, and along the banks of the river, towards the scene of the battle. The Indians regarded the expedition as a religious rite and guided the troops with awe and in profound silence. The soldiers were affected with sentiments not less serious, and as they explored the bewildering labyrinths of those vast forests, their hearts were often melted with inexpressible sorrow; for they frequently found skeletons lying across the trunks of fallen trees—a mournful proof to their imaginations, that the men who sat there had perished of hunger, in vainly attempting to find their way to the plantations.
>
> Sometimes their feelings were raised to the utmost pitch of horror by the sight of bones and skulls scattered on the ground—a certain indication that the bodies had been devoured by wild beasts; and in other places they saw the blackness of ashes among the relics—the tremendous evidence of atrocious rites. (Galt's *Life of West.*)
>
> The unknown and innumerable cruelties of the French savages, as has already been mentioned, can never be demonstrated; and imagination itself can but faintly picture their horrors.

In reply to his anxious questions, one of his tawny guides had already told Halket, that he recollected during the combat to have seen an officer fall beneath such a remarkable tree as he should have no difficulty in recognising; and that at the same moment another rushing: to his side was instantly shot down and fell across his comrade's body. As they drew near the spot, the detachment was halted, and the Indians peered about through the trees to recall their memories of the scene. With speaking gesture, they briefly discoursed in their own tongue. Suddenly and with a shrill cry, the Indian of whom we have spoken sprang to the well-remembered tree.

While the troops rested on their arms in a circle around, he and his companions searched among the thick-fallen leaves. In a moment, two gaunt skeletons were exposed lying together, the one upon the other, as they had died. The hand that tore away their scalps had not disturbed their position; but no sign remained to distinguish the relics from the hundred others that strewed the ground. At the moment Sir Peter remembered him of a peculiar artificial tooth which his father bore. The bones were then separated, and an examination of those which lay undermost at once solved all doubts.

"It is my father!" exclaimed the unhappy youth, as he sunk into the arms of his scarce less affected friends.

Brief and stern, as befits a soldier buried upon the battlefield, were the rites that followed. Wrapped in a Highland plaid, the twain who "in death were not divided," were interred in a common grave. In lieu of solemn dirges and the passing bell, the rattling sounds of musketry awoke the long-slumbering echoes of the mountains as the customary volleys were fired above their breasts. As the chasm was being closed, a stone was brought from the hill-side and placed within its mouth. Overgrown now with tall grass, this and the waning memories of a few old men alone point out the spot where for nine-and-ninety years have slept well the brave, the accomplished, the unfortunate representatives of a chivalrous line.

Thus, remote from the dust of their fathers, in unnoted, unhonoured graves, rest the bones of Braddock and of his scarce less unfortunate subordinate. A forest oak appropriately points out the sepulture of the first; but this memorial will not long serve to fulfil its task, since its system is already touched by the finger of decay, and its blasted crest seems to relate with a melancholy significance to not only his fate to whom it owes a name, but to its own prospective doom.

★★★★★★

The wood-cut in this volume gives a very accurate representation of this tree. The original drawing was made, during the summer of 1854, by that skilful artist, Mr. Weber: by whom it was presented to the Historical Society of Pennsylvania.

★★★★★★

Less perishable than the productions of nature, the handiworks of art have remained to link the interest of later times with the associations of the past. The sash in which the body of the general was carried from the field, is said to be yet preserved in the family of the late President Taylor, to whom it was presented during the Mexican

BRADDOCK'S GRAVE

campaign through the intervention of General Gaines. Of its history during the interim, nothing is said; but a detailed description of its present appearance and the circumstances under which it came into General Taylor's hands are given us. (De Hass: *Hist. Western Virg.*)

The reader will recollect that for a long period it was the custom of officers to wear with their uniform a sash of scarlet silken network, the use of which was to bear them, if wounded, from the ground. On that of Braddock the date of its manufacture (1707) is wrought in the wool; and the dark stains upon its texture still exist, mute but unfailing witnesses of the fatal stroke.

After the burial of the Halkets, in a large shallow pit hard by were cast what remained of about four hundred soldiers; this done, the troops returned to Fort Pitt, satisfied with having at least removed from sight so many of the most melancholy testimonials of their misfortunes. But the work was incomplete: twenty-one years after, when Jasper (subsequently Mr. Justice) Yeates visited the field, he found it strewed with skulls and bones, and the trees around, to the height of twenty feet from the earth, scarred with musket bullets and cannon balls. (Galt's *West.*; VI. *Haz. Reg.*)

★★★★★★

In 1854 I was accompanied to this spot by a garrulous old man alleging himself the son of one of the party who buried the Halkets. He was possessed with the vulgar idea that there was considerable treasure upon the bodies, and only needed a little countenancing to explore the ground. It is hoped that the discouragement he received will preserve this grave from such an unhallowed violation as attended Braddock's. It is singular what an infatuation on this subject obtains in the common mind. The accidental discovery by an Irish labourer on a railway cutting of twenty golden guineas among a mass of bones sufficed to set in a ferment the souls of many of the lower classes about Braddock's Field. If these may be relied on, it would seem that a little harvest of dollars was once fished from the river where they had laid since his defeat, by a neighbouring farmer.

But probably the tale is entirely the creature of a clumsy imagination. There have, however, been found other and more interesting relics of the French occupation of Du Quesne. Some of their artillery they appear to have sunk in the Ohio, when they evacuated the fort: and M'Kee's Rocks, just below the mouth of Chartier's Creek, is pointed out as the particular spot. One of their gun-carriages was not long since discovered here; and in the siege of Fort Henry (Wheeling), in 1782, by the British and Indians, the defendants found their account in the possession of a cannon similarly obtained. De Hass.

★★★★★★

When peace returned and the farmer's plough was passed over the spot, the scene of the thickest of the fight became known as the Bullet Field. But fifty years of cultivation have wrought their customary effect; and where once the hillsides ran red with blood down to the stream below, now

Peaceful smiles the harvest,
And stainless flows the tide.

A more tranquil, rural landscape than that at this day presented by the battle-ground of the Monongahela cannot well be imagined. The ploughman no longer turns up in his labours the evidences of war; and it is difficult, at first blush, to recognise the features of the scene. As yet, however, swale and valley and ravine remain to mark the various courses of the fray; but ere long these too will be obliterated or concealed by the growing hamlet that lies hard by; and the physical traces of the event we have sought to chronicle will be lost to sight forever.

Appendix No. 1

BRADDOCK'S INSTRUCTIONS, ETC.

(The first paper that ensues is printed from a contemporaneous copy in II. *Penn. Arch.* which more than probably was given to Gov. Morris, if not by the general himself, at least by one of his family; by Shirley or Orme. It naturally differs materially from the copy translated from English into French and back again into English, published in the American version of the French Memoire. (II. *Olden Time.*)

The second document is that taken from the *Mémoire* as above, collated with the garbled fragments in XXVI. *Gent. Mag.*)

G. 11. *Instructions for* our Trusty & well beloved *Edw'd Braddock, Esq'r. Major General of all our Forces*, and whom We have appointed Gen¹ & Commander of all & singular our Troops & Forces yᵗ are now in North America, & yᵗ shall be sent or raisd there to vindicate our just Rights & Possessions in those Parts. Given at our Court, at Sᵗ James, yᵉ 25ᵗʰ day of Novʳ, 1754, in the 28ᵗʰ Year of our Reign.

Whereas, We have by our Commission, bearing date the 24ᵗʰ day of Septʳ last past, appointed you to be Gen¹ & Commander of all & singular our Forces, yᵗ are or shall be in North America. For your better direction in discharge of yᵉ Trust thereby reposed in You, We have judged it proper to give You the following Instructions.

1ˢᵗ. We having taken under our Royal & serious Consideration the Representations of our Subjects in North America, & yᵉ present State of our Colonies, in order to vindicate our just Rights and Possessions from all Encroachments, & to secure yᵉ Commerce of our Subjects, We have given direction yᵗ Two of our Regiments of Foot now in Ireland, commanded by Sʳ Peter Halket & Col. Dunbar, & likewise a suitable Train of Artillery, Transports & Store Ships, together with a certain Number of our Ships of War, to convey the same, shall forthwith repair to North America.

2ᵈ. You shall immediately, upon yᵉ Receit of these our Instructions, embark on board one of our Ships of War, and you shall proceed to North America, where you will take our said Force under your Command. And We having appointed Aug. Keppel, Esqʳ., to command yᵉ Squadron of our Ships of War on yᵉ American Station, We do hereby require & enjoin you to cultivate a good understanding & correspondence with yᵉ sᵈ Commander of our Squadron during your continuance upon yᵉ Service, with which you are now entrusted. We having given directions of yᵉ like nature to yᵉ sᵈ Commander of our Squadron, with Regard to his conduct & correspondence with you.

3ᵈ. And Whereas, there will be wanting a number of men to make up yᵉ designed complements of our said Regiments, from 500 to 700 each: And Whereas, it is our Intention yᵗ Two other Regiments of Foot, to consist of 1000 men each, shall be forthwith raised & comanded by Govʳ Shirley and Sʳ Wᵐ. Pepperell, whom We have appointed Colˢ of yᵉ same in our Provinces & Colonies, in North America, and have given directions yᵗ yᵉ Regiment under yᵉ command of yᵉ former should rendezvous at Boston, & yᵗ under yᵉ command of yᵉ latter at New York and Philadelphia; and Wᵉ having given orders to our several Governors to be taking the previous steps toward contributing, as far as they can, to have about 3000 men in readiness to be enlisted for these Purposes, & to be put in Proportion as they shall be raised under your command, & be subject to your distribution into the corps above mentioned. And We having thought proper to dispatch Sir John Sᵗ. Clair, our deputy Quarter Master Genˡ, & Jaˢ. Pitcher, Esqʳ., our Commissary of yᵉ musters, in North America, to prepare every thing necessary for yᵉ arrival of yᵉ Two Regiments from Europe, and for yᵉ raising of yᵉ Forces above mentioned, in America. You will inform yourself of such of our Governors as you can most conveniently upon your arrival, & of all of them in due time, & likewise of our sᵈ deputy Quarter Master Genˡ & Commissary of yᵉ musters, concerning yᵉ Progress they shall respectively have made in yᵉ Execution of our commands above mentioned, in order yᵗ you may be enabled without delay to act accordingly.

4ᵗʰ. Whereas, it has been represented to Us yᵗ yᵉ Forces, which are to go from Cork under your command, may be in want of Provisions upon yⁿ arrival in America, We have caused in consideration thereof 1000 Barrels of Beef and 10 Tons of Butter, to be put on board the Transport Vessels, & to be delivered to you upon your arrival in America, in case you shall find yᵉ same to be necessary in order to be distributed among yᵉ officers & Troops, & yᵉ several Persons belonging to yᵉ Train of Artillery. But it is our Royal Will & Pleasure, yᵗ in case yᵉ Govʳˢ of our Colonies shall have provided a proper Quantity of Provisions for our Troops upon their arrival, you will then signify yᵉ same to yᵉ Commander in Chief of our Fleet in those Parts, yᵗ yᵉ sᵈ 1000 Barrels of Beef and 10 Tons of Butter, or such Part thereof as shall not be expended may be applied to yᵉ Use of our Royal Navy.

5ᵗʰ. Whereas, We have given Orders to our said Govʳˢ to provide carefully a sufficient Quantity of fresh victuals for yᵉ use of our Troops at their arrival, & yᵗ they should also furnish all our officers who may have occasion to go from Place to Place, with all necessaries for travelling by Land, in case there are no means of going by Sea; & likewise, to observe & obey all such orders as shall be given by You or Persons appointed by you from time to time for quartering the Troops, impressing Carriages, & providing all necessaries for such Forces as shall arrive or be raised in America, and yᵗ the sᵈ several Services shall be performed at the charge of yᵉ respective Governments, wherein the same shall happen. It is our Will & Pleasure yᵗ you should, pursuant thereto, apply to our sᵈ Governors, or any of them, upon all such Exigencies.

6ᵗʰ. And Whereas, We have further directed our said Govʳˢ to endeavour to prevail upon yᵉ Assemblies of their respective Provinces to raise forthwith as large a sum as can be afforded as their contribution to a common Fund, to be employed provisionally for yᵉ general Service in North America, particularly for paying the charge of levying yᵉ Troops to make up yᵉ complements of yᵉ Regiments above-mentioned. It is our Will & Pleasure yᵗ you shou'd give them all yᵉ advice & assistance you can towards effectuating these good Purposes, by establishing such a common Fund as may fully supply yᵉ intended Service; But you will take particular Care to prevent yᵉ Payment of any money whatever to yᵉ Troops under your command, except such as shall be, pursuant to yᵉ Returns, made to yₒᵤ of effective men.

7ᵗʰ. We having likewise directed our sᵈ Govʳˢ to correspond, advise & confer with you about all such matters as may tend to yᵉ promoting the said Levies in their respective Provinces, you are hereby required to be aiding & assisting to them in yᵉ Execution of our sᵈ Instructions, for which purpose you will not only keep a constant & frequent correspondence in writing with them, but will likewise visit the sᵈ Iⁱ inces, or any one of them yᵗ you shall think it necessary for our Service so to do. And you will remind our said Governors to use all possible dispatch, that yᵉ Execution of our design may not be retarded by yᵉ Slowness of Levies to be made in their respective Provinces, or for yᵉ Want of Transports, Victuals, or any other necessaries, at such times & Places as you shall think fit to appoint for their General Rendezvous. And if any Preparation should be necessary for carrying on our Service, which is not contained in these our Instructions, you shall, with yᵉ concurrence of the Governors who are to assist in any such Service, make any such Preparations, provided yᵗ yᵉ same shall appear to you absolutely necessary for yᵉ Defence of our just Rights and Dominions; and you will, in all such Emergencies & occurrences yᵗ may happen, whether herein mentioned or not provided for by these Instructions, not only use your best Circumspection but shall likewise call to your assistance a Council of War when necessary, which We have thought fit to appoint upon this occasion, consisting of yourself, yᵉ Commander in Chief of our Ships in those Parts, such Governors of our Colonies or Provinces, & such Colonels & oth.r of our Field officers as shall happen to be at a convenient distance from our s⁴ Gen¹ & Commander of our Forces, and you shall with yᵉ advice of them or a majority of them, determine all Operations to be performed by our said Forces under your command, and all other important points relating thereto, in a manner yᵗ shall be most conducive to yᵉ Ends for which yᵉ s⁴ Forces are intended, & for yᵉ faithful discharge of yᵉ great Trust hereby committed to you.

8ᵗʰ. You will not only cultivate yᵉ best Harmony & Friendship possible with yᵉ several Governors of our Colonies & Provinces, but likewise with yᵉ Chiefs of yᵘ Indian Tribes, & for yᵉ better Improvement of our good Correspondence with yᵉ s⁴ Indian Tribes, you will find out some fit & proper Person agreeable to the Southern Indians to be sent to them for this purpose, in like manner as we have orderd Col. Johnson to repair to yᵉ Northern Indians, as yᵉ person thought to be most acceptable to them, to endeavour to engage them to take part & act with our Forces, in such operations as you shall think most expedient.

9ᵗʰ. You will inform yourself from time to time, of yᵉ Nature & Value of yᵉ Presents yᵗ shall be voted or orderd by yᵉ Assemblies of our different Colonies & Provinces, in yᵉ accustomed manner of the inviting & engaging yᵉ Indian Tribes to our Alliance & Interest, and you will be very watchful yᵗ a just & faithful distribution be made of yᵉ same, by all such Persons who shall be entrusted therewith, and you shall assist yᵉ s⁴ Persons with your best advice in yᵉ s⁴ distribution. You will likewise give a particular attention to yᵉ prudent disposal of such Presents as shall be made upon any Occasion, or such as shall have been prepared by Lieut. Governor Dinwiddie, for yᵉ said Indians, out of yᵉ money already vested in his Hands or otherwise.

10ᵗʰ. Whereas, it has been represented to Us, yᵗ an illegal Correspondence & Trade is frequently carried on between the French & our Subjects in yᵉ several Colonies, you will diligently take all possible measures to prevent the continuance of all such dangerous Practices, particularly that the French should not, upon any account whatever, be supplied with Provisions, &c°.

11ᵗʰ. Whereas, We have thought it necessary upon this occasion to establish & ascertain the Rank that shall be observed between the officers bearing our immediate Commission, & those who act under the Commissions of our Governors, Lieut or Deputy Governors, or yᵉ Presidents of our Colonies, for the Time being. We have orderd several printed Copies thereof to be put into your Hands, to be affix'd or dispersd as you shall judge proper in America.

12ᵗʰ. You will herewith receive a Copy of yᵉ early directions that were sent by our Order on yᵉ 28ᵗʰ August, 1753, to our several Governors, enjoining & exhorting our Colonies & Provinces, in North America, to unite together for their common & mutual defence, & you will see by our direc-

234

tions of 5ᵗʰ July, Copies whereof are now also delivered to you our repeated commands, for enforcing the Observance of our said orders of yᵉ 28ᵗʰ August, 1753, and yᵗ We were graciously pleased to order the Sum of £10,000 to be remitted in Specie to Lieuᵗ Govʳ Dinwiddie, to draw Bills for a farther Sum of £10,000, upon yᵉ conditions mentioned in our Warrant of the 3ᵈ July last, & tran 'tted to yᵉ sᵈ Lᵗ Govʳ Dinwiddie, on yᵉ 27th Septʳ following, by our Ord   or yᵉ general Service & Protection of North America, and yᵉ several other Letters of October yᵉ 25 & 26, & of Novʳ yᵉ 4ᵗʰ, to our Govʳˢ, to Sir Wᵐ. Pepperell & Col. Shirley, Copies of which will be delivered to you herewith, will fully acquaint you with our Orders & Instructions which have been signified to our officers & Governors upon this Subject, at those respective Times, will enable you to inform yourself what Progress has been made in the Execution thereof; And as Extracts of Lieuᵗ Govʳ Dinwiddie's Letters of May 10ᵗʰ, June 18ᵗʰ, & July 24ᵗʰ, relating to the Summons of the Fort which was erecting on yᵉ Forks of yᵉ Monongahela, and yᵉ Skirmish yᵗ followed soon after, & likewise of yᵉ action in the Great Meadows, near the River Ohio, are herewith delivered to you, you will be fully acquainted with what has hitherto happened of a hostile Nature upon the Banks of that River.

13ᵗʰ. You will not fail to send Us by the first, & every occasion that may offer, a full and clear account of your Proceedings, & of all material Points relating to our Service, by Letter, to one of our Principal Secretaries of State, from whom you shall receive, from time to time, such farther Orders as may be necessary for your Guidance and Direction.

G. R.

A LETTER WRITTEN BY COLONEL NAPIER AND SENT TO GENERAL BRADDOCK BY ORDER OF THE DUKE OF CUMBERLAND.

London, November 25th, 1754.

Sir,

His Royal Highness the Duke, in the several audiences he has given you, entered into a particular explanation of every part of the service you are about to be employed in; and as a better rule for the execution of His Majesty's instructions, he last Saturday communicated to you his own sentiments of this affair, and since you were desirous of forgetting no part thereof, he has ordered me to deliver them to you in writing. His Royal Highness has this service very much at heart, as it is of the highest importance to his majesty's American dominions, and to the honour of his troops employed in those parts. His Royal Highness likewise takes a particular interest in it, as it concerns you, whom he recommended to his majesty to be nominated to the chief command.

His Royal Highness's opinion is, that immediately after your landing, you consider what artillery and other implements of war it will be necessary to transport to Will's Creek for your first operation on the Ohio, that it may not fail you in the service; and that you form a second field train, with good officers and soldiers, which shall be sent to Albany and be ready to march for the second operation at Niagara. You are to take under your command as many as you think necessary of the two companies of artillery that are in Nova Scotia and Newfoundland as soon as the season will allow, taking care to leave enough to defend the Island. Captain Ord, a very experienced officer, of whom his Royal Highness has a great opinion, will join you as soon as possible.

As soon as Shirley's and Pepperel's regiments are near complete, his Royal Highness is of opinion you should cause them to encamp, not only that they may sooner be disciplined, but also to draw the attention of the French and keep them in suspense about the place you really design to attack. His Royal Highness does not doubt that the officers and captains of the several companies will answer his expectation in forming and disciplining their respective troops. The most strict discipline is always necessary, but more particularly so in the service you are engaged in.

Wherefore his Royal Highness recommends to you that it be constantly observed among the troops under your command, and to be particularly careful that they be not thrown into a panic by the Indians, with whom they are yet unacquainted, whom the French will certainly employ to frighten them. His Royal Highness recommends to you the visiting your posts night and day; that your colonels and other officers be careful to do it; and that you yourself frequently set them the example; and give all your troops plainly to understand that no excuse will be admitted for any surprise whatsoever.

Should the Ohio expedition continue any considerable time, and Pepperell's and Shirley's regiments be found sufficient to undertake in the mean while the reduction of Niagara, his Royal Highness would have you consider whether you could go there in person, leaving the command of the troops on the Ohio to some officer on whom you might depend, unless you shall think it better for the service to send to those troops some person whom you had designed to command on the Ohio; but this is a nice affair, and claims your particular attention. Colonel Shirley is the next commander after you, wherefore if you should send such an officer he must conduct himself so as to appear only in quality of a friend or counsellor in the presence of Colonel

Shirley: and his Royal Highness is of opinion that the officer must not produce or make mention of the commission you give him to command except in a case of absolute necessity.

The ordering of these matters may be depended on, if the expedition at Crown Point can take place at the same time that Niagara is besieged.

If after the Ohio expedition is ended it should be necessary for you to go with your whole force to Niagara it is the opinion of His Royal Highness that you should carefully endeavour to find a shorter way from the Ohio thither than that of the lake; which however you are not to attempt under any pretence whatever without a moral certainty of being supplied with provisions, &c. As to your design of making yourself master of Niagara, which is of the greatest consequence, His Royal Highness recommends to you to leave nothing to chance in the prosecution of that enterprise.

With regard to the reducing of Crown Point, the provincial troops being best acquainted with the country, will be of the most service.

After the taking of this fort His Royal Highness advises you to consult with the governors of the neighbouring provinces, where it will be most proper to build a fort to cover the frontiers of those provinces.

As to the forts which you think ought to be built (and of which they are perhaps too fond in that country), His Royal Highness recommends the building of them in such manner, that they may not require a strong garrison. He is of opinion that you ought not to build considerable forts, cased with stone, till the plans and estimates thereof have been sent to England and approved of by the government here. His Royal Highness thinks that stockaded forts, with pallisadoes and a good ditch, capable of containing 200 men or 400 upon an emergency, will be sufficient for the present.

As Lieutenant Colonel Lawrence, who commands at Nova Scotia, hath long protracted the taking of Beau-Sejour, his Royal Highness advises you to consult with him, both with regard to the time and the manner of executing that design. In this enterprise His Royal Highness foresees that his majesty's ships may be of great service, as well by transporting the troops and warlike implements, as intercepting the stores and succours that might be sent to the French either by the Baye Françoise, or from Cape Breton by the Baye Verte on the other side of the Isthmus.

With regard to your winter quarters after the operations of the campaign are finished, his Royal Highness recommends it to you to examine whether the French will not endeavour to make some attempts next season and in what parts they will most probably make them. In this case it will be most proper to canton your troops on that side, at such distances, that they may easily be assembled for the common defence. But you will be determined in this matter by appearances, and the intelligence, which it hath been recommended to you to procure by every method immediately after your landing. It is unnecessary to put you in mind how careful you must be to prevent being surprised. His Royal Highness imagines that your greatest difficulty will be the subsisting of your troops. He therefore recommends it to you to give your chief attention to this matter, and to take proper measures relative thereto with the governors and with your quartermasters and commissaries.

I hope that the extraordinary supply put on board the fleet, and the 1000 barrels of beef destined for your use, will facilitate and secure the supplying of your troops with provisions.

I think I have omitted nothing of all the points wherein you desired to be informed: if there should be any intricate point unthought of, I desire you would represent it to me now, or at any other time; and I shall readily take it upon me to acquaint His Royal Highness thereof and shall let you know his opinion on the subject.

I wish you much success with all my heart; and as this success will infinitely rejoice all your friends, I desire you would be fully persuaded that nobody will take greater pleasure in acquainting them thereof, than him, who is, &c.

(Signed.)   Robert Napier.
(A. D. C. to the Duke.)

Appendix No. 2

Fanny Braddock.
Goldsmith's Miscellaneous Works, Vol. III. (Life of Richard Nash.)

Miss Sylvia S—— was descended from one of the best families in the kingdom and was left a large fortune upon her sister's decease. She had early in life been introduced into the best company and contracted a passion for elegance and expense. It is usual to make the heroine of a story very witty and very beautiful, and such circumstances are so surety expected, that they are scarce attended to. But whatever the finest poet could conceive of wit, or the most celebrated painter imagine of beauty, were excelled in the perfections of this young lady. Her superiority in both was allowed by all who either heard or had seen her. She was naturally gay, generous to a fault, good-natured to the highest degree, affable in conversation, and some of her letters and other writings, as well in verse as prose, would have shone amongst those of the most celebrated wits of this, or any other age, had they been published.

But these qualifications were marked by another, which lessened the value of them all. She was imprudent. But let it not be imagined that her reputation or honour suffered by her imprudence: I only mean, she had no knowledge of the use of money; she relieved distress by putting herself into the circumstances of the object whose wants she supplied.

She was arrived at the age of nineteen, when the crowd of her lovers and the continued repetition of new flattery had taught her to think she could never be forsaken, and never poor. Young ladies are apt to expect a certainty of success from a number of lovers; and yet I have seldom seen a girl courted by a hundred lovers that found a husband in any. Before the choice is fixed, she has either lost her reputation or her good sense; and the loss of either is sufficient to consign her to perpetual virginity.

Among the number of this young lady's lovers was the celebrated S——, who, at that time, went by the name of 'the good-natured man.' This gentleman, with talents that might have done honour to humanity, suffered himself to fall at length into the lowest state of debasement. He followed the dictates of every newest passion; his love, his pity, his generosity, and even his friendships were all in excess; he was unable to make head against any of his sensations or desires; but they were in general worthy wishes and desires, for he was constitutionally virtuous. This gentleman, who at last died in a gaol, was at that time this lady's envied favourite.

It is probable that he, thoughtless creature, had no other prospect from this *amour* but that of passing the present moments agreeably. He only courted dissipation, but the lady's thoughts were fixed on happiness. At length, however, his debts amounting to a considerable sum, he was arrested and thrown into prison. He endeavoured at first to conceal his situation from his beautiful mistress; but she soon came to a knowledge of his distress and took the fatal resolution of freeing him from confinement by discharging all the demands of his creditors.

Nash was at that time in London, and represented to the thoughtless young lady, that such a measure would effectually ruin both; that so warm a concern for the interests of Mr. S—— would in the first place quite impair her fortune in the eyes of our sex, and what was worse, lessen her reputation in those of her own. He added, that this bringing Mr. S —— from prison would be only a temporary relief; that a mind so generous as his would become bankrupt under the load of gratitude; and instead of improving in friendship or affection, he would only study to avoid a creditor he could never repay; that though small favours produce good-will, great ones destroy friendship. These admonitions, however, were disregarded; and she found, too late, the prudence and truth of her adviser. In short, her fortune was by this means exhausted; and, with all her attractions, she found her acquaintance began to disesteem her in proportion as she became poor.

In this situation she accepted Nash's invitation of returning to Bath. He promised to introduce her to the best company there, and he was assured that her merit would do the rest. Upon her very first appearance, ladies of the highest distinction courted her friendship and esteem; but a settled melancholy had taken possession of her mind, and no amusements that they could propose were sufficient to divert it. Yet still, as if from habit, she followed the crowd in its levities, and frequented those places where all persons endeavour to forget themselves in the bustle of ceremony and show.

Her beauty, her simplicity, and her unguarded situation soon drew the attention of a designing wretch, who at that time kept one of the rooms at Bath, and who thought that this lady's merit, properly managed, might turn to good account. This woman's name was Lindsey, a creature who, though vicious, was in appearance sanctified, and, though designing, had some wit and humour. She began by the humblest assiduity to ingratiate herself with Miss S; shewed that she could be amusing as a companion, and, by frequent offers of money, proved that she could be useful as a friend.

Thus, by degrees she gained an entire ascendency over this poor, thoughtless, deserted girl; and in less than one year, namely, about 1727, Miss S——, without ever transgressing the laws of virtue, had entirely lost her reputation. Whenever a person was wanting to make up a party for play at dame Lindsey's, Sylvia, as she was then familiarly called, was sent for; and was obliged to suffer all those slights which the rich but too often let fall upon their inferiors in point of fortune.

In most, even the greatest minds, the heart at last becomes level with the meanness of its condition; but in this charming girl, it struggled hard with adversity, and yielded to every encroachment of contempt with sullen reluctance. But though in the course of three years she was in the very eye of public inspection, yet Mr. Wood, the architect, avers, that he could never, by the strictest observations, perceive her to be tainted with any other vice than that of suffering herself to be decoyed to the gaming-table, and at her own hazard playing for the amusement and advantage of others. Her friend Nash, therefore, thought proper to induce her to break off all connections with dame Lindsey, and to rent part of Mr. Wood's house, in Queen's square, where she behaved with the utmost complaisance, regularity, and virtue.

In this situation, her detestation of life still continued. She found that time would infallibly deprive her of a part of her attractions, and that continual solicitude would impair the rest. With these reflections she would frequently entertain herself and an old faithful maid in the vales of Bath, whenever the weather would permit them to walk out. She would even sometimes start questions in company, with seeming unconcern, in order to know what act of suicide was easiest, and which was attended with the smallest pain. When tired with exercise, she generally retired to meditation, and she became habituated to early hours of sleep and rest; but when the weather prevented her usual exercise, and her sleep was thus more difficult, she made it a rule to rise from her bed, and walk about her chamber, till she began to find an inclination for repose.

This custom made it necessary for her to order a candle to be kept burning all night in her room; and the maid usually, when she withdrew, locked the chamber door, and pushing the key under it beyond reach, her mistress, by that constant method, lay undisturbed till seven o'clock in the morning, when she arose, unlocked the door, and rang the bell as a signal for the maid to return.

This state of seeming piety, regularity, and prudence continued for some time, till the gay, celebrated, toasted Miss Sylvia was sunk into a housekeeper to the gentleman at whose house she lived. She was unable to keep company, for want of the elegancies of dress, which are the usual passports among the polite; and was too haughty to seem to want them. The fashionable, the amusing, and the polite in society now seldom visited her; and from being once the object of every eye, she was now deserted by all, and preyed upon by the bitter reflections of her own imprudence.

Mr. Wood and part of his family were gone to London, and Miss Sylvia was left with the rest as governess at Bath. She sometimes saw Mr. Nash, and acknowledged the friendship of his admonitions, though she refused to accept any other marks of his generosity than that of advice. Upon the close of the day upon which Mr. Wood was expected to return from London, she expressed some uneasiness at the disappointment of not seeing him, took particular care to settle the affairs of his family, and then as usual sat down to meditation. She now cast a retrospect over her past misconduct, and her approaching misery; she saw that even affluence gave her no real happiness, and from indigence she thought that nothing could be hoped but lingering calamity. She at length conceived the fatal resolution of leaving a life in which she could see no corner for comfort and terminating a scene of imprudence in suicide.

Thus resolved, she sat down at her dining-room window, and with cool intrepidity wrote the following lines on one of the panes of the window:

'Death! thou pleasing end of human woe!
Thou cure for life, thou greatest good below!
Still mayst thou fly the coward and the slave
And thy soft slumbers only bless the brave.'

She then went into company with the most cheerful serenity, talked of indifferent subjects till supper, which she ordered to be got ready in a little library belonging to the family. There she spent the remaining hours preceding bedtime, in dandling two of Mr. Wood's children on her knees. In retiring from thence to her chamber, she went into the nursery to take her leave of another child, as it lay sleeping in the cradle. Struck with the innocence of the little babe's looks, and the consciousness of her meditated guilt, she could not avoid bursting into tears, and hugging it in her arms; she then bid her old servant a goodnight, for the first time she had ever done so, and went to bed as usual.

It is probable she soon quitted her bed, and was seized with an alternation of passions, before she yielded to the impulse of despair. She then dressed herself in clean linen and white garments of every kind, like a bride-maid. Her gown was pinned over her breast, just as a nurse pins the swaddling clothes of an infant. A pink silk girdle was the instrument with which she resolved to terminate her misery, and this was lengthened by another made of gold thread. The end of the former was tied with a noose, and the latter with three knots, at a small distance from one another.

Thus prepared, she sat down again and read; for she left the book open at that place, in the story of Olympia, in the *Orlando Furioso of Ariosto*, where, by the perfidy and ingratitude of her bosom friend, she was ruined and left to the mercy of an unpitying world. This fatal event gave her fresh spirits to go through her tragical purpose; so, standing upon a stool, and flinging the girdle, which was tied round her neck, over a closet-door that opened into her chamber, she remained suspended. Her weight, however, broke the girdle, and the poor despairer fell on the floor with such violence, that her fall awakened a workman that lay in the house, about half an hour after two o'clock. Recovering herself, she began to walk about the room, as her usual custom was when she wanted sleep; and the workman imagining it to be only some ordinary accident, again went to sleep.

She once more, therefore, had recourse to a stronger girdle, made of silver thread, and this kept her suspended till she died. Her old maid continued in the morning to wait as usual for the ringing of the bell, and protracted her patience, hour after hour, till two o'clock in the afternoon; when the workmen at length entering the room through the window, found their unfortunate mistress still hanging and quite cold. The coroner's jury being impanelled, brought in their verdict lunacy;

and her corpse was next night decently buried in her father's grave.

Thus, ended a female wit, a toast, and a gamester; loved, admired, and forsaken; formed for the delight of society, fallen by imprudence into an object of pity. Hundreds in high life lamented her fate, and wished, when too late, to redress her injuries. They who once had helped to impair her fortune, now regretted that they had assisted in so mean a pursuit. The little effects she had left behind were bought up with the greatest avidity, by those who desired to preserve some token of a companion that had once given them such delight. The remembrance of every virtue she was possessed of was now improved by pity. Her former follies were few, but the last swelled them to a large amount; and she remains the strongest instance to posterity, that want of prudence alone almost cancels every other virtue.

In all this unfortunate lady's affairs Nash took a peculiar concern: he directed her when they played, advised her when she deviated from the rules of caution, and performed the last offices of friendship after her decease, by raising the auction of her little effects.

Appendix No. 3

THE FRENCH REPORTS OF THE ACTION OF THE 9TH JULY, 1755.

The ensuing three papers are taken from copies procured by Mr. Sparks from the originals in the Archives of the War Department at Paris: and it is to his kindness that they are now for the first time published *en bloc*. Their gist has indeed been given in the second volume of his *Washington*.

I.

RÉLATION DU COMBAT DU 9 JUILLET, 1755.

Monsieur de Contre-cœur Capitaine d' Infanterie commandant au fort Duquesne sur la belle rivicre, ayent été informé que les Anglois armoient dans la Virginie pour le venir attaquer, fût averti peu de temps àprès qu'ils étoient en marche, il mit des découvreurs en campagne que s'informerent fidellement de leur routte. Le Sept du courant il fût averti que leur armée composée de 3000 hommes de troupes de la vieille Angleterre étoient à Six lieux de ce fort: Cet officier employa le landemain a faire ses dispositions, et le neuf il détache Monsieur de Beaujeu et lui donna pour second Monsieur Dumas et de Lignery, tous trois Capitaines, avec quatres Lieutenants, 6 Enseignes, 20 Cadets, 100 Soldats, 100 Canadiens et 600 Sauvages, avec ordre de s'aller embarquer[1] dans un lieu favorable qu'il avoit fait reconnoitre la vieille. Le détachement se trouva en presance de l'ennemi a trois lieux de ce fort avant d'avoir pû gagner son poste. Monsieur de Beaujeu voyant son embuscade manquée prit le parti d' attaquer: il le fit avec tant de vivacité que les ennemis qui nous attendoient dans le meilleur ordre du monde en parurent étonnées, mais leur artillerie chargée a cartouche ayent commencé à faire feū, notre trouppe fût ébranlée a son

---

[1] Embusquer ?

245

tour. Les Sauvages aussi, éprouvantés[1] par le bruit du canon plutôt que par le mal qu'il pouvoit faire, commencoient à perdre leur terrain. Lorsque Monsieur de Beaujeu fût tué, Monsieur Dumas s'appliquà aussitôt a ranimer son détachement: il ordonna aux officiers qui conduisoient les Sauvages de s'étandre sur les aisles pour prendre l'ennemi en flanc, dans le temps que lui, Monsieur de Lignery, et les autres officiers qui etoient a la tête des françois attaquoient de front. Cet ordre fût executé si promptement que les ennemis qui poussoient deja leurs cris de Vive le Roi ne furent plus occuppés que de bien deffendre. Le combat fût opiniatre de part et d'autre, et le succès longtemps douteux, mais enfin l'ennemi pliat. Il chercha inutillement de mettre quelques ordres dans sa retraite: les cris des Sauvages, dont les bois rétantissoient, porterent l'épouvante dans tous les cœurs des ennemis. La deroute fût complette: le champ de bataille nous resta avec six pieces de canons de fonte de douze et de Six, quatre affuts a bomb de 50, 11 petite Mortiere à grenade Royale, touttes leur munitions et generalement tous leurs bagages. Quelques déserteurs qui nous sont venus depuis nous ont dit que nous avions eû affaire qu'a 2000 hommes, le reste de l'armée étant à quatre lieux plus loin. Ces mêmes déserteurs nous ont dit que les ennemis se retiroient en Virginie, et des découvreurs qu'on à envoyé presqu'a la hauteur des terres nous l'ont confirmeés en nous rapportant que les milles hommes qui n'avoient point combatû avoient également pris l'épouvante, et abandonnes vivres et munitions en chemin, sur cette nouvelle l'on a envoyé un détachement sur la routte qui a détruit ou brulé tout ce qui pouvoit rester en nature. Les ennemis ont laissés plus de 1000 hommes sur les champs de bataille. Ils ont perdu vué[2] grande partie d'artillerie et de munitions de vivres, ainsi que leur général nommé Monsieur Bradork et presques tous les officiers. Nous avons eus 3 officiers de tués et 2 de blessés; 2 Cadets blessés. Un tel succès que l'on avoit pas lieu de se promettre, vu l'inégalité des forces, est le fruit de l'experiance de Monsieur Dumas et de l'activité et de la valeur des officiers qu'il avoit sous ses ordres.

---

[1] Epouvantés ?   [2] Une ?

II.

RÉLATION DEPUIS LE DÉPART DES TROUPPES DE QUEBEC, JUSQU'AU 30 DU MOIS DE SEPTEMBRE, 1755.

Les regimans partagés par division de quatre et cinq compagnies etoient partis pour se rendre en partie au fort frontenac ou nous devions former un camp et dela aller faire le siege de chozen; ce projet n'a pu avoir son exécution, ayant été obligé de les faire marcher pour empecher les ennemis de faire se lui du fort St. fréderie, et on fut dans l'obligation de faire redescendre le régiment de la Regne et notre première division qui étoit deja fort avancée. Les ennemis avoient trois corps d'arinée, l'une étoit desti-

246

née pour les trois Riviéres, ou ils ont échoués. Le corp étoit de trois mils hommes commandés par le Général *Braudolk ;* Leurs intentions étoit de faire le Siege du fort *du Quesne.* Ils avoient beaucoup d' artillerie, beaucoup plus qu'il nén faut pour faire le Siege des forts de ce pais, la plus part ne valent rien, quoiqu'il ayent beaucoup couté au Roi. Monsieur *de Beaujeu* qui commandoit dans ce fort prevenu de leurs marche et fort embarassé de pouvoir, avec le peu de monde qu'il avoit, empecher ce Siège, se détermina a aller au devant de l'ennemi. Il le proposa aux Sauvages qui etoient avec lui, qui dabord rejetterent son avis, et lui dire quoi, mon père, tu veux donc mourir et nous sacrifier, les Anglois sont plus de quatres Mils hommes et nous autres nous ne Sommes que huit cent, et veux les aller attaquer ; tu vois bien que tu n'a pas d'esprit : Nous te demandons jusqu'a demains pour nous déterminer. Ils tinrent conseil entre eux ils ne marchent jamais qu'il ne fussent de même. Le landemain matin Monsieur de Beaujeu sorti de son fort avec le peu de troupes qu'il avoit et demanda aux Sauvages qu'elles avoient été leurs délibérations. Ils lui répondirent qu'ils ne pouvoient marcher. Monsieur de Beaujeu, qui etoit bon, affable et qui avoit de l'esprit, leur dit : Je suis déterminé à aller au devant des ennemis : quoi — laisserez-vous aller notre[1] pere seul ? Je suis sur de les vianere. Ils ce déciderent àlors à le Suivre. Ce détachement étoit composé de 72 hommes de troupes, de 146 Canadians et 637 Sauvages : La rencontre s'est faitte à 4 lieux du fort le 9 du Juillet à une heure apres midi ; la faire[2] a duré jusqu'a cinq. Monsieur de Beaujeu à été tué a la premiére discharge. Les Sauvages qui l'amoient beaucoup vangerent sa mort avec toutte sa[3] bravoure imaginable. Ils obligerent l'ennemi a prandre la fuitte après un perte considerable. Cela n'est pas extraordinaire ; leur façon de se battre est bien différente de celle de nous autres Européens, la quelle ne vaut rien en ce pais. Ils se mirent en battaille, présanterent un front, a qui, a des hommes cachés derrière des armes[4] qui chaque coup de fusil en culbutoient un ou deux : c'est ainsi qu'ils défirent presque entierèment les Anglois et cela presque tous de vieilles troupes qui arvient passé l'hiver dernier. On fait monter la perte des ennemis à 1500 hommes. Monsieur de Braudolk leur général y a été tué et quantité d'officiers. On leur a pris 13 pièces d'artillerie, beaucoup de boulets et de bombes, cartouches et poudres, et farines, 100 bœufs, 400 chevaux tués, ou pris, tous leur chariots pris ou cassés. Si nos Sauvages ne S'étoient pas amusés a piller, il ne s'en seroit pas retourné un. Il y a grande aparence qu'ils ne tanteront plus rien pour cette partie, puis qu'en se retirant ils ont brulé un fort qu'ils avoient établis pour leurs retraites. Nous avons perdus trois officiers, dont Monsieur de Beaujeu, 25 Soldats, Canadiens, ou Savages, environ autant de blesse. Nous n'avons pas été aussi heureux dans notre partie : revenons à nous autres.

---

[1] Votre ?   [2] L'affaire ?   [3] La ?   [4] Arbres ?

III.

DE MONSIEUR LOTBINIERE À MONSIEUR LE COMTE D'ARGENSON.

Au camp de Carillon, le 24 Octobre, 1755.

Dès l'automne dernière comme j'eus l'honneur de vous le marquer, l'Anglois commença un fort au pied des montagnes d'Aliganai qu'il nomma fort de *Comberland :* le fort est éloigné du nôtre sur la Belle rivière de 110 miles suivant leur estime. Ils ont fait partir d'Europe dans l'hiver deux régimens de troupes réglés de 500 hommes chacun sous le commandement de Monsiur Braddock qui est arrivé à Alexandrie en Virginie le 24 fevrier. Ce roi lui avoit donné la commission de général de toutes les forces du nord de l'Amérique et c'est lui qui devoit présider aux opérations préparées à la Cour de Londres tandis qu'on amusoit la cour de france de Mille propositions de paix pour être un état d'Envahir plus surement ce pays. Le général Braddok, sitot son arrivée en Virginie, fit ses préparatifs pour se mettre en campagne dans le premiers jours d'Avril. Il se réserva la réduction du fort de l'Ohio, et asemblé prendre toutes ses précautions pour s'assurer de la réussite. Cependent comme il n'a pas été servi par les provinces de la nouvelle Angleterre suivant ses désirs et qu'on la fait attendre un temps infini pour les chariots et autres choses qui devoient lui être fourni par les provinces il n'a pû laisser le fort de Comberland que dans les premiers jours de juin. Nos sauvages nous ont rapporté dans l'hiver qu'il se fasoit de grands préparatifs chez l'Anglois, mais Monsieur Duquesne, a qui cette nouvelle fut raporté, bien des fois traita ce la de fanfarronade et dit que ce n'étoit qu'un feu de paille. En consequence, il ne prit aucun des précautions nécessaires pour un mouvement si général.

Monsieur de Vaudreuil arriva dans le mois de Juin, a qui l'on dit que le gouvernement étoit dans un etat mervillieux. Monsieur Duquesne, arriva dans les derniers jours de juin qui confirma à son successeur ce qu'il lui avoit déja écrit et deux jours après on sut la prise de Beauséjour. Monsieur Duquesne, qui avoit sû son fort ménacé, avoit envoyé a son secours, négligeant totalement les autres cotés. Secours arriva a point nommé et le Général de Guillet sachant que l'ennemi n'étoit qu'a trois lieux du fort Duquesne, on fit partir 891 hommes dont 250 français le reste sauvage sous le commandement de Monsieur de Beaujeu, Capitaine de nos troupes, qui se trouva vis-a-vis de l'ennemi a 11 heures du matin. Il l'attaqua avec beaucoup de chaleur et après 5 heures de combat notre detachment réussit a mettre totalement en déroute un avant-garde de 13 cents et quelques hommes, non compris les voituriers, on se trouva le général Braddock. Son arriere-garde de 700 hommes étoit a environ huit lieux et ne fut point attaqué. Il se trouva dans cet avant-garde le régiment d'halke, completté depuis son arrivée en Virginie à 700 hommes, 3 compagnies franches de 100 hommes chacune, le reste étoit troupe de province. Il resta sur la place plus de 600 morts, un nombre tres grand de blessés qui sont mort au retour : le général lui même y fut blessé et mourut à quelques lieux du Champs de Bataille. En un mot il n'a rétourné de ces 1300 hommes qu'environ 300 hommes dont 11 officiers de plus de 150 qu'ils étoient. Nous n'y perdimes que le commandant avec deux autres officiers, 30 et quelques Canadiens et sauvages, et a peu près même nombre de blessé. Toute l'Artillerie de l'ennemi, ces chariots et tous ses équipages resterent au champs de battaille : ce qui fit un pillage considerable qui arreta notre troupe. On eut les papiers du Général Braddock parmi lesquelles se retrouverent les instructions du Roi donné avec réserve, qui se trouverent plus étendu par une lettre de Colonel Napier adjutant Général ecrite par ordre du Duc de Comberland pour lui servir de conduite dans toutes ses opérations.

Appendix No. 4

BRADDOCK'S LAST NIGHT IN LONDON.

Since the preceding pages were in press, the editor has been referred to a passage in the "*Apology for the Life of George Anne Bellamy*" of too interesting a character to be entirely omitted; though, unfortunately, it is now impossible to introduce it in its proper connection. It seems that from her earliest youth Braddock had been the constant friend of this beautiful and accomplished, although sometimes frail, actress. He had, at her request, given the agency of his regiment to her putative husband, Mr. Calcraft; and on the eve of his departure he came, with Colonel Burton and Captain Orme, to take a last farewell. Miss Bellamy was at this time living, under a contract of marriage, with Mr. John Calcraft, as his "domesticated wife," and the mistress of an establishment in Brewer Street. She continues:

> Before we parted, the general told me he should never see me more; for he was going with a handful of men to conquer whole nations; and to do this they must cut their way through unknown woods. He produced a map of the country, saying, at the same time, 'Dear Pop, we arc sent like sacrifices to the altar.' The event of the expedition too fatally verified the general's expectations. On going away, he put into my hands a paper, which proved to be his will. As he did not doubt my being married to Mr. Calcraft . . . . he made *him* his sole executor; leaving me only the plate which he had received as the usual perquisite from government on his nomination. (Vol. I.,Vol.V.)

This plate, which had, "besides the royal arms, a greyhound for the crest," the Treasury officers were so mean as to endeavour afterwards to recover but were cast in the courts. What were the grounds of their demand is not known. The value of Braddock's estate was £7000 (Vol.

V.) Certainly, the fate of "her second father" would appear to have brought no common shock to the mind of the fair Apologist; and we are indebted to her memoirs for a further anecdote:

> This great man having been often reproached with brutality, I am induced to recite the following little anecdote, which evidently shows the contrary. As we were walking in the park one day, we heard a poor fellow was to be chastised; when I requested the general to beg off the offender. Upon his application to the general officer, whose name was Dury, he asked Braddock, How long since he had divested himself of brutality and the insolence of his manners? To which the other replied, 'You never knew me insolent to my inferiors. It is only to such rude men as yourself that I behave with the spirit which I think they deserve.' (Vol. III.)

In the same work (Vol. II., Vol. III.), may be found some notices of Colonel Burton's first wife (Miss St. Leger, of Ireland) and her family. After her death, and while yet in this country, he became enamoured of an Indian beauty; but he seems to have subsequently married an American lady.

LEONAUR

ALSO FROM LEONAUR
AVAILABLE IN SOFTCOVER OR HARDCOVER WITH DUST JACKET

THE FALL OF THE MOGHUL EMPIRE OF HINDUSTAN *by H. G. Keene*—By the beginning of the nineteenth century, as British and Indian armies under Lake and Wellesley dominated the scene, a little over half a century of conflict brought the Moghul Empire to its knees.

LADY SALE'S AFGHANISTAN *by Florentia Sale*—An Indomitable Victorian Lady's Account of the Retreat from Kabul During the First Afghan War.

THE CAMPAIGN OF MAGENTA AND SOLFERINO 1859 *by Harold Carmichael Wylly*—The Decisive Conflict for the Unification of Italy.

FRENCH'S CAVALRY CAMPAIGN *by J. G. Maydon*—A Special Correspondent's View of British Army Mounted Troops During the Boer War.

CAVALRY AT WATERLOO *by Sir Evelyn Wood*—British Mounted Troops During the Campaign of 1815.

THE SUBALTERN *by George Robert Gleig*—The Experiences of an Officer of the 85th Light Infantry During the Peninsular War.

NAPOLEON AT BAY, 1814 *by F. Loraine Petre*—The Campaigns to the Fall of the First Empire.

NAPOLEON AND THE CAMPAIGN OF 1806 *by Colonel Vachée*—The Napoleonic Method of Organisation and Command to the Battles of Jena & Auerstädt.

THE COMPLETE ADVENTURES IN THE CONNAUGHT RANGERS *by William Grattan*—The 88th Regiment during the Napoleonic Wars by a Serving Officer.

BUGLER AND OFFICER OF THE RIFLES *by William Green & Harry Smith*—With the 95th (Rifles) during the Peninsular & Waterloo Campaigns of the Napoleonic Wars.

NAPOLEONIC WAR STORIES *by Sir Arthur Quiller-Couch*—Tales of soldiers, spies, battles & sieges from the Peninsular & Waterloo campaingns.

CAPTAIN OF THE 95TH (RIFLES) *by Jonathan Leach*—An officer of Wellington's sharpshooters during the Peninsular, South of France and Waterloo campaigns of the Napoleonic wars.

RIFLEMAN COSTELLO *by Edward Costello*—The adventures of a soldier of the 95th (Rifles) in the Peninsular & Waterloo Campaigns of the Napoleonic wars.